Beeronomics

"*Beeronomics: How Beer Explains the World* is a significant book. It covers diverse aspects of the economics of beer in world history, providing fascinating reading for beer enthusiasts and others alike. Each chapter is a revelation. Drawing it all together leaves us with a much changed view of this wonderful, historically important beverage."

Julian M. Alston, Distinguished Professor and Director of the Robert Mondavi Institute Center for Wine Economics, UC Davis, and author of *The Effects of Farm and Food Policies on Obesity in the United States*

"This impressive, all-encompassing, and accessible book is a tour de force and must-read for anybody interested in history, economics, and obviously beer. Cheers!"

Bart Minten, Senior research fellow, International Food Policy Research Institute

"For several years now, Jo Swinnen has been devoting serious scholarly attention to a neglected topic, and uncovering intriguing stories along the way. Finally, these insights are made available to a broader public in this refreshing read."

Koen Deconinck, Former Management Consultant at Bain & Company; Economist at Organisation for Economic Co-operation and Development

"This is a fascinating book on beer, history, and economics by the leading beer economists from the world's beer capital. In fifteen chapters, Swinnen and Briski tell the story of how the world has shaped beer and how beer has shaped the world."

Karl Storchmann, New York University, Managing Editor of the *Journal of Wine Economics*

"For much of human history beer was central – a safe source of fluids, calories that fed the work force, and tax revenues that reshaped the political world. Monks, generals, scientists, kings, and robber barons are all part of the book's journey that ends with craft beer. A must on all business schools list of case studies and your holiday gift list!"

Professor Harry de Gorter, Cornell University

"*Beeronomics* provides an excellent addition to the literature. It addresses and explores multiple aspects and issues related to beer and brewing worldwide, using several interesting approaches to highlight new trajectories and trends in the field. Definitely worth a read!"

Professor Ignazio Cabras, Chair in Entrepreneurship and Regional Economic Development and Faculty Director (International Development), Newcastle Business School, Northumbria University

Beeronomics

How Beer Explains the World

Johan Swinnen and Devin Briski

OXFORD
UNIVERSITY PRESS

Great Clarendon Street, Oxford, OX2 6DP,
United Kingdom

Oxford University Press is a department of the University of Oxford.
It furthers the University's objective of excellence in research, scholarship,
and education by publishing worldwide. Oxford is a registered trade mark of
Oxford University Press in the UK and in certain other countries

First Edition published in 2017
Impression: 1

Published in the United States of America by Oxford University Press
198 Madison Avenue, New York, NY 10016, United States of America

British Library Cataloguing in Publication Data
Data available

Library of Congress Control Number: 2017932968

ISBN 978-0-19-880830-5

Printed in Great Britain by
Clays Ltd, St Ives plc

This book is dedicated to friends and colleagues from all over the world with whom, over the past decades, I have had the pleasure of discussing the economics of everything—"how the world works"—while enjoying wonderful beers.

Jo Swinnen

This book is dedicated to my mom who always believed in my storytelling and taught me to love beer, and my dad who introduced me to the unexpected bounty and emotional rewards of sobriety. I'd also like to thank Casey's Pub in Detroit, Michigan and Pizzeria Castello in Leuven, Belgium for nourishing me during this process.

Devin Briski

Contents

List of Figures   ix
List of Tables   xi
About the Authors   xiii

Introduction: From Monasteries to Multinationals and Back   1

1. The World's Oldest Profession: Brewing in the Cradle of
   Civilization   7

2. A Revolution Every Thousand Years: How Hops Jump-Started
   Commercial Brewing in Medieval Europe   15

3. The Brew that Launched a Thousand Ships: How Porter Paid
   for the British Royal Navy   23

4. A Revolution Every Thousand Years, Part II: How Bottom
   Fermentation Made Beer the Darling of the Scientific and
   Industrial Revolutions   37

5. How TV Killed the Local Brewery   47

6. Beer Monopoly: How the Belgian Beer Barons Dethroned
   the King   55

7. Socialist Lubricant: Liberalization, Takeovers, and
   Restructuring the East European Brewing Industry   63

8. The Belgian White: Reincarnation of an Old World Brew   73

9. The *Reinheitsgebot*: Protection against Competition or
   Contamination?   83

10. From Land to Brand: How Nineteenth-Century Nationalist
    Politics Planted the Seeds for the Global Trademark Battle
    over "Budweiser"   93

11. The Great Convergence: The Fall of the Beer-Drinking
    Nation and the Rise of the Beer-Drinking World   103

Contents

12. From Vodka to Baltika: Deciphering Russia's Recent Love
    Affair with Beer   113

13. Trading Water or Terroir? The Changing Nature of the
    Beer Trade   119

14. Craft Nation: How Belgium's "Peasant Beers" Became the
    Best in the World   129

15. Hop Heads and Locaholics: Strategies of the American Craft
    Beer Movement   145

Conclusion: How Beer Explains the World   161

Selected Bibliography   171
Index   173

List of Figures

0.1   Global consumption of beer and wine in value (US$ billion), 1960–2013   5

3.1   Indirect tax revenue in Britain (£ millions), 1750–1850   27

3.2   Production of strong beer in London by top twelve brewers (in 1,000 barrels), 1750–1810   35

4.1   Beer production in Germany, UK, and USA, 1860–1960 (billion liters)   45

5.1   Number of breweries in the USA, 1950–80   48

9.1   German beer imports, 1985–2015 (% of total beer consumption)   91

11.1   Total beer consumption by country (billion liters), 1960–2010   104

11.2   Per capita beer consumption, 1960–2010   106

11.3   Share of beer in total alcohol consumption, 1960–2010 (%)   110

12.1   Beer consumption in Russia (liters per capita), 1960–2012   114

13.1   Share of beer imports in US beer consumption, 1970–2014 (%)   121

13.2   Beer trade in the world (billion liters, % of production), 1960–2013   126

14.1   Belgian beer exports and domestic consumption (million liters)   131

15.1   Number of craft brewers and craft market share in the US (%), 1980–2014   147

List of Tables

4.1 Number of breweries and average brewery size, 1900–1980   43

7.1 Market share (%) of multinational breweries in Eastern
Europe in 2000   68

11.1 Top five beer markets in the world, 1960–2010   105

About the Authors

Johan Swinnen is Professor of Economics and Director of the LICOS Center for Institutions and Economic Performance at the University of Leuven in Belgium. He is also Senior Research Fellow at the Centre for European Policy Studies (CEPS) in Brussels and a Visiting Scholar at Stanford University. Earlier he was Lead Economist at the World Bank, Economic Advisor at the European Commission, and President of the International Association of Agricultural Economists. He is a regular consultant for international organizations and governments and has written extensively on food policy, institutional reforms, economic development, and the economics of beer (and wine, chocolate, and sports). He is the President of the Beeronomics Society (http://www.beeronomics.org) and holds a PhD from Cornell University.

Devin Briski is a print and audio journalist focusing on food, ideas, and technology. She serves as content marketing manager for the events team at Vox Media, which produces Code Conference and Vox Conversations. She is also host of the podcast *One Man's Trash* about the collectibles market. Devin began her career in Silicon Valley, where she worked on the publishing and marketing team of *Stanford Social Innovation Review* and co-founded online magazine *The Ventured Life*. She holds a bachelor's degree in sociology and a master's degree in journalism, both from Columbia University.

The mention of the history of beer always brings a laugh. The history of beer for most people is not a serious topic of study. Beer, after all, is a drink for leisure.

That perception of beer is a case of historical myopia, of an inability of many people at the beginning of the 21st century to conceive of a world where beer was a necessity, a part of everyday life, from breakfast to dinner—and where beer taxes made up a major share of revenues for towns and governments.

R. Unger, 2004

The dramatic consolidation that took place in the brewing industry [after World War II] and the equally dramatic increase in the number of craft brewers [in recent decades] are one of the most radical structural transformations to take place in any American industry.

K. Elzinga, C.H. Tremblay, and V. Tremblay, 2016

SABMiller's board has backed a revised £79bn takeover bid by Anheuser-Busch InBev, paving the way for the third-biggest corporate takeover in history.

Financial Times, July 29, 2016

Introduction

From Monasteries to Multinationals and Back

True beer connoisseurs get stars in their eyes at the mere mention of Westvleteren Abt 12. It's served as the "Best Beer in the World" five years out of the past decade at RateBeer.com. But it's as notoriously difficult to obtain as it is prestigious. The Trappist monks who brew the beer in the small village of Westvleteren in rural Belgium prefer to sell as little as needed to operate their decidedly no-frills monastery. The beer is only sold at the gate of the monastery, one case at a time, upon appointment and with the promise by the buyer to drink it, not to sell it. The bottles come in old wooden cases, without any label.

Needless to say, the promise not to sell is not always kept beyond monastery gates where eBay-enabled lucrative global markets await. The popularity of Westvleteren has not been lost on other brewers and monasteries more willing to respond to growing consumer demand for high-end Trappist ales. Just down the road from Westvleteren, St. Bernardus of Watou is one of the many small, traditional Belgian breweries to capitalize on the growing interest in pre-industrial brewing recipes. On every bottle of St. Bernardus' Belgian abbey ale, a cartoon abbot shoots a knowing glance out of the corner of his eye, presumably at the drinker about to indulge. The medieval iconography and telltale monastic robes don't just serve as a quality guarantee; they also stake a claim to the historic authenticity of the production methods.

The market share of abbey ales like St. Bernardus has exploded in recent years, both in Belgium's domestic market and as exported goods to nations as disparate as Japan and Costa Rica. Beers like St. Bernardus are served for eighteen dollars per bottle at high-end restaurants like Monk's Kettle in San Francisco, paired with dishes to bring out the flavor as part of the emerging practice of beer gastronomy. The restaurant's name refers to the monks of the Low Countries (modern-day Belgium and the Netherlands) as "the first craft brewers."

The popularity of Trappist and abbey ales can be seen as a sort of consumer counterrevolution to the century of consolidation that preceded it. During the twentieth century, the number of breweries worldwide plummeted, while a few savvy macrobreweries producing lager beer cornered the market in beer-drinking nations, undercutting local breweries and prompting a massive global shakeout. By 1990, the top three US breweries were responsible for more than 90 percent of US beer consumption. In traditionally beer-drinking Belgium, Stella Artois and Jupiler cornered the export and domestic consumption markets, respectively. And then the era of global integration began. Today, three multinationals produce more than half of the world's beer. Their advertising is strategic, their distribution channels are extensive, and they report to their shareholders first and foremost.

These brewers are a far cry from today's Trappist monasteries in Belgium, refuges for men to voluntarily enter a life of solitude, celibacy, and faith. The Westvleteren motto of "We aren't monks who brew beer, we brew beer to be monks" references how some breweries serve a holier purpose than the profit of multinationals. But this is also their primary marketing point. In the mind of a burgeoning movement of beer connoisseurs, the modern monastery is the anti-multinational. The medieval iconography of breweries like St. Bernardus of Watou calls upon a mythological prehistory for today's craft beer movement—a time when brewing was necessarily small-scale, local, and labor-intensive— a true craft.

But these crafty exporters fail to provide historical context: monasteries were actually the large-scale brewers of their day. Their establishment by Emperor Charlemagne, the "Father of Europe," during the eighth century was the first time in history that beer had been brewed on anything close to a commercial scale. The establishment of these early centralized brewing operations preceded industrial brewing. The specifics of how brewing beer came to be centralized, commercialized, and exploited for tax revenue by political bodies in flux has influenced not only the styles of beer we enjoy today but also the very course of history.

How Beer Explains the World

This book explains how beer markets have shaped history, and vice versa. Throughout history—from ancient Mesopotamia to today's craft beer explosion—the production and consumption of beer have played a pivotal role in economics and politics on a local, national, and even global scale.

Because beer brewing requires the adoption of an agrarian lifestyle, it has long been associated with the transition to "civilized" society. Chapter 1 describes the first recorded political economy of brewing, which can be traced back to ancient Mesopotamia, the so-called cradle of civilization. Beer regulations were recorded in the earliest codified law. Beer also played a major role in ancient Egypt, where cereal grains were used as a form of currency.

Chapter 2 describes a crucial turning point in brewing history: the introduction of hops. Hops provided more than just an appealing flavor—in fact, early evidence shows medieval denizens actually didn't like the flavor. But hops acted as a preservative for beer, which enabled brewers to begin brewing on a larger scale and storing beer. Therefore, the introduction of hops coincided with the beginning of commercial (non-monastic) brewing and a medieval export market.

In economics, economies of scale is the principle that commodities with high fixed costs are more profitable when produced in large batches. This has been especially important to the economic history of beer, where the fixed costs of operating a brewery are high. Chapters 3 and 4 discuss two developments that paved the way to fully industrialized breweries. Chapter 3 analyzes how an oligopoly of porter brewers in eighteenth-century London was so profitable that high taxation rates paid for centuries of successful British imperialist conquests. Chapter 4 examines how a scientific revolution in brewing paved the way for bottom-fermented lager beer and the dramatic transformation of global beer markets.

While scientific and mechanical developments like pasteurization, refrigeration, and automated bottling played a major role in the consolidation of the brewing industry and the dominance of lager during the twentieth century, another technology is frequently forgotten: television. Chapter 5 explores the role that television advertising played in the spectacular consolidation of the brewing industry during the second half of the twentieth century.

The world was shocked when Belgian-Brazilian multinational InBev announced the hostile takeover of American behemoth Anheuser Busch (AB). AB's Budweiser brand claimed 50 percent market share of the largest beer market in the world, after all. But the executives at AB had failed to note a major shift in the structure of the beer market. Chapter 6 narrates the change from domestic consolidation to the current age of global integration through the hostile takeover no one saw coming.

The fall of the Berlin Wall in 1989 catalyzed major changes in global beer markets. The demise of communism brought in foreign direct investment (FDI) dollars to previously nationalized breweries. Chapter 7 explores how investments by Western breweries in Eastern Europe eased the transition from socialism to a capitalist state for barley farmers.

Chapters 8 through 10 explore the transition from land to brand as the primary regulating and marketing device in beer markets. Chapter 8 looks at the history of white beer, native to the tiny Flemish village of Hoegaarden. The unique style developed there gained popularity during the Middle Ages due to a tax exemption bestowed upon the village. Centuries later, there was popular outrage when multinational AB InBev purchased the only remaining brewery brewing white beer, registered Hoegaarden as a trademark, and proceeded to move production of the beer outside of the city to save costs.

Chapter 9 explores the history and modern-day consequences of the world's oldest food law, the Bavarian *Reinheitsgebot*, which limits the brewing of beer to water, barley, hops, and yeast for all beer served in Germany. The *Reinheitsgebot* came under fire when the European Court of Justice claimed that the law no longer served to protect consumers but rather was functionally a tariff that protected German beer brewers from foreign competition.

Chapter 10 examines the oldest international trademark dispute in recent memory: the battle between American beer behemoth Budweiser and Czech brewery Budweiser Budvar, from the city of České Budějovice (German: Budweis). This trademark dispute gets to the intersection of language, ethnicity, and the limits of geographical indication over the course of the twentieth century.

It's not just the brewing industry and regulations that are changing— so are consumption patterns. As Figure 0.1 illustrates, over the past fifty years consumption expenditures on beer have increased significantly and have been the highest of all alcoholic beverages—they are typically double those on wine. However, the nature of the beer which consumers buy has changed dramatically—and so have the beer consumers themselves. There have been major changes in the geography of beer consumption in the world. When one thinks about beer-drinking nations, one imagines countries like Germany, Britain, and Belgium. However, a look at global trends actually shows that beer consumption is decreasing in these countries. The fastest-growing markets are in Spain, Russia, China, and Brazil. Since 2003, China has overtaken the US as the world's largest beer market. Chapter 11 explores the "global convergence of tastes" and the effect economic growth and globalization is having on traditional alcohol consumption habits.

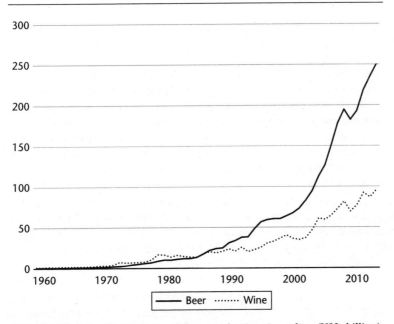

Figure 0.1 Global consumption of beer and wine in value (US$ billion), 1960–2013

FAOstat

Chapter 12 takes an up-close look at this trend in Russia. Traditionally a vodka-drinking nation, Russia observed a "hockey stick" spike in beer consumption during the mid-1990s before the trend flattened out in 2008. This can be attributed, among other factors, to a law that banned alcohol advertising on television. The law had a loophole: beer wasn't officially considered "alcohol."

Widely touted by its slogan "Australian for Beer," outrage spread among Americans on the internet when it was popularly discovered that Foster's is actually "imported" from Canada, where it is brewed under license. Chapter 13 examines the beer trade, a market wrought with idiosyncrasies. With high transportation costs, global brands like Stella Artois and Heineken must cash in on the cultural cachet of an "import." Still, American markets can't get enough of it. And beer trade is growing rapidly, transformed by global mergers and consumer demand for specialty beers and "terroir."

Belgium is renowned for the highest quality beers in the world. However, in the mid-twentieth century, the fine sour beers, abbey ales, and white beers were considered obscure "peasant" styles that would eventually be wiped out by the dominance of German-style lager, namely Stella Artois. Chapter 14 recounts how a few Belgian brewers shifted their strategy and rebranded their products as high-end exports. It was a long shot then, but one that's paying off handsomely today as Belgium has rebranded itself as the "craft nation."

After a century of shakeout in the American brewing industry, culminating in the ascendance of the holy trinity of Bud, Miller, and Coors, the American beer market has undergone another radical shift. In the past two decades, demand for higher-end beers produced by smaller, local craft breweries has exploded. Chapter 15 explores the factors underlying these dramatic shifts in the American brewing industry.

1

The World's Oldest Profession

Brewing in the Cradle of Civilization

> The Germanic tribes on no account permit wine to be imported to them, because they consider that men degenerate in their powers of enduring fatigue, and are rendered effeminate by that commodity.
>
> Julius Caesar, *De Bello Gallico* (Book 4, Chapter 2)

No course on the history of Western civilization is complete without one text: *The Epic of Gilgamesh*. The collection of half-destroyed stone tablets is the oldest known narrative work, originating in ancient Mesopotamia in 2000 BC. What looks to be a slog is actually an easy and entertaining read, once you get used to the disjointed, half-missing narrative style that comes from four millennia of wear and tear. Literary critics may read it as a mythical allegory for man's transition to civilization, but the best parts of the *Epic* are the moments when it's clear that despite 4,000 years and half a hemisphere between them and us, when it comes down to it, humans really haven't changed much at all. Take the protagonist, a beast named Enkidu, and his first sip of beer:

> Enkidu knew nothing about eating bread for food
> And of drinking beer he had not been taught
> The harlot spoke to Enkidu saying:
> "Eat the food, Enkidu, it is the way one lives
> Drink the beer, as it is the custom of the land"
> Enkidu ate the food until he was sated
> He drank the beer—seven jugs!—and became expansive and sang with joy!
> He was elated and his face glowed
> He splashed his shaggy body with water
> And rubbed himself with oil, and turned into a human
> He put on some clothing and became like a warrior.

Enkidu starts as pre-civilized man, both allegorically and literally. He wanders among animals, suckling from the teats of cows for sustenance. But the goddess Ishtar needs him to slay the beast Humbaba of the Cedar Forest, so she sends her priestess, the prostitute Shamhat, to lure him into civilization using her feminine wiles. After six nights and seven days of coupling, Enkidu agrees to accompany Shamhat to Uruk and experience civilization for himself. The rite of passage for Enkidu is eating bread and drinking beer—the fruits of planned agriculture that distinguished Sumerians from their nomadic predecessors.

The tablets fictionalize an important turning point in the history of both humans and beer: the Neolithic Revolution. At several points around the world between 9000 and 7000 BC, a gradual transition from nomadic life (the "extractive economy") to a more settled life as farmers (the "agrarian economy") began to take hold.

It is possible, and even probable, that before this revolution, "beer," loosely construed, was already brewed to some extent. Fermentation materials such as sugar in tree saps and fruit were available in sufficient quantities to the nomadic humans living before the Neolithic Revolution. Archaeologists seem to agree with the narrative in *Gilgamesh*: once humans settled down, brewing took off. Uruk is known as the cradle of civilization, where the "fertile crescent" created by the Tigris and Euphrates rivers facilitated one of the earliest known agrarian societies. It's also here that one of the oldest known beer recipes was found, recorded on a clay tablet and dating back to 6000 BC. Beer was more than a commodity—it was currency. Records show people traded grain and beer for timbers, metals, and precious stones.

But the true masters of beer were the Egyptians. The remarkable civilization of ancient Egypt can't be understood without the political economy of cereals. Life was based around the annual flooding of the Nile River, and barley and wheat grew so plentifully that they were able to cultivate a significant export market. A highly sophisticated system of storage at all levels of political organization and an unusually dry climate facilitated conditions for the preservation of cereals and their value as currency. Stored raw grains served as both currency and trading commodities, while bread and beer were used as payment between social classes. Rulers or political officials received a harvest payment. They were then responsible for passing this down through a system of patronage to support a vast network of workers and dependents. Scribes were charged with developing a system of equivalencies between jugs of beer, loafs of bread, and raw grains.

Egyptians in every social class drank beer. It is said that Ramses III, one of Egypt's greatest pharaohs, found beer to be such a noble drink that he and his guests drank it in golden cups. At the height of the Egyptian Empire, beer was the drink of choice for both festive and ordinary dining occasions. It was only (much) later, i.e. after Egypt had been conquered by the Roman Empire, that wine became widespread and the Egyptian elite began to prefer wine over beer. However, even then, beer remained the drink of choice for the Egyptian masses.

Beer was brewed every morning and consumed throughout the day. Like Sumerians, Egyptians drank unfiltered beer—beer that had not gone through any sieving or settlement phase—directly from large jars through straws in order to avoid the sediment. The straw was used to get through the layer of yeast and hulls floating on the surface of the beer. Both cultures had a variety of beers and breads, affording preferences and a significant trade sector with other peoples.

The World's Oldest Profession

But let us not forget Shamhat: the prostitute with whom Enkidu sleeps before transitioning from bestial humanoid to civilized man. The interesting thing about Shamhat is that some translations refer to her as a priestess but most as a harlot or prostitute. In reality, she's both. She is a priestess of Ishtar, the goddess associated with sex and fertility. Her job as a priestess is to do Ishtar's bidding, which usually involves seducing men. It's no accident that she's the one to introduce Enkidu to beer.

The production and consumption of beer has always been a gendered division, though a surprising amount of diversity exists regarding the actual gender roles. Many taverns doubled as brothels in the ancient Near East, where women worked as brewmaster by day, madam by night. From the beginning, beer has been associated with sex. The earliest Sumerian art shows women drinking from cylindrical jars in seductive positions and during the act of intercourse. The same is true of Egypt, where drinking to excess for both genders was portrayed as both positive and festive. Hieroglyphs displayed women vomiting from overconsumption as a celebration of wealth.

In ancient Mesopotamia, brewing was considered a domestic—and thus female—chore. Sumerians and Egyptians both also assigned specifically female deities to alcohol production. The Egyptian goddess Hathor was a giant cow that forgot her mission to destroy human society when she became intoxicated. She was known as "Lady of drunkenness, music and dance." In the case of Sumerians, the goddess Ninkasi, or "Lady of the inebriating fruit," specifically protected those who brewed the beer. Brewing was the only profession to be assigned to a female deity. Ninkasi was mother of nine sons, all named after symptoms of drunkenness: "the boaster," "the brawler," "he of frightening speech," etc. She lived on legendary Mount Sabu, or "The mount of the taverner."

But the liberality afforded by Sumerians with respect to alcohol and female sexuality eventually gave way to a more conservative approach among the Babylonians. Though taverns were still operated by women, documentary evidence begins to emerge of the marginalization of women from ritualistic drinking. Babylon is also the source of the earliest known legal document, The Code of Hammurabi, famous for its brutal "eye for an eye" logic. Interestingly enough, the four laws that address beer consumption are all addressed to female pronouns. None of them condemn drunken unruliness; rather, they place blame on the management of taverns. Brew-mistresses were responsible for making sure that taverns did not become meeting places for thieves. Restrictions meant to maintain quality standards in brewing and honest business practices also applied specifically to women. One interpretation of the female pronoun is that male tavern owners were exempt from punishment under such laws; another is that the laws specifically targeted female-operated tavern–brothels. However, the law pointed to a clear distinction between religious women and tavern owners. One disturbing law declared, "If a priestess enters a tavern, she will be burned alive."

The Great Wine Divide

Where does the perception of wine as a more civilized drink than beer come from? Like many tropes of Western civilization, we can blame the ancient Greeks. At the beginning of the Greek empire (around 500 BC), the Greeks indeed brewed beer. However, this was soon surpassed by wine production. The popularity of wine coincided with the increasing notion that wine was a drink that was more "suitable for the gods." Greeks thought so little of beer that ancient Athenians are likely the first civilization to produce cereal grains but not ferment them, opting instead to drink their alcohol exclusively in the form of wine. Primitive beers of other cultures from this period were associated with excess and barbaric behavior, as portrayed in the ancient literature. In Plato's *Laws*, the Athenian describes the Scythians, Persians, Carthaginians, Celts, Iberians, and Thracians as the six "bellicose races," indiscriminate with their intoxicants, and lacking in civilized customs: "Both women and men take all of it [their drink] unmixed and pour it down over their clothes, and they consider the custom to be beautiful and pleasant," chides Plato, father of Western philosophy. He contrasts this with the moderate wine consumption of the Athenian symposiums, where the mastery of desire brings participants closer to higher knowledge. Aristotle wrote that wine made drinkers "heavy-headed," while beer had a "stupefying" effect.

While many Greek writers saw beer as the drink of barbarians, inferior to wine, some early Greek writers and philosophers adopted a more neutral position toward the qualities of beer versus wine, sometimes even attributing positive qualities to beer. Sophocles in particular was accommodating. He thought beer to be "healthy," even conducive to a "diet of moderation" consisting of meat, bread, vegetables, and beer. Xenophon described beer as "very good" once people got used to it.

However, discrimination against beer was reaffirmed by the Romans. According to the historian Pliny the Elder (23–79 AD), the Romans learned brewing techniques from the Egyptians. Nevertheless, the Romans generally drank only wine, and they despised beer and its drinkers, whom they referred to, like the Greeks, as "barbarians" and "uncivilized" people. As the Roman Empire expanded across Europe, so did viticulture and the consumption of wine. While the Indo-European tribes in modern-day France, Spain, Portugal, and northern Italy had been beer drinkers for millennia, Roman conquest spread wine culture and (later) production to northern Italy (above the Po River) and southern Gaul (France), and then to the Iberian Peninsula (Spain and Portugal), and later still to northern Gaul (northern France and Belgium). The introduction of wine consumption and production was usually to the detriment of the local beer-drinking cultures conquered by the Romans—especially for the upper classes. But some Celtic tribes stayed used to drinking beer. Especially in the outer, northern areas of the Roman Empire where the influence of Germanic tribes was strong and where wine was difficult to obtain, i.e. in what is now called Britain, Belgium, and Germany, beer was still consumed in large quantities during the period of Roman rule.

In the fifth century AD, the Germans took control over large parts of the Western Roman Empire, which heralded a "great beer revival." The early German tribes drank beer in considerable quantities. After half a millennium of wine-drinking rulers, beer-drinking rulers took over again, and the negative perception of beer and beer-drinking people as being uncivilized—commonplace under Roman rule— became rare.

But production of beer remained a primarily domestic task—in the sphere of women—until one Emperor Charlemagne came along.

Of Monks and Men

Charlemagne is considered the Father of Europe, and his rule the beginning of early modern Europe. He came to power on the eve of the ninth century, drawing up rules on how towns should be organized. Brewers factored prominently in his "ruling hierarchy." Carolingian influence took hold among a loose confederation of Germanic tribes living in Gaul (modern-day Belgium and France), but soon expanded to other regions in what is now Germany, Italy, and Spain. One of his main societal contributions was the establishment of monasteries as centers for brewing. Initially, most monasteries were located in Southern Europe, where the climate permitted the monks to grow grapes and make wine for themselves and their guests. However, when later monasteries were established in the northern regions of Europe, where the cooler climate made it easier to grow barley instead of grapes, the monks started to brew beer instead of wine. This led, throughout the early Middle Ages, to the spread of the principle of "monastic brewing" through the British Isles and to many parts of Germany and Scandinavia. In fact, the growth in brewing in the Low Countries (modern-day Belgium and the Netherlands) in the ninth and tenth centuries was mainly due to this extension of Carolingian authority northwards.

Prior to the twelfth century, these monasteries were the only places where beer was brewed on anything close to a commercial (large) scale. The beer brewed by the monks was used for their own consumption as well as given to pilgrims and the poor. The oldest known drawings of a "modern" brewery were found in the monastery of St. Gall, in present-day Switzerland, and were dated 820 AD. The plans of the St. Gall monastery show three breweries, all producing beer but for different groups of consumers: one brewery for the guests, one brewery for the pilgrims and the poor, and one for the monks in the monastery. The beer that was produced for the guests was of a better quality than that brewed for the pilgrims, the poor, and the monks.

Monasteries also played an important social policy role for the rich and unmarriageable. The equation was simple: sons with no inheritance and no shot at finding a respectable wife were sent to the monasteries. In this sense, they were big money-makers for the Catholic Church. Upon admission of a son, a family would pay an endowment for lifelong living expenses. If the son died early, the monastery got to keep the endowment. Monasteries were glorified frat houses, and wealthy ones at that. They bore some similarities in expenditures as well. In the grand tradition of what happens when a bunch of guys decide to live together, they spent much money, time, and energy brewing beer. And they drank a lot of it—sometimes three or four liters per day per monk.

There were several reasons for this. First, like everybody else, monks preferred beer over water, as the available water in the Middle Ages was often polluted. Second, apart from nutritional reasons, beer was often used in monasteries for spiritual and medicinal purposes. Third, an average meal in the monasteries of the early Middle Ages was rather frugal, and beer provided a welcome nutritious addition for the monks and their guests. Fourth, although beer contained alcohol, it was seen as a liquid like water, and was, as such, not forbidden during a fasting period. Beer was the ubiquitous social lubricant and this not only because it was an essential part of the—often dire—medieval diet, but also because during the Middle Ages every even remotely social occasion called for a drink.

But the general medieval population consumed far less beer on a daily basis than did the monks. Medievalist Richard Unger estimates that citizens of the Low Countries of Europe were likely consuming not much more than half a liter to one liter per day per capita. What's more, class and age determined just how strong the beer would be. Children drank beer, but only beer with a very low alcohol percentage. Barley and a mixture of additives would be rebrewed two, three, and sometimes four times until all that remained was essentially boiled water with a hint of beer and an alcoholic content of as little as 2 percent. Called "table beer," third and fourth brews were consumed by children, paupers, and for breakfast. Averaging about 250 liters per capita per year, people during the early Renaissance did drink much more beer than we do today—but not necessarily more alcohol.

As religious organizations, monasteries were exempt from taxes; however, they were also forbidden from selling beer at a profit. Monastic brewing played an important role in the social fabric rather than the economics of medieval continental Europe. The monks later started to brew beer for noblemen and began to provide their produce for church celebrations and feasts where peasants could drink for free, but it was never a for-profit organization. Around the fourteenth century, the introduction of one spice to the brewing process changed all of that.

2

A Revolution Every Thousand Years

How Hops Jump-Started Commercial Brewing in Medieval Europe

Perhaps it's the overlap between drinking and storytelling traditions, but the origin of brewing is steeped in mythology. Even more mystical than fermented cereal beverages is its ubiquitous additive—hops. Roman botanist Pliny the Elder was the first to write about *humulus lupus*, identifying medicinal properties such as use as a diuretic. During the high Middle Ages, the vine plant, which grew freely across central Europe, was linked to the occult—it was said to be associated with fertility and female magic, sometimes witchcraft. Outside of the monasteries, brewing and folk medicine were considered female jobs, making it probable that women were the first to experiment with including hops as part of the brewing process. But how and why hopping beer became such a widespread practice has remained a matter of speculation. Was it because beer drinkers universally preferred hopped beer? Far from it—in fact, there's a gap of several centuries between the earliest documentation of hopped beer and the point at which it spread across Europe. And yet today the hop is so ubiquitous in brewing that it's arguably beer's defining ingredient. After all, despite being etymologically rooted in "barley," beer refers to fermented wheat and oat styles as well. But virtually all beer contains hops.

The spice's mystique can mask the material role it played in the development of commercial brewing. Rumors and myths are easy to find, but it's harder to dig up the cold, hard facts. Literally—the facts on the origins of hopped beer can be found in cold library basements, and are available as hard copies only. They're hard to read as well, as they are largely pre-Gutenberg-era handwritten records in antiquated and highly localized German and Dutch lexicon.

Luckily for us, Richard Unger of the University of British Columbia has done the heavy lifting. He's already penned two archival excavations on the brewing industry—*Beer in the Middle Ages and Renaissance* and *The Brewing Industry in Holland*—both complete with meticulously compiled charts and numbers and period quotations on trade and tax data available in the dustiest corners of card-catalog-searchable archives. And from these heterogeneous data points, he's pieced together the overarching trends in the development of the commercial brewing industry from disparate markets of early medieval, feudalist Europe. A formidable endeavor, and yet when we commented on the breadth of his work he responded with a prompt, "Well, I chopped out a lot of detail."

Unger's scholarly pursuits began with his study of medieval technology and trade, eventually leading him to the brewing industry. He quickly learned that the medieval political economy of beer was about much more than the beer itself. Political power and economic development were frequently rooted in and around the innovation and regulation of the brewing industry. "What I didn't know was how much material there is. It's absolutely massive. The first records of taxing beer are from 5,500 years ago," he says. "Every town, province, everybody, taxed beer, always. And they kept records. And the records survived." The records tell us the story of the numbers behind beer's transition from source of nourishment and intoxication to source of wealth and government revenue—and thus political power. The transformation of brewing cannot be understood without exploring the politics and economics of medieval cities. Both are inextricably tied to the one additive that enabled commercial brewing and the globalization of beer: hops.

All About the Additives

As we've discussed, beer wasn't always brewed with hops, though its use as a preservative had been known for some time. One of the earliest mentions of hops from medieval Europe is a document stating that Pepin the Short, the father of Emperor Charlemagne, gifted a church with a hops garden in 768 AD. Archaeological evidence indicates that the spice was commonly grown in monastery gardens in those days but not actively used in brewing. Unger dug up some records from 822 and 830 written by abbots that do mention the use of hops in brewing, but there isn't much. Unger concludes that prior to 1200 AD, brewers in the monasteries had known of and likely experimented with hops, but the practice did not catch on until centuries later.

Why didn't they prefer hops from the beginning? Most likely because they didn't like the taste. The advantages hops lent in terms of preservation were not necessary or necessarily appealing to monks and abbots that brewed frequently and exclusively for internal consumption. It was not until beer took on a more important economic and political role that the use of hops spread. Even then, it spread unevenly.

Following the decline of Charlemagne's empire, a considerable source of income for the Catholic Church and local rulers came from the regulation and taxation of beer additives, or *gruit*—a blend of spices used for brewing. The system was known as the *gruitrecht*. Around the tenth century across the Low Countries and Germany, *gruitrecht* began as the exclusive right of the Catholic Church. Bishops maintained a monopoly on *gruit*, and its recipe was kept secret to prevent tax fraud, though we know bog myrtle was a major component. Those outside the monasteries who wanted to brew beer were required to bring their barley to a central authority and mix it with *gruit* before brewing to prevent them from diluting the recipe and evading taxes.

By the twelfth and thirteenth centuries, the *gruitrecht* was decentralized and secularized at the discretion of its original arbiter—bishops and counts found it easier to pass along the responsibility to local officials than to collect taxes from towns. On one hand, the *gruitrecht* was a fundamentally regressive tax, serving as an excise tax on frequently the poorest sectors of the population for whom beer was a source of nutrition and a safe beverage. But on the other hand, a basic principle of the *gruitrecht* was that anyone had the right to brew beer, as long as they could afford the *gruit* for it.

The arrival of hops changed all that. With this new additive anybody could brew beer without paying taxes for *gruit*. Hops were also much better at preserving beer. This enabled brewers to produce larger batches and merchants to travel with and trade beer over much longer distances than had previously been possible. The spread of hops marks the spread of true commercial brewing and beer as an industry. By the fourteenth century, the *gruitrecht* was on the path to obscurity—but the politics of beer and local taxation remained a strong point of resistance to these globalizing forces.

Brauhaus der Hansa

In 1284, a great fire tore through the trade city of Hamburg in modern-day northern Germany, all but destroying it. What was a great tragedy for Hamburgers came with the silver lining of eerily fortunate timing for the burgeoning merchant class—it was just becoming clear that mass-producing and exporting beer could be a profitable venture, and the timing was perfect for rebuilding facilities to maximize this new approach to brewing beer. The rebuilt Hamburg was nicknamed "Brauhaus der Hansa"—the Brewing House of the Hanseatic League.

The growth of Hamburg as a center of an emerging international beer industry necessitated two preconditions: the Hanseatic League, and a reconsideration of the usefulness of hops. By the late twelfth century, merchants in port cities realized that trade routes could only be maintained with a quasi-military network protecting traders from pirates and thieves. In response to these conditions, they established the Hanse, a confederation of merchant guilds in designated towns that facilitated trade routes from the Baltic to the North Sea. Safety encouraged investment in tools of trade—craftsmen built ships and liquid-proof barrels to transport clothes and spices. In Hanse towns, the mass production and export of such items carried the potential for profit—salt, wax, and clothing were all elevated to industrial levels of production and sold abroad at a profit to traders.

Unger also points to the thirteenth-century appearance of records of hopped beer. Traders in northern German towns began to cast a critical eye on the brewing practices of the monasteries. Of particular interest was hops—the spice may not have made for the best-tasting beer, but its preservation qualities were recognized as the key to heretofore unrealized profit from large-scale brewing and trade. Hamburg was well positioned as a center of brewing since it could easily source the raw materials: the surrounding Elbe Valley provided brewers with grains, while hops were imported from small Baltic towns to the north. Hamburg shed the antiquated *gruitrecht* early on and began to mass-produce and export hopped beer to less-developed beer markets in the Low Countries, southern Germany, and Britain.

The total destruction of Hamburg actually benefited these efforts. Breweries were rebuilt with an eye on new lucrative export markets— with wide cellars, roomy floors, high ceilings, and the latest copper kettle technology. These facilities were constructed strategically near waterways. From the beginning, hopped beer was designed for profitable export. The fourteenth century marked Hamburg's crowning success: Unger estimates that some 40 to 50 percent of the city's income came from beer exports.

But the success of Hamburg brewers did not go unnoticed. Brewers from other northern German trade towns such as Wismar, Bremen, and Hannover started producing hopped beer and capitalizing on lucrative export markets. One of those towns was Einbeck, 150 miles south of Hamburg—today it is a small town compared to Hamburg but in the Middle Ages it was part of the Hansa trading system and one of the major cities in northern Germany. Einbeck's wealth was based on its production and export of beers—a reputation which today is still reflected in "Bock beer," a beer style popular in Germany and parts of the United States which derives its name from Einbeck ("Ein Bock" in southern German dialect where the beer became popular).

Walking around the old city center of Einbeck, largely untouched by the bombings of the world wars which destroyed many German old city centers, one cannot but notice the large rounded doors of many of the historic houses. These doors tell an amazing story of "homebrewing *avant la lettre.*" The doors were large to allow brewing kettles to be rolled in and rolled out. In its heyday as a brewing center around 900 houses were owned by families who would take turns brewing beer. The families supplied the ingredients for the brewing and the town, which owned the brewing rights, provided the infrastructure and knowledge. Sixteen large brewing kettles were rolled around from one house to the next during the brewing season, and town brewmasters followed the kettles. The brewmasters oversaw the brewing and were in charge of quality control—which they applied rigorously. The bottom of barrels with low-quality beer was chopped to pieces to prevent side-selling of bad beer. This was to maintain Einbeck's beer reputation in its overseas markets, from the north to the south of Europe.

Hence, Hamburg brewers found themselves in fierce competition with brewers in their fellow northern German trade towns. The municipal government of Hamburg reconfigured its brewing laws and regulations to capitalize on its advantage as a major port and brewing center and maintain the position of their export market. Brewers couldn't just hop beer—Hamburg brewers had to produce high-quality, desirable hopped beer that citizens abroad would pay good money for. By the end of the fourteenth century, city government officials were dedicating considerable time and energy to ensuring only high-quality beer was exported under the name Hamburg. From 1381 onwards, the town council's official blessing was needed to export hopped Hamburg beer. Export-oriented breweries faced completely separate regulatory guidelines from those filling domestic demand. The hopped beer that Hamburg had become known for was rarely consumed within the city itself.

The year 1411 brought even more stringent regulations: the city revoked the exporting rights of several breweries, effectively increasing the average size of those that continued to export. They passed guidelines delineating a minimum time between brews and mandated export of subpar beer to be a punishable offense. They even set up an office at the harbor with officials whose job it was to taste test every batch of beer for quality.

But regulations could only do so much to maintain the German Hansa towns' exclusive claim to high-quality, efficiently brewed hopped beer. The fifteenth century brought the slow decline of the Hanse export heyday as brewers in their destination markets began to imitate the north German brewers' model.

The Low Countries: Stuck in a *Gruit*

Retired historian Raymond Van Uytven knows the history of small towns in the southern Low Countries, modern-day Belgium, like the back of his hand. His Dutch-language scholarship on medieval brewing has informed much of American scholar Richard Unger's work. He's able to read the political economy of medieval cities from the architectural details of the preserved buildings the way one might analyze a poem.

Towns in the southern Low Countries were prime competition for imported hopped beer during the fourteenth century. It's hard to say in retrospect whether the influx of imported hopped beer was perfect timing or disastrous timing for modern-day Belgium's Flanders and Brabant; whatever value judgment is placed on the events that occurred, they definitely provided the impetus for some major changes in the taxation structure.

Prior to the fourteenth century, these duchies had their own thriving, profitable export market—for textiles, not beer. Cities such as Bruges, Ghent, Brussels, and Leuven grew wealthy during the twelfth century by manufacturing textiles from raw British wool and exporting them to countries along the Black Sea coast. Today's ornate cathedrals and government halls in these cities are testament to just how much wealth the textile export trade brought. But there's no better articulation of what happened next than Van Uytven's blunt statement: "They built all this with textiles. Fourteenth century, there was no more textiles. All they had was beer."

The fourteenth century brought big changes to cities that had grown wealthy from textile exports. The decline of the textile trade came from the rising price of wool and improved manufacturing of cloth in Britain itself. Cities could no longer rely on tax revenue from textile manufacturing for public revenue, so they turned to their second biggest industry: beer. The *gruitrecht* became the main source of tax revenue. Just as cities in Brabant and Flanders were dealing with the decline of their textile industries, the influx of imported hopped beers from Hamburg and Bremen began. Complicating things even more, the imported hopped beers were untaxable by the *gruitrecht* that was in place.

Governments imposed heavy trade taxes on imported beer or made imports illegal, but consumers complained that the foreign beers were of much higher quality. Some local brewers started experimenting themselves with hops. Cities in the northern Low Countries, such as Amsterdam and Haarlem, were quicker to catch on to the new hopped beer and large-scale production style. Amsterdam brewers quickly began imitating the strategies of those in Hamburg.

Once they did, brewers in the southern Low Countries faced increased economic pressure as they struggled to compete with hopped beer from even more cities. The pressure grew as proximate cities such as Amsterdam began exporting hopped beer, reducing travel costs and the chance that merchandise would be stolen en route. The pressure was adding up.

In 1380 part of the southern Low Countries, including Brabant, came under the control of Philip the Good, Duke of Burgundy. Their duke was also the King of France. One of his first measures was to replace the *gruitrecht* with a general excise tax on all beer. The law changed several times as authorities experimented with the balance between raising tax revenue, stimulating the local brewing industry, and keeping consumers happy. This tax reform transformed the local brewing industry. Leuven rose to prominence as the major brewing center of Brabant. In 1378, just before the tax change, records showed that brewers made seventy-seven times as much *gruit* beer as hopped beer. Fifty years later, by 1436, they had switched completely to hops. Leuven produced almost five million liters of hopped beer by the late fifteenth century.

With the shift to hopped beer, commercial brewing and consumption of beer grew. The ability to store beer for longer periods of time made brewing a profitable way to maximize calorie intake—always the foremost concern among medieval folk. Unger identifies a correlation between the spread of hops around the continent and what he refers to as the "golden age of brewing."

During this golden age of the 1500s the capacity of brewing kettles for commercial brewers significantly increased. In economic terms, it's the first recorded indication that economies of scale were bringing about an early consolidation of brewing—a precursor of what would happen at a much larger scale during the industrial revolution (discussed in Chapter 4). Smaller brewers were undercut by larger ones that could afford the capital investment in bigger capacity kettles.

Of course, by today's standards there were still a lot of brewers and these early commercial ventures were by no means the industrial brewing we have today. But the brewing industry had definitely become more commercial, more centralized, and bigger in scale compared to the *"gruit* era." It also remained a key source of interest for local and central governments looking to increase tax revenue. The consequences would be huge.

3

The Brew that Launched a Thousand Ships

How Porter Paid for the British Royal Navy

Every Economics 101 teacher explains David Ricardo's principle of comparative advantage within the first two weeks of class. Most of them also use his original example: the long-standing and mutually beneficial wool–wine trade between Britain and Portugal. Britain can produce wool more efficiently than wine; Portugal can produce wine more efficiently than wool. But even if Portugal can also produce wool more efficiently than Britain, it is still in both nations' best interest to specialize and trade with each other. The principle of comparative advantage is now a central tenet of economic theory. But according to economic historian John Nye, Ricardo's example makes no sense in practice.

"Portugal's wine was garbage," he says bluntly. "No one else bought Portuguese wine." The Portuguese wine industry actually better serves as a historic example of how the antiquated mercantilist theory of trade misguided production. Sure, Portuguese wine was better than English wine. But at any period in European history, by any metric, the nation with the absolute advantage in wine production has always been France. In fact, the fruitful Portuguese–British wine trade heralded by Ricardo can be traced back to the 1703 Methuen Treaty guaranteeing Portuguese wine lower tariffs than French wine in exchange for the preferential treatment of British textile imports.

In eighteenth-century British politics, mercantilist economic philosophy drove debates on trade—or lack thereof. The main principle was that any trade deficit brought a total loss of income to the nation by preventing development of domestic industries. Members of the British Parliament believed that in order to achieve wealth and greatness, they had to limit their nation's dependence on products from competing European nations. Instead, they should expand the United Kingdom through conquests of new lands abroad and import raw materials from their colonies. This belief guided foreign policy. Then, in 1776, Adam Smith published *The Wealth of Nations*, a brick of a book with a detailed critique of mercantilism that would change the way the entire world thought about trade—eventually. On his heels were Ricardo and David Hume: the new paradigm of free markets was in its infancy.

Today, Smith, Hume, and Ricardo are canonical thinkers in economic theory. But back then they were advocating a break from dominant thought—one that, they believed, if enacted would bring about a period of both peace and greater wealth. They argued that mercantilist policies both inhibited wealth and encouraged war. Rather than trade with France, Britain fought with her over trade routes and colonies abroad. Following the wool–wine trade example, Ricardo argued in his 1817 work *On the Principles of Political Economy and Taxation* that free trade would "diffuse general benefit and bind together by one common tie of interest and intercourse, the universal society of nations throughout the civilized world."

Economists found a platform for arguing theoretical truths on trade, wealth, and welfare in Britain's Corn Laws, a number of tariffs designed to protect domestic agriculture from foreign competition. At its core, Smith's proposition was deeply moral: all ships rise with a rising tide. He knew that competition brought on by free trade would bring about greater economic inequality, but he was observing a world where peasants couldn't afford the calories necessary to survive and aristocrats had no idea exactly how their estate in the abstract paid for their day-to-day luxuries. As England industrialized, the school of Manchester Liberalism continued in the tradition of Smith, arguing that free trade and efficient markets would make the necessities of life affordable for a growing urban proletariat. The Anti-Corn Law League advocated the repeal of these tariffs with cries for "Cheap bread!"

The rest is history: in 1846, after continued advocacy, policymakers slowly came around to the new school of thought and repealed the mercantilist-era Corn Laws. This watershed moment marked Britain's unilateral move toward free trade. At least, the rest was history—until trade historian John Nye decided to take a second look at the archives.

The Myth of Free-Trade Britain and Fortress France

Nye's investigation into British trade policy began on a whim. "As a historian, I had read over and over about how after Britain repealed the Corn Laws, they became free trade while the rest of Europe still had its head in the sand," he explains. "But I noticed that no one had actually ever conducted a substantive comparison of the trade policies of Britain and France."

This was in the early 1990s, when digging through archives still meant braving dusty filing cabinets, but a curious Nye pursued the task. What he found debunked a narrative that political historians had come to treat as common sense. Britain actually had much higher tariffs than France in the early nineteenth century, and they still had higher tariffs after the repeal of the Corn Laws. Britain's overlooked tariffs were on particular goods, notably French wine. Parliament did not touch the long-standing wine tariffs until the bilateral Anglo-French Treaty of 1860. In fact, earlier attempts by the British to promote "free trade" with France had been rebuffed because Britain refused to lower its tariffs on wine and spirits.

Nye's first paper, published in 1991, sparked much academic controversy. The "myth of free-trade Britain and fortress France" had been treated as an assumption in history, political science, economic theory, and international politics. Britain's unilateral tariff repeal has been used for theories of hegemonic stability, arguing that the Corn Law repeal was possible because Britain had obtained enough economic and geo-political power to act as an economic hegemon. Its position afforded it the possibility of single-handedly bringing about a new paradigm.

But Nye's analysis argued that the repeal of the Corn Laws was more of a symbolic gesture than anything else. Except for lowering tariffs on imported grain, most of the tariffs they repealed were on industry, and at that point Britain was the world's industrial leader. This could be compared to modern-day Japan unilaterally repealing its tariff on American compact cars.

"People just looked at the way people talked about trade during this period without looking at what was actually happening," explains Nye. "The way something is discussed politically or journalistically is often not the way it's working economically." But now Nye was tasked with answering a far more interesting question: what function did these taxes serve in Parliament's foreign policy? Next, he did what every good investigator does—he followed the money.

"A big part of the struggle over trade with France was the struggle over wine," says Nye. "But wine was tied to the big picture of alcohol." He soon learned that he couldn't understand international trade and domestic tax policy on French wine without considering its foremost domestic substitute: beer.

It became the passion project he never anticipated. "No one had ever linked wine and beer policy to tax and trade policy." He dedicated nearly two decades to researching and writing his magnum opus, *War, Wine and Taxes: The Political Economy of Anglo-French Trade, 1689–1900.*

The story gets even more remarkable. In his book, Nye not only challenges the basic assumptions of international economic history, but also identifies Britain's alcohol protectionist and taxation policy as an important factor in the country's military success during the eighteenth century. Drawing on his calculations of beer taxes and wine tariffs, Nye was able to piece together a much greater historical puzzle. Far from being inconsequential, wine tariffs and beer taxes were the lynchpin of British mercantilist strategy. Their stated reasoning was to deprive Britain's rival France of wealth, but their real power came from the strategic protection and taxation of a burgeoning oligopoly of London beer barons capitalizing on the industrial revolution. In effect, Parliament was able to fund its imperialist conquests overseas by price-gouging London's growing urban proletariat on their post-work pints.

Protestantism, Constitutional Government, and Beer

The British weren't always beer lovers. During the high Middle Ages, wine was the glorified drink. The marriage of Henry II and Eleanor of Aquitaine in 1152 gave the English crown control of France's Bordeaux region. Its dark, bitter red wines, Anglicized as "clarets," shaped the tastes of the British aristocracy in the following centuries. And, in fact, claret continued to be imported in large quantities throughout the seventeenth century.

But all of this changed in 1688 with the Glorious Revolution. A primarily Protestant Parliament had grown frustrated with the rule of absolutist King James II and his pro-French policies, Catholic reign, and ill-advised tax policy. Members of Parliament conspired with Dutch republican leader William of Orange to invade Britain and steal the crown. In exchange for their support, William of Orange imparted to Parliament the power to administer and enforce taxes.

Following the Glorious Revolution, Britain's constitutional monarchy more closely resembled the representative model of the Dutch Republic than its absolutist peers in the Catholic regions of Southern Europe. A powerful Parliament gave Britain's growing bourgeoisie—the class of increasingly wealthy trade merchants and industrialists with no noble blood—greater say in political affairs. Social power could be obtained through bottom lines rather than bloodlines. But the rift between Protestant Britain and Catholic France was about more than religion and government. On the eve of European imperialism, mercantilist ideology led both nations to colonize lands in the New World so they could ship raw materials back to the homeland. The two great powers of Europe were revving up for centuries of competitive expansion, ready to battle for control of new markets overseas. The battles would be numerous and bloody. They would also be very expensive.

From 1689 to 1815, Britain was at war for ninety-one years—an astonishing 80 percent of one-and-a-quarter centuries—mostly fighting against the French House of Bourbon, followed by the French Republic during the Napoleonic Wars. Britain either won or fought on equal terms with France in all of these wars. By the nineteenth century, the United Kingdom had come to be known as the "Empire where the Sun Never Sets," with colonies all over the world and trade routes protected by their formidable navy.

But these fortunes had changed tremendously over a century and a half. In the seventeenth century, at the dawn of the Glorious Revolution, France was a far more powerful political entity than Britain. So how was Britain able to raise enough money to fund all their warring?

During the eighteenth century, the British Parliament oversaw the quadrupling of its tax revenue, and its navy grew vastly more powerful (see Figure 3.1). As Britain's fleet of battleships grew more fearsome, so

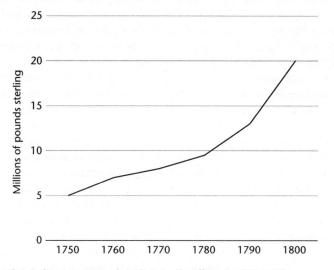

Figure 3.1 Indirect tax revenue in Britain (£ millions), 1750–1850

Nye, J. (2007). *War, Wine and Taxes: The Political Economy of Anglo-French Trade, 1689–1900*. Princeton University Press, based on Brien, P.K. and Hunt, P.A. (1993). The Rise of a Fiscal State in England, 1485–1815. *Historical Research*, 66(160): 129–76.

did its fleet of tax collectors. In *Sinews of War*, John Brewer gives an account of Britain's military supremacy dealing "with bookkeeping, not battles, with ink-stained fingers rather than bloody arms." He attributes British naval power to the success of its tax bureaucracy, documenting its internal system of checks and balances and meticulous accounting practices. But the tax bureaucracy doesn't tell the whole story, according to Nye. It wasn't just the efficiency of tax collectors; it was the taxes themselves. Britain was able to pay for more than a century of almost non-stop warring through the strategic regulation and taxation of beer and wine.

After the Glorious Revolution, the British were faced with a problem: they didn't want to continue lining the pockets of their Catholic rivals by importing French wine. But they weren't exactly prepared to put down the bottle. Sir Thomas Moore stepped up with a series of pamphlets on alternatives to French wine. Titled "England's Interest, Or, The Gentleman and Farmer's Friend," Moore's pamphlets instructed British citizens to plant fruit trees in order to increase national wealth. He promised that ciders made from apples, pears, crabapples, cherries, currants, gooseberries, and mulberries had the potential to be just as "strong, wholesome and useful as French Wines."

King William of Orange and the Protestant merchant elites were concerned with how their citizenry's taste for French wine was filling the war coffers of their rivals in the House of Bourbon. France's public revenue relied heavily on export taxes levied on wine. In 1689, when France declared war on the new Protestant alliance, Parliament seized the opportunity to enact an embargo on French imports. The thirteen-year War of Spanish Succession followed quickly on its heels. When peace was finally declared in 1714, Britain kept customs duties on French wine prohibitively high. By this point, lines had been drawn—literally.

Alcohol was at the center of the conflict, fueling the new British nationalist paradigm. Historian Peter Mathias describes the symbolism of "'Protestantism, constitutional government and beer' as a triumvirate which faced the alliance of 'Catholicism, autocracy and wine'." Drinking songs that accused French wines of "spoiling the products of our land | and of her Coin disrobe her" encouraged Brits to drink beer as a patriotic way of increasing national wealth.

A crucial element was that the tariff on wine was based on volume, not value. This had the important economic effect of shifting demand almost exclusively to high-end wines, as low-quality wines became too expensive for the masses. Prior to the Glorious Revolution, cheap French wine was imported in barrels to Britain. But the volume tariff had all but ended the profitability of cheap wine imports. The British aristocracy continued to import high-end clarets from Bordeaux, while the working-class poor searched for a replacement. The porter beer style was quick to satisfy their after-work needs during the dramatic industrialization and urban expansion of London in the century that followed.

Rise of the Brewgeoisie

When thirteen-year-old Ralph Thrale began working as a brewer for six shillings a week, little could he have known that in three decades he'd serve as a member of Parliament, or that his son would attend Oxford University and be spoiled on a yearly allowance of three thousand pounds. In 1711, Thrale had traveled from the English countryside to work for his uncle, Edmund Halsey, at the midsized Anchor Brewery by the River Thames.

Tracing its roots back to 1650, Anchor was one of London's older "common brewers." Distinguished from on-site publican-brewers, common brewers produced beer en masse and sold it to public houses around the city. Thrale worked as a clerk for Anchor Brewery for twenty years, where his records serve as the earliest detailed accounting sheets available on the early London brewing industry.

By Henry Thrale's death in 1788, the profitability of the porter industry had become apparent and Anchor was still a formidable market force. But as Thrale's close friend Samuel Johnson said during the execution of his will, "We are not here to sell a parcel of boilers and ales, but the potentiality of growing rich beyond the dreams of avarice." The brewery was sold to manager John Barclay and accountant David Perkins for 135,000 pounds. In fifty-nine years, the brewery had close to quadrupled in value. But this was still only the beginning.

Eighteenth-century London was the site of the earliest industrial revolution to shape the modern world. The British gentry and poor working class migrated en masse to London to find work in the industrial expansion, which was booming thanks to new technologies that dramatically increased the efficiency of production. The principles guiding large-scale industrial production were very different from those of the previous era, in which craftsmen were dispersed across the countryside. Scientific innovations enabled economies of scale in brewing. Producing goods on a larger scale lowered the production costs for each individual unit. This business model meant large profits were possible.

In the early days of the eighteenth century, the migration of the English gentry from the countryside brought about the popularity of pale ale. Malt producers learned how to dry barley using coke, enabling brewers to produce lighter, more delicate ales. The preferred recipe of the migrating English gentry, pale ale was best produced on a small scale because coke-malted barley was more sensitive to heat. To compete with publican-brewers, common brewers like Anchor began taking advantage of their size. They produced highly hopped brown ale and stored it in giant vats called butts. This became known as "common butt-beer." A second, stronger recipe was called "stout butt-beer." Eventually, the popularity of this style among the shipyard workers of London's ports earned it the nickname "porter."

Technically, porter was a regression rather than an improvement. Porter relied on wood-malted barley, which was of inferior quality to the coke-malted barley used for pale ales. Pale ales were higher quality and better tasting, but porter was more conducive to large-scale brewing. Pale ale clouded if stored for a long period of time, while porter's strong taste masked impurities in the brewing process. This beer actually tasted better after it had aged. Wood malt could also withstand greater temperature variation when brewed on a large scale, while the batch size leveled out minor inconsistencies. With cheaper inputs and the advantage of size, one pint of porter began selling for three pence, undercutting pale ale.

Until then, brewing had been a craft. In the eighteenth century, the first scientific treatises attempted to standardize the brewing process. Published in 1738, *The London and Country Brewer* was the first book-length guide to brewing and the earliest to recognize how London's new urban character had fundamentally changed beer production. London brewers were no longer craftsmen but industrialists. Their profit depended not on the quality of their craftsmanship but on the strategy of their operation. The guide touts the benefits of economies of scale, "'Tis certain, that the great Brewer can make more Drink, and draw a greater Length in proportion to his Malt, than a Person can from a lesser Quantity, because the greater the Body, the more is its united Power in receiving and discharging, and he can brew with less charge and trouble, by means of more convenient Utensils." In economic terms, this principle holds that by brewing on a larger scale, every unit of beer is cheaper to produce. For the common brewers, this meant that porter was the more profitable style of beer to invest in. By brewing on a large scale, they could make a little bit of profit on a lot of units.

A key enabler of the industrial revolution in brewing was neither vat nor thermometer. Rather, it was the "big ledger"—the all-important record of production and sales data diligently maintained by clerks at successful porter breweries. Records from pre-industrial publican-brewers combined personal and business finances, the accounts approximated both out of carelessness and to evade taxes. The success of porter industrialists lay in precise record-keeping, which allowed them to calculate profit points and expand strategically. When Ralph Thrale took ownership of Anchor Brewery, it was an early instance of what became the new norm: the brewery's clerk, rather than its brewmaster, was considered second in line for ownership. Henry Thrale did not demonstrate the same business prowess as his father and the brewery foundered early under his lead, falling behind the similar porter breweries of business-savvy Benjamin Truman and Samuel Whitbread.

In the early stages of Britain's industrial revolution, the few common brewers that strategically invested in increasing the size of their production facilities saw their profit margins grow as a result. In 1699, London's 194 common brewers collectively produced 6,700 barrels of strong ale. By 1760, the top five porter brewers were producing 50,000 barrels annually, while the top twelve brewers produced 47.9 percent of London's strong ale. Never before in recorded history had the market been so concentrated. One of the results of this market concentration was that the large-scale brewers began to set prices together.

The industrial porter brewers didn't just achieve market power, they also came into political power. Ralph and Henry Thrale were the earliest line of what would come to be known as London's "beerage"—the multigenerational politician-brewer peer networks of London's major porter families. Historian Robert Walcott described Southwark, center of the hops and malt trade, as a land where "wealthy beer barons with hireling armies of draymen battled for the representation." Southwark was represented by at least one brewer in Parliament from 1695 to 1837, with only one twelve-year interruption.

The unprecedented wealth of London's porter brewers was matched by an equally unprecedented rise in tax revenue from the beer excise tax. The growing concentration of London's porter oligopoly enabled the tax bureaucracy to collect excises more efficiently. Prior to the industrial revolution, the beer excise didn't generate much revenue for two reasons: evasion and inefficient collection. It was easy for publican-brewers to lie about how much beer they produced and sold, and just as easy for tax collectors to pocket the money. Even assuming the complete honesty of tax collectors and brewer-publicans, the cost of paying excisemen to collect taxes from every small business dispersed across the countryside ate a huge chunk of potential revenues.

Beer Cartel

During a performance of Shakespeare's *Winter's Tale* with King George III in attendance, the line, "Here's to good English stingo, mild and stale," was interrupted by a cry from the audience: "At threepence a pot, Master Garrick, or confusion to the brewers." The heckler was referencing Parliament's latest tax increase, the Beer Act of 1761, which raised the duty on beer from five shillings to eight shillings per barrel. Two-penny ale, the traditional cheap strong brew sold at a fixed price of two pence, now cost 3.5 pence. British beer drinkers were not happy. Four pence had been the established maximum price of beer since 1266. Two-penny ale had always been available for two pence. The price increase felt symbolic—an attack on tradition. The stated reasoning behind the tax increase was none other than more war.

By the mid-eighteenth century, the Spanish and French crowns united under the House of Bourbon as a formidable mercantilist competitor to Britain. Tensions again came to a head in 1756 when the Seven Years' War broke out. The two world powers battled for colonies in North America, the Caribbean, India, West Africa, Sweden, Prussia, and Austria simultaneously. When conflict subsided in 1763, Britain had chased the Bourbons out of every colony. But the carnage took its toll on the war coffers, and Parliament was again faced with the question of how to pay for inevitable future wars.

Following the tax increase, outrage was widespread among London's urban working class. One anonymous editorial included a back-of-the-envelope calculation to show that homebrewing two-penny ale would cost seventeen shillings per barrel, while the new retail price was forty-two shillings. The regressive function of the tax was not lost on the writer. "I do not pretend to be an expert in brewery accounts; but this difference between the man who can afford to advance a small sum of money to purchase utensils and malt to brew his own strong beer with, and the laboring poor who buy it at the public house, must be obvious to everyone who benefits," he wrote.

A crucial development of British fortunes (and those of the brewing industry) was when the porter oligopoly and Parliament realized their closely aligned interests: porter brewers would rather pay their taxes than compete with cheap wine, and Parliament would rather generate revenue from a domestic industry than one based in their geopolitical rival. It was in the interest of Parliament to encourage the concentrated market structure—they paid the salaries of fewer excisemen to keep more diligent watch on fewer operations.

By 1761, the porter industrialists had begun to operate as a cartel. The top twelve brewers collectively agreed to raise their wholesale price per barrel for publicans from twenty-three shillings to thirty shillings. These twelve produced almost half of London's beer, giving them tremendous market power. Faced with this increase, publicans had little leeway for their own competitive pricing. They could only lower their price by half a penny, which came with the risk of cutting into their already thin profit margins.

The big twelve were compelled to stick together because the nature of profit in a cartel is different from a competitive market. In a competitive market place, producers have the incentive to keep prices lower than their competitors so that consumers will buy their goods. It is always most profitable for producers to band together and artificially inflate prices, but the problem with this is cheating: if one producer begins charging a competitive price, then he will profit while everyone else tanks. The most important component to running a profitable cartel is being able to trust the other parties. For the eighteenth-century porter brewers, this wasn't an issue—the prices were legally fixed by Parliament itself. Usually industry representatives protest against high taxes on their goods because they decrease consumption, but in this case the porter brewers were willing to pay high taxes in exchange for the assurance that Parliament was enforcing inflated fixed prices and keeping cheap wine out of the country with high tariffs.

Eventually, protests following the 1761 price increase subsided, but inflation during the Napoleonic Wars brought about a whole new slew of price increases. With each one, the Committee of Porter Brewers unanimously decided to raise the price based on supply shocks. The "traditional" retail price of porter was raised to four pence in 1799 and 4.5 pence in 1802, with temporary peaks at six pence in 1804 and 1813. Though there are reports of infighting among the big twelve breweries regarding price changes, they always stuck together, raising the price each time only through unanimous vote.

When Britain again needed revenue to fight the French and Indian War, followed by the American Revolution, they began cracking down on tax fraud and levying significant fines. The big twelve managed to avoid the steady stream of evasion charges coming through the courts. The "honesty" of the big brewers also checks out in historic hindsight. Mathias cross-referenced sales and tax records for a representative selection of period brewers, finding that evasion persisted among midsize and publican-brewers, but that major porter brewers followed the law. Their intentions, of course, weren't so selfless. At any point, Parliament could vote to repeal the wine tariff.

The looming threat of competition with cheap wine meant that tax evasion was just too big of a risk to take—and the government's potential punishment too severe.

Opposition from Unlikely Bedfellows

Nineteenth-century Great Britain was an imperialist superpower abroad and an industrial powerhouse at home. The century between the defeat of Napoleon and the beginning of World War I has been dubbed "Pax Britannica," a period of relative peace in European history brought about by Britain's apparent invincibility. Pax Britannica stands in stark contrast to Dickensian London, the dark flipside of wealth and world power. The abject poverty of the British working class, unsanitary living conditions, and harsh treatment at factories during the industrial revolution have been reference points for criticism of the emerging industrial capitalist system. The rhetoric of urban poverty is haunted by the trope of the habitual drinker and perennial debtor. In *David Copperfield*, Charles Dickens models the character of Mr. Micawber after his own father, who was sent to debtors' prison. When a young Dickens visited his father in debtors' prison, he received what has become the famous advice of poor Mr. Micawber: the difference between being happy and wretched comes down to one shilling over or under annual income every year.

Friedrich Engels wrote extensively on the condition of the English working class from a socialist perspective during the nineteenth century. In *Conditions of the Working Class in 1845*, he portrays the pub-going of textile workers as the escapist necessity of an exploited class; sobriety would follow naturally from a non-exploitative social organization. But few studies referenced how the tax structure disproportionately burdened the working class by way of alcohol consumption. After all, it's easier to sympathize with exploited workers than exploited alcoholics.

It took the unlikeliest of bedfellows to loosen the monopolistic hold of porter brewers on alcohol consumption: the brief alliance of ideological free-trade advocates and temperance activists during the early nineteenth century. Rather than petition for a wholesale ban on alcohol, early temperance activists were interested in reducing the price of beer to discourage consumption of hard liquor among the lower classes. One unintended consequence of the beer excise was the widespread illegal distillation of gin and the unfortunate health consequences that accompanied it. The same free traders opposing the Corn Laws on ideological grounds took similar issue with the high beer excise. After the defeat of Napoleon in 1815, Parliament no longer had war as the go-to excuse for such high beer taxes. Under increased pressure from anti-monopoly advocates, Parliament passed the Beer Act of 1830, which loosened alcohol license restrictions and reduced the beer and malt excises. But by then, the top twelve London porter brewers were producing 85 percent of the city's strong beer and the tied house system was well established (Figure 3.2). In practice, the Beer Act did little to address the industrial organization that permitted monopolistic pricing; in fact, it added to brewers' profit by reducing the malt excise. The protectionist tariff on French wines was not touched until the Anglo-French Treaty of 1860 and not fully repealed until 1870. By this point, the United Kingdom was adept at deriving tax revenue from the alcohol consumption of its imperialist conquests—Ireland and India provided two major sources of revenue.

The narrative of British fiscal exceptionalism strips a history long-shrouded in both gore and glory to the bare bones of boring numbers and naked self-interest. Prior to the Glorious Revolution and the rise of industry, tax revenues from beer were low because they were difficult to enforce. Dispersed pubs lied about how much beer they sold to evade taxes. Tax collectors pocketed the money. There was no way to enforce the law and prevent these happenings.

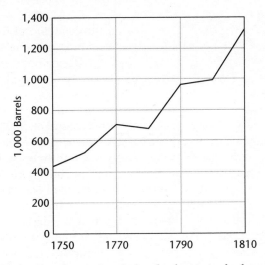

Figure 3.2 Production of strong beer in London by top twelve brewers (in 1,000 barrels), 1750–1810

Mathias, P. (1959). *The Brewing Industry in England 1700–1830*. Cambridge University Press.

This changed dramatically in the eighteenth century. The combination of scale economies in beer production, a government-tolerated beer cartel, and the credible threat of eroding brewers' revenues by lowering wine tariffs, created massive rents for eighteenth-century porter brewers and for the British Parliament and its imperial ambitions. The world has never been the same since.

4

A Revolution Every Thousand Years, Part II

How Bottom Fermentation Made Beer the Darling of the Scientific and Industrial Revolutions

Citizens of the Czech lands have always held their brewers to a high standard of craftsmanship. But in the medieval period, they had some weird ways of showing it. "Because beer is sticky, they believed that when beer is really sticky, it is really good," says Tomáš Raboch, press representative for Pilsner Urquell. He describes a medieval ritual test of quality in his hometown: brewers would brew their beer and spread it on a bench. Members of the city council wearing leather trousers would then sit down on the bench for a designated period of time. The clincher: "If they didn't stick, if they could stand up, the beer was not perceived as good." Unsurprisingly, the public test's impact on the quality of beer was just as questionable. "Because they didn't know at that time how to achieve it, they were adding weird stuff to beer," he continues. "They believe, if we add the bones of dead people, it will allow the beer to be better. But how could they do it? They didn't have any tools or any methods. They just had to try."

Raboch's anecdote illustrates just how much beer lovers everywhere owe to the past brewers of the Bohemian city of Plzen in the modern-day Czech Republic. Plzen became a city in 1295 when Bohemian King Wenceslaus II gave 260 citizens the right to brew and sell beer, protecting their sales up to nine kilometers from the city center. The right to brew beer was passed down through families. As power shifted to the Habsburgs in Austria, the official name became the German Pilsen, though the city was a diverse mix of German-speaking middle-class burghers and Czech-speaking peasants from the countryside migrating during the industrial revolution.

Pilsen was always a beer city. But in 1838, it made beer history when pub-goers famously took to the streets, stealing thirty-six barrels of beer and dumping them in front of city hall. This was a protest against the inconsistent quality of the top-fermented beers that were the norm. After that, several town brewers decided to band together and try their hand at the Bavarian practice of lagering (German for "to store") beer in a cold space for an extended fermentation period. First, they needed to dig a gigantic underground cellar where they could store their beer in cold conditions. They chose a space by the Radbuza River directly above a sandstone foundation in which they could carve tunnels for additional storage space. Next, they needed an expert in the new practice. So they called upon Josef Groll, a Bavarian brewer, to obtain some yeast from his region and develop a recipe for bottom-fermented beer to be brewed in Pilsen.

In 1842, Groll brewed the first batch of clear, light-colored, bottom-fermented beer using the lager method. Bavarian lagers were dark in color due to the malting process, but the Pilsen burghers had invested in technology that allowed Groll to toast barley without burning it. Groll also mashed the barley four times over to bring out the highest percentage of fermentable sugars. A new, slow-acting Bavarian yeast sunk to the bottom of the barrels during the lagering period, allowing the brewers to filter them out easily. These technical improvements, in combination with the famously pure Bohemian spring water and Saaz hops, yielded a uniquely golden-colored product of consistent quality. According to Raboch, the recipe worked the first time and has been unchanged since 1842.

Of course, the citizens of Pilsen were happy, but by this point the aspirations of the burgher collective had extended beyond their medieval nine-kilometer domain. Word of the clear, light-colored lager being brewed in western Bohemia spread to Prague as people anticipated the opportunity to try this new style of beer called "Pilsner." To distinguish itself from a growing number of copycats, the original burghers' brewery trademarked this recipe as "Pilsner Urquell," or "the original source of Pilsner."

The experimentation is thankfully over in Pilsen. Raboch reflects on the creation story with a certain pride: "Today, we can say that seventy percent of all beer production in the world is a copy of Pilsner Urquell." The relentless experimentation of brewers trying to pass the sticky test eventually paid off, with pilsner-style beer shaping the tastes of generations to come, and creating the second "golden age of brewing" since hops had jump-started the beer trade. The story of the pilsner-style beer (or "pils") is the link between twin engines of modern European history: the scientific and industrial revolutions. The nineteenth century is a time when the population migrated from the countryside to cities, the economy shifted from agricultural to industrial, and brewers shifted from craftsmen to scientists. The development and perfection of bottom-fermented pils beer would secure beer's status as a widely consumed beverage in the twentieth century and beyond for one simple reason: the possibility and profitability of large-scale, consistent industrial production.

From Monks to Scientists

The Technische Universität München, a research university specializing in the natural sciences in Freising, Germany, is translated to English as "TUM" or "TU Munich." The reasoning behind this marketing choice is a distinctly German approach to meaning and translation: the closest English meaning of "technische" would likely be "technical." But the German word has a more complex meaning, referencing the interplay between the technical application of knowledge and the more abstract tutelage of technique. It's a distinction that Dr. Martin Zarnkow, laboratory manager at the school's Weihenstephan Research Brewery, tellingly emphasizes. "Technology is using the technique in a practical way," he describes. It's safe to call Weihenstephan the Harvard of brewing schools, churning out brilliant food scientists responsible for today's most important innovations in brewing and beer technology. Zarnkow's reluctance to translate "technische" points at the mission statement: the goal is not to train brewers to make great beer, but rather to train scientists to answer practical questions about manipulating the natural world.

When most beer geeks see the name "Weihenstephan," they don't think white lab coats and test tubes. Rather, they recognize Bavarian blue-and-white labeled bottles as top-notch imported beers: the fruity Vitus wheat beer nicknamed "lady-killer" among staffers for its 7.7 percent alcohol content, the sweet yet complex doppelbock Korbinian, and the impeccably crisp Kristallweiss have all worked their way on to the favorites lists of beer enthusiasts around the world. But the brewery's origins lie neither in scientific research facility nor industrial factory: the Weihenstephan Benedictine monastery obtained the right to brew and sell beer in 1040. The monks that founded Weihenstephan surely did not anticipate the future of beer, as best evidenced today by their chosen site on top of a huge hill. "There's no room to expand!" jokes Zarnkow.

At Weihenstephan, the decline of brewing-as-craft can be traced to 1803, when the monastery was secularized as a result of negotiations with Napoleon's occupying armies. At that point, monasteries were important components of the agricultural sector, spreading knowledge on farming and harvesting practices. Forced secularization served to alter the purpose of monastic breweries as centers of knowledge. These would serve the impending scientific revolution, when Munich became the center of knowledge on the science of beer. Zarnkow can't help but look back on Weihenstephan's brewing history with wistfulness. "For a thousand years, we have a good feeling for this product, but now we have an understanding: what really happens."

The scientific revolution utilized deductive reasoning and controlled experimentation as a means of establishing certain principles about the natural world. It wasn't long before scientists became interested in how and why alcohol happened. Antoni Van Leeuwenhoek, George Ernst Stahl, and Hermann Boerhaave contributed theories on how yeast facilitated the fermentation of beer. Their studies were continued by Antoine Laurent Lavoisier, who outlined for the first time what was happening at a molecular level: sugar molecules are broken down into alcohol and carbon dioxide, thus explaining how sweet barley mash becomes the beverage, both carbonated and alcoholic, we all love. By 1818, scientists had discovered that the beer fermentation process could be split up into a first phase, in which sugars were transformed into alcohol and carbon dioxide, and a second phase, in which the beer ripened and the remaining impurities were removed.

"Pasteurization" is associated with milk today, but Louis Pasteur's interest in fermentation and preservation actually began with alcohol. During the 1850s, Pasteur conducted a series of experiments on wines, which led him to the theory that yeast are living cells responsible for the fermentation process. The pasteurization method he is famous for involves heating fermented products to a certain temperature and cooling immediately, thus killing bacteria and allowing products to be preserved.

Other important work had also been done on yeast to produce new beers by manipulating the yeast's environment. Traditional Bavarian brewing practices involved lagering beer by storing it in cold environments (usually caves in the hilly mountainside). But all lagered beer is not necessarily bottom fermented: "Bottom fermentation" refers to beer brewed with slow-acting yeast that grows heavier over the course of the fermentation process, falling to the bottom of the storage barrel so that brewers can easily filter the beer. Spaten brewer Gabriel Sedlmayr owned one of the many Munich *brauhauses* experimenting with different strains of yeast to find slow-acting ones conducive to the lagering process. In the 1830s, he decided to take his research on the road. Sedlmayr and Austrian brewer Anton Dreher famously traveled to an already industrialized ale- and porter-drinking England, taking notes and swiping yeast cultures from brewers they visited. The lessons they learned in England inspired their experiments, and Dreher is credited with brewing the first light-colored lager in 1840 by coke-malting barley, the technique used for British pale ale.

Danish scientist Emil Christian Hansen, and cousin of Dreher, took knowledge about yeast a step further. At the newly founded Carlsberg Laboratories in Copenhagen, Hansen succeeded in isolating yeast for the first time. Other breweries could now also produce lager beer with the preferred bottom-fermenting yeast.

Just one more scientific innovation was all the beer world needed to really take lager production to the next level: in 1876, Carl von Linde, a lecturer at TU Munich, pioneered refrigeration technology on commission from Munich brewery Paulaner, producing self-cooling vats to lager beer. This one invention cut out the need for caves, for underground cellars, for chipping giant ice blocks from lakes: all became costs and physical burdens of brewing's past.

Collectively, these insights were necessary preconditions for the industrialization of brewing. Prior to the scientific and industrial revolutions, brewing had been a craft. Brewers estimated measurements, time, and technique. But with the profitability of large-scale brewing on the horizon, these brewer-scientists saw the incentive to produce a highly standardized product.

Another Revolution is Brewing

The industrial revolution also offered a number of technological aids to the increasingly concentrated brewing industry. The refined Watt's steam engine not only made it possible to use more complicated, steam-operated machinery during the brewing process, but also reduced transportation costs. With trains and steamboats, it became much cheaper to export beer throughout Europe and to the US, Canada, and even Australia. Pilsner Urquell was one of the earliest to take advantage of these new technologies. Raboch describes how a friend of the brewer, Mr. Pinkas, requested one barrel of the new Pilsner shortly after the first batch was brewed. He then took it to Prague to share. The results were so successful he quit his job to start a new restaurant, the now-historic U Pinkasu. His strategic advantage was being the first in the city with a connection to the new, golden pils beer.

Pils-style beer also became popular in America during this period, primarily as a result of German immigrants brewing their native style of beer in new American cities. Most famously, in 1865, Bavarian immigrant Ebenhard Anheuser founded the Bavarian Brewing Company—the predecessor to Anheuser Busch—in St. Louis, where he began brewing Budweiser beer. Of course, his signature style was named after the Bohemian city of Budweis, which had a robust export market to rival Pilsner. The name duplication would come to a head many decades later (see Chapter 10). But at this point, consolidation and competition was not quite global, though it was certainly on its way.

Another technological advance was also critical: glass bottles were known for their superiority over casks for preserving beer on long journeys, but in the seventeenth century glass beer bottles were handblown and therefore expensive. The invention of the chilled iron mold meant that, by the 1890s, glass bottles could be produced relatively cheaply and in mass quantities. Equally important was the invention of new methods to close beer bottles. Glass beer bottles were initially closed with a cork held in place with wire. In 1882, Henry Barrett invented the screw stopper, while twenty years later, William patented the crown cork, at last enabling automated bottling machines to be developed. In the first half of the twentieth century, metal beer cans were invented and introduced in the US, where they soon became popular, though their widespread use in Europe did not materialize until much later.

Brewers were on the crest of the industrialization wave, and they were being rewarded handsomely in Munich and Plzen. The innovations of the nineteenth century benefited the Pilsner Urquell and the Spaten breweries—large enough to have the capital to invest in upgrades—more than the small breweries scattered across the Bavarian and Bohemian countryside. In Munich, the market was dominated by seven famous *brauhauses* that still today sponsor tents at the city's annual Oktoberfest. These breweries honed their recipes for bottom-fermented pils-style beer, enabling them to offer a relatively inexpensive, standardized product that quickly became popular among the urbanizing populations.

In this way the industrial revolution paved the way for a massive consolidation in the global beer industries in the first part of the twentieth century. Between 1900 and 1940 the number of breweries declined rapidly and the size of breweries grew, as many small breweries closed or merged into larger ones. The number of breweries fell by more than 60 percent in the US (from 1,816 to 684), in Belgium (from 3,223 to 1,120),

Table 4.1 Number of breweries and average brewery size, 1900–1980

	Number of breweries		
	Belgium	UK	US
1900	3,223	6,447	1,816
1920	2,013	2,914	Prohibition
1940	1,120	840	684
1960	414	358	229
1980	123	142	101
	Average brewery size (million liters)		
	Belgium	UK	US
1900	0.4	0.9	2.5
1920	0.5	1.9	Prohibition
1940	0.9	4.9	9.4
1960	2.4	11.6	48.4
1980	11.6	48.1	219.1

Swinnen, J. (2011). *The Economics of Beer*. Oxford University Press.

and most dramatically in the UK, with a decline of almost 90 percent (from more than 6,000 to just 840 breweries) (Table 4.1). The average size of the breweries became four to five times larger over this time.

Turbulence in Twentieth-Century Beer Markets

The late nineteenth century was characterized by strong and continuous growth in beer production. Production increased sharply the last quarter of the century and up until the eve of World War I—a change enabled by a strong decline in global grain prices and the development of technologies permitting far more efficient industrial production. By the early twentieth century, the beer markets of Germany, the UK, and the US were the largest in the world and of similar size: between five and seven billion liters each (Figure 4.1).

However, the twentieth century would bring trials and tribulations to the beer barons. While the scientific and industrial revolutions were transforming brewing and causing the closure of many small breweries, brewing was not the only industry experimenting with the ways in which food could be manipulated and preserved. Apart from the competition from the New World with tea and coffee, carbonated beverages were also establishing themselves as formidable competitors. In 1767, after experiments in his Leeds brewery, the Englishman Joseph Priestly had invented artificially carbonated water. Hungarian scientist Ánios Jedlik was the first to produce a consumable soda water. Then in 1886, the American John S. Pemberton expanded on Jedlik's invention with some now famous caramel coloring and the notorious addition of a now-illegal South American stimulant to the mix and—Coca Cola was born. In the following decades, consumption of Coca Cola and copycat sodas grew rapidly. One of the primary advantages of beer had previously been its ability to be preserved. But all these new substances were changing the game: beer now had to be a drink people wanted to drink.

However, it was not Coca Cola, but rather enemy bombs that would forever change the brewing industry as Europe knew it. In 1915, what would come to be known as World War I swept the European continent, destroying many things, breweries included.

In Europe, beer production fell by 70 percent during World War I. The brewing industry faced particular losses in occupied nations, including Belgium and France. The mobilization scattered many workers in the brewing industry, which led to a shortage of employees in the breweries. Moreover, metal materials (such as copper), vehicles, and draft animals were claimed by the occupying forces. As a consequence, a lot of breweries had to close down their businesses. German occupation did introduce these areas to pils-style beer for the first time—an introduction that would pave the way for shakeout and consolidation following the war. The beer industry also suffered in Germany as other industries (especially war industries) were given priority in the allocation of resources. Moreover, grains were scarce and expensive, with food and feed shortages throughout Europe.

After the war, the scarcity of raw materials persisted for several years. Breweries that wanted to start up again or increase production had to manage with what they could find. All kinds of grains, peas, beets, and beans were used to produce beer. Yet beer production recovered strongly in some postwar European countries. For example, in France beer production increased fourfold between 1918 and the late 1930s. Recovery was slower in Germany and the UK (Figure 4.1).

But production declined again dramatically in the 1940s. During World War II, food was rationed and raw materials for the European breweries were again scarce and expensive. As during earlier shortages, breweries tried to cope by using substitutes for their normal brewing ingredients. Examples of substitutes include several types of malt that had been flavored or aromatized, beets (which are rich in sugar content), and several flavoring substances, such as coriander seed, chamomile blossom, and the skins of lemons and oranges. As the war continued,

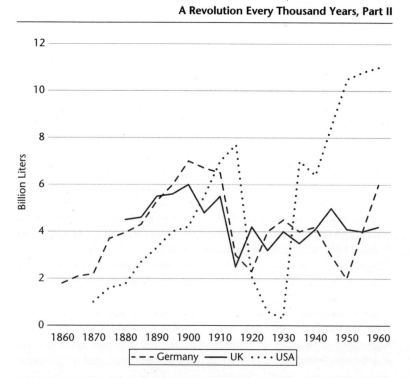

Figure 4.1 Beer production in Germany, UK, and USA, 1860–1960 (billion liters)
Mitchell, B. (1998). *International Historical Statistics: Europe 1750–1993*. Springer.

metal and cork—necessary to close the beer bottles—became scarce as well. Cork was increasingly substituted by cardboard with an added layer of paper, by recycling used crown caps, or by using swing-top bottles that had rubber rings made of used and rejected car or plane tires to close the bottle.

The impact of the two world wars was smaller in the US. During World War I, American beer production decreased approximately 10 percent. Wartime grain rationing induced American brewers to brew beer with a lower alcohol content—only 2.75 percent on average.

A much more radical decline in beer production was caused by government regulation. In 1919, temperance activists succeeded in securing the nationwide prohibition of alcohol from 1919 to 1933. During this period, the sale, manufacture, and transportation of alcohol of more than 0.5 percent was banned. As a result, the US had no legal beer production for fourteen years. There was some illegal beer production during this period, but it was minimal, with moonshiners opting to direct their illegal efforts toward more efficient means of intoxication. Total beer output collapsed and many American breweries closed down (Figure 4.1). Some sold their plants and equipment as soon as possible at substantial losses. Others, who expected the prohibition to be temporary, tried to use their equipment to produce related products, including beer containing less than 0.5 percent alcohol. Sure enough, the prohibition was repealed in 1933, and the manufacture and sale of alcoholic beverages—including beer—was once again legal.

But American woes were far from over. The decade following prohibition, American brewers were faced with the Dust Bowl and the Great Depression. Grain prices skyrocketed due to the drought in the American South, causing massive migration of "Oakies" to the West to seek better times. Though some scholars suggest the Dust Bowl reduced production in the 1930s, official numbers suggest that beer production increased to pre-prohibition levels. In fact, the Dust Bowl affected the nature of the brewing process rather than the amount of beer produced. As during World War I, US breweries reacted to high grain prices by switching ingredients. Instead of barley, cheaper grains such as corn and rice were used as adjuncts to brew lager beer. And thus the famously scorned "light lager" style popularized by Budweiser, Miller, and Coors—what one could call the holy trinity of Super Bowl brands and the three largest to this day—was born.

While World War II would once again curb production and consumption in the beer-drinking world, a new golden age of brewing took off when peace finally came to Europe and the world again. Czech- and German-style pilsner beer, along with its bastard New World cousin the light lager, became the darlings of the world's beer markets. This style of beer could be produced efficiently, on a large scale, automatically bottled and canned, then transported long distances. Imbibers preferred it to the inconsistent top-fermented ales being brewed by local publican-brewers. The growing popularity of these beers stimulated a further consolidation of the beer industry in the postwar period. The arrival of a new technology would again play a dramatic role in the closure of many local and regional breweries from the 1950s onwards.

5

How TV Killed the Local Brewery

The Brooklyn Dodgers earned their team name from borough residents' famous prowess dodging trolley cars. In 1947, the team made history by signing Jackie Robinson, the first African American player to be recruited by a major-league baseball team. After a year of racist death threats and national controversy, the Dodgers emerged victorious with their third World Series pennant. But the 1947 season was significant for another reason that would come to change the future of baseball dramatically: broadcast television was now possible in New York, with more cities pending Federal Communications Commission (FCC) approval every day. Commercial producer James C. Beach smelled an opportunity for his client Schaefer Brewery. In an editorial for *Television Magazine* published in 1947, he wrote: "Customers were lined up at bars all over New York watching telecasts of Brooklyn Dodger baseball games from Ebbets Field. Now—to get those fans to order Schaefer Beer." His idea employed techniques unique to filming with camera: "We make the television camera the 'I' character—the guy standing at the bar. Then we have the camera 'drink' a foaming glass of Schaefer." The goal: "To make his [the viewer's] salivary glands spring a leak, and let him carry on from there."

Breweries were among the first American industries to recognize the potential of television advertising to expand their business. "They just got it—that this could really change the market," says Lisa George. George didn't set out to study beer. As an economist at CUNY Hunter, George specializes in media markets. Specifically, she studies how the introduction of new media technologies influence product markets. And once she set her sights on broadcast television, it wasn't long before she identified its co-evolution with the brewing industry. "The more I learned about it, the more I realized: these industries grew up together," she says. "Television made a huge difference in what the brewing industry looks like."

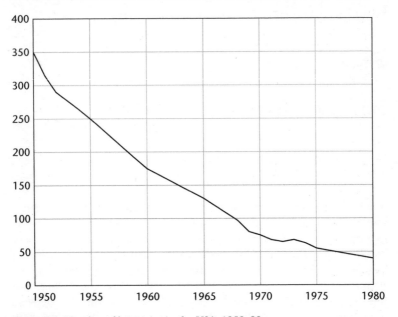

Figure 5.1 Number of breweries in the USA, 1950–80

Tremblay, V. and Tremblay, C. (2005). *The US Brewing Industry: Data and Economic Analysis.* MIT Press.

The rapid and spectacular consolidation of the American beer industry in the postwar period had held the intrigue of industrial organization economists for some time. From 1950 to 2000, the US beer market changed dramatically: the number of mass-producing brewers in the US fell from over 350 to only twenty-four, and the market share of the four largest brewers rose from 20 to 90 percent (Figure 5.1). By the 1990s, the era of regional breweries was all but a memory, as sports fans divided along the branded lines of Anheuser Busch, Miller, and Coors. In 2000, at 54 percent domestic market share, the leading brewery, Anheuser Busch, brewed a higher percentage of America's beer than the leading eight German breweries combined brewed for their own domestic market.

Since this dramatic change, economists have generally fallen into two camps on why the American brewing industry consolidated so quickly. Some credit the introduction of packaging and assembly-line technologies that permitted the more efficient production and price competition of larger firms. Others cite strategic advertising expenditures by the largest brewers. George points out the underlying connection between the two explanations, offering a more sophisticated cause and effect: broadcast television.

From Public Houses to Levittown

There is a trope of postwar America: identical ticky-tacky boxes with picket fences, the nuclear family, TV dinners, and the five o'clock network news. With Europe destroyed by World War II, America established itself as a beacon of capitalist hard work and individual liberty in the cultural branch of the Cold War, heading off the Soviet Union's socialist doctrine. The face of America became the "Levittown": sprawling suburbs where assembly-line-built houses filled small lots and became affordable to any family with a blue collar income. George notes how demographic trends in America during the postwar period distinguished American social life from that of traditional Europe. "Television diffused here more quickly. The US was suburbanizing at the same time, so people actually got TVs in their homes really quickly in the US," describes George. "People are all of a sudden spending more time at home, moving out of cities, a lot of people at the same time having babies, watching TV at home, so they were exposed to more advertising."

This became known among scholars as the Fordist age, where division of labor was applied to more than just cars. The postwar iteration of the American Dream was born. For every family, a house, a car, and a television set as the centerpiece in the living room. All produced on an assembly line, identical to the neighbor's, but within reach for the gainfully employed. With efficient production came consolidation, and national brands emerged. Postwar America saw the rise of the now-iconic McDonald's, Coca Cola, and of course Budweiser.

It's no exaggeration to say that a unified American culture was mediated through the introduction of widespread access to television programming. Shows like *Leave it to Beaver* and *I Love Lucy* became reference points for millions of families, shaping the childhood impressions of the baby boomer generation against which they would later revolt during the late 1960s. "People love to dis television, but it had an impact on American culture," describes George. "The next day at work you would talk about what you saw on TV about Lucille Ball, it was something that connected people not just when they got home."

Prominent cultural historians have argued that broadcast TV played a central role in facilitating the civil rights movement when footage of police brutalizing peaceful protestors shocked members of the nation who had never traveled south of the Mason–Dixon line. But George is right that television certainly had its haters. The one with the longest sentences was certainly German Jew Theodor Adorno. Exiled from Nazi Germany and witness to the role of mass media in fascism, he wrote extensively on how the cultural industry in postwar America led consumers tacitly to conform to the homogeneous norms espoused by Fordist manufacturing and capitalist consumerism. Art had died; the age of kitsch was upon us.

George is of the opinion that cultural criticism can learn a lot from the field of industrial organization: "What is lacking is an understanding of where markets come from," she notes. "You can talk about the good and the bad, but all of what drives this are the fundamentals of technology and how technology interacts with the market." Likewise, George's peers in the field of industrial organization have had more success analyzing numbers than deconstructing commercial jingles—preferring to think of Sunday styles as "unobservable heterogeneity." As an economist with a focus on the material consequences of culture, George decided to conduct a study that would give both fields some food for thought.

The Great American Pastime

While Schafer capitalized on Dodgers' victories in Brooklyn, Detroit-based Goebel Brewing Company offered their services to the Detroit Tigers, bringing baseball games to the masses. They began sponsoring the broadcast of Tuesday and Thursday games in 1947 in exchange for planned showings of several short commercials between innings. They also pioneered what would become a common approach: corporate scorecards. Goebel constructed a wooden structure with their name and slogan to offer viewers inning roundups: hits, runs, and errors, followed by live updates on scores of other American league games happening simultaneously. A 1947 article in *Television Magazine* lauded this innovative approach, offering valuable market research: "Two separate surveys have shown that viewers do not regard any of these between inning activities as commercial—this, in spite of the fact that the word Goebel appears twice on cards each time and the bottle and glass are always in full view."

Goebel's tactics quickly spread in popularity. The Boston brewery Narragansett announced that it would sponsor telecasts of Red Sox games. St. Louis Cardinals fans that crowded around whatever TV was available became familiar with Hyde Park Brewery's "Albert the Stick Man." In Chicago, breweries Keely, Peter Fox, and Canadian Ace competed for viewers' attention on television. Early-comers of the 1940s also included National Bohemian Beer in Baltimore and Sunshine Beer in Reading, Pennsylvania.

Television was a natural and obvious advertising platform for publicity thanks to its long-standing association with watching sports. Prior to television, breweries sponsored minor-league baseball games, advertising on jerseys and selling beer at concession stands as the primary source of getting the word out about their product. The introduction of television presented the opportunity for Americans to watch baseball games rather than just listening to them on the radio. Minor leagues faded to irrelevance as access to the pros became more widespread than ever before. As the sports-watching habits of Americans changed, the new potential for TV advertising benefited some breweries while disadvantaging others.

"National brands could advertise, potentially get their product to people in a whole TV market," explains George, but "the smaller guys, they'd have to pay to advertise to the whole TV market, but they couldn't really serve them—they'd have to expand." As George explains, the issue at hand was a new distinction in the product market and the media market. In a competitive advertising market, equilibrium prices are determined per viewer. But if a firm can only serve a fraction of the viewing population, the effective price per customer is much higher. In markets where all firms operate on the same local scale, advertising prices might increase but not advantage particular firms. However, in markets where some firms can service larger geographies than others, advertising prices per customer rise for small firms compared to large firms.

Large producers took full advantage of this change in relative costs, increasing advertising expenditure dramatically during the television expansion period. Advertising expenditure per barrel roughly doubled from 1950 to 1960, from about $100 to $200 per barrel. Throughout this process, television lowered the cost of advertising for large regional and national brewers relative to their local counterparts. As long as some viewers switched from local media (such as newspapers) to television and television advertising, the medium itself was likely to have increased economies of scale in advertising and hasten the spread of national— relative to local—products.

Determining Cause and Effect

In the decade from 1950 to 1960, ownership of televisions grew from under 10 percent to almost 90 percent. The introduction of television broadcasting to American life and the growth of television advertising expenditures went hand in hand with the postwar consolidation of the brewing industry. But does this mean that one caused the other?

The difficult thing about history is unraveling the causes and correlations of historic threads. Historians may argue about the interplay between certain movements, for example the role of television in facilitating the civil rights movement using archival data. But making a scientific case for cause-and-effect relationship between these two phenomena is trickier. It's the basic issue that correlation is not causation. Just because civil rights and television happened at the same time and were implicated in the same conversations doesn't mean TV caused the civil rights movement. Historic changes tend to grow slowly, building on, feeding off of, and reacting to each other in the process.

Lisa George explains the challenge of determining cause and effect: "When you do a statistical type of economic study, relating historical data to one another, you're never really sure: is it causing it, or is it just related?" George searched for other ways to find a cause-and-effect relationship between the spread of network television and the consolidation of the brewing industry. But, as any economist or statistician will tell you, this is difficult. To conduct an econometric analysis of the past, she needed to figure out a way to isolate the variables of television and consolidation of the brewing industry. "What you really need is for the world to conduct an experiment for you. What you look for is something that happens in the world that lets you say: this happened for totally different reasons than the one I want to study, so let me go and look at the consequences," she explains. "If I had just linked the spread of TV with the decline of local beers, people would have said 'Interesting, but it's just technology.' So one way you can pin down the causality is because of these shocks."

George found one such shock in the spread of television advertising. The FCC issued the first commercial broadcast licenses on July 1, 1941. Television had only penetrated New York, Philadelphia, Chicago, and Schenectady before America found itself embroiled in World War II and expansion was curtailed. Living up to its postwar reputation, the true spread of television came at the end of World War II. In the first three years following the war, forty-two cities hosted seventy-one broadcasting stations. But in September of 1948, the FCC froze station licensing briefly to study signal interference, color standards, and spectrum allocation. What was supposed to be a temporary freeze was extended when infighting in the FCC met with the outbreak of the Korean War. No new licenses were issued until 1952. After the freeze ended, television spread rapidly, with 440 VHF stations reaching about 95 percent of the US population by 1960.

George recognized this idiosyncratic nature of expansion as a unique opportunity to apply the tools of econometrics to history. The wartime construction ban and the FCC freeze created three distinct sets of markets: markets with stations licensed before Pearl Harbor, which were able to resume commercial broadcasts immediately after the war; markets with stations licensed after the war but before the freeze; and markets with stations licensed after the freeze. This natural historic experiment is exactly what George needed to study the cause-and-effect relationship between television and the consolidation of the brewing industry.

Her analysis showed that greater television penetration is indeed associated with a decline in local beer production. The introduction of television advertising appears to have influenced tastes in the long term. After seeing one commercial, drinkers might not automatically switch to a national brand from a local one. But a few years after the introduction of TV into a market, a pattern of decline in the production levels of local breweries emerges. George estimates that increasing television access from 0 to 100 percent in a market appears to reduce local production by almost 30 percent. Since locally produced beers were generally consumed locally, the results suggest that television played a crucial role in the decline of local production. When considered along with historical evidence that national brewers were expanding output, these results further support the hypothesis that television hastened the decline of local beer.

The US: Leader in Television and Macrobrewing

The postwar consolidation of the brewing industry in the United States was rapid and spectacular. An interesting comparison arises when we look at how the concentration of the US beer market compares to that of other countries. In 1958, the top four US firms controlled 24 percent of US market share, while the top four German firms controlled 12 percent of the market share in Germany. By 2000, the top four US firms controlled 94 percent of the market share, while the top four German firms controlled 29 percent of the market share. In short, the US beer market grew significantly more concentrated and at a much faster pace than beer markets in other countries such as Germany.

Can television advertising explain the slower consolidation in European beer markets? Economist William James Adams of the University of Michigan thinks it did play a role in comparison to the US. Before 1990, European brewers were very unlikely to advertise on television for a number of reasons, the most important one being that there was very little commercial TV. Almost all TV channels were state-owned, with very little or no commercial advertising. However, in the late 1980s the situation changed. Commercial TV channels sprang up all over Europe and TV advertising spread rapidly. And the brewers' advertising dollars followed. In 1990, less than one-third of German brewers' advertising budgets were spent on television. By 1999, that number had doubled to two-thirds of all advertising. Like in America, this change was disproportionally comprised of large, national brewers. In 2000, the top ten German brewers spent 84 percent of their advertising budgets on television commercials.

While consolidation in both Europe and the US had started in the early twentieth century with the industrial revolution, the extreme concentration with the demise of many local and regional brewers came earlier in the United States, coinciding with national advertising strategies on commercial TV. In Europe, where public TV dominated in the 1960s through much of the 1980s, this process was delayed until commercial TV and beer advertising spread rapidly from the late 1980s onwards.

6

Beer Monopoly

How the Belgian Beer Barons Dethroned the King

If Julie MacIntosh can deliver anything with finesse, it's an anecdote that encapsulates a big personality in a few small details. The personality: August Busch III, former CEO of the iconic American firm Anheuser Busch. MacIntosh relates a story of an employee with the fearsome task of please-don't-shoot-me messenger: delivering news to the CEO that a Super Bowl commercial of him discussing the history and quality standards of Budweiser beer was not testing as well with market research groups as one of a lizard and ferret singing a duet. A few Americans remembering the commercial giggle, but the anecdote doesn't quite resonate with Belgian family business owners comprising most of the audience.

MacIntosh is the keynote speaker at a conference on family firms in Brussels, co-headlining with Wolfgang Riepl, reporter for the Flemish industry paper *Trends*. The pairing is inspired. MacIntosh published a book on the Busch family, *Dethroning the King*, while Riepl wrote *The Belgian Beer Barons*, a book on the families behind Interbrew, the Belgian part of AB InBev, the multinational brewer of unprecedented size. In 2008, InBev shocked the world by announcing it was planning a hostile takeover of iconic American brewery Anheuser Busch. But where Super Bowl jokes go over Belgian heads, MacIntosh's anecdotes describing the volatile father–son relationship between August Busch III and August Busch IV that brought the biggest brewing company in the world to its knees send a tangible quiver of fear running through the audience of family business owners. She has no shortage of material. *Dethroning the King* is a story of intrigue and drama, beer models, coke binges, and authoritarian personalities. Following the forced retirement of Busch III, full-out screaming matches between father and son clouded every boardroom meeting. Busch III wasn't ready to rescind control, and Busch IV didn't have the necessary board backing to aggressively seize the reins. Americans can look forward to its production on the silver screen.

Riepl's spiel is decidedly less dramatic. As he narrates in *The Belgian Beer Barons*, Interbrew also started as a family business. In 1987, Belgium's competing macrobreweries Jupiler and Stella Artois merged to form Interbrew after years of secret collaboration and price fixing. They had previously both been operating as family businesses, but ones that pursued a decidedly different management style from that of the Busch's. The families retained controlling shares of the new firm but stepped back from any and all roles in its management, opting instead to guide the direction of the company from a distance and let a CEO make strategic decisions. In the following two decades, Interbrew went on a mergers and acquisitions spree as seldom seen before.

Following every acquisition, the families appointed a new CEO. The strategy paid off. In 1987, the year of the merger as Interbrew, Anheuser Busch was twenty times the size of Interbrew. Two decades later, Jupiler-Stella had grown through acquisitions and one merger into InBev, a global beer multinational able to purchase a controlling share in the King of Beers. It's a story of the mouse eating the elephant.

What's fascinating is that it appears the dominant firm in the world's biggest beer market did not see this acquisition coming. There was something rotten in the state of Anheuser Busch, to be sure, but the Hamlet-esque story belied what had been going on for some time. At the end of the day, the hostile takeover of Anheuser Busch is not a story of Budweiser's fall from grace—it's a story of globalization. Budweiser didn't lose its clout as the King of Beers in America, and it still hasn't. The problem was that amid all the father–son fighting, the firm was so focused on its domestic power-play for control of the world's largest beer market (America) that it neglected to notice that the game had fundamentally changed: they were no longer competing on a national playing field but on a global one.

Why Anheuser Busch Didn't See it Coming

Budweiser didn't inherit its crown as the King of Beers. Anheuser Busch's rise to fame was earned the old-fashioned way, by building new facilities to increase production and distribution efficiency, prioritizing sharp advertising, and producing consistent quality. They were a central player in the consolidation of the American brewing industry.

The postwar shakeout saw local brands exit the market en masse, while big regional breweries grew to national giants. By the 1970s, Budweiser, Miller, and Coors had safely claimed their spots as the holy trinity of American brand dominance. For the most part, this consolidation process didn't happen through mergers and acquisitions but through the growth of a few regional brands into dominant national brands. One of the primary reasons for this was the advertising economies of scale afforded by broadcast television, as elucidated in Chapter 5. It made more sense for breweries to expand their brands than to buy up rights to pre-existing local ones. By the 1980s, the Big Three easily claimed more than 90 percent of the world's largest beer market. This was the beer market that August Busch III knew. Under his tight hold on Anheuser Busch, Budweiser had beat perennial number two Miller and cornered the American beer market.

America led the world both in market size and concentration. The industrial revolution, the introduction of new technologies, TV advertising, and the rise of cheap and widespread canned lager had brought about a shakeout in all traditional beer-drinking nations (further described in Chapter 11). But nowhere else did a beer market consolidate so rapidly. Both the consolidation and the size of the American beer market meant that the biggest American firms were also the biggest firms in the world. As the 1990s approached, Anheuser Busch maintained position number one, while Miller and Coors followed behind. Even long-straggling Pabst and Stroh were of formidable size on the global playing field.

Busch III had ridden the wave of consolidation in the world's largest beer market for a long time. The domestic beer market afforded the brewery continued growth, and as such, the firm held an exceptional place among American firms. They were treated like royalty in the St. Louis area, where high-level careers brought privileges and respect. The legacy of "Budweiser" was deeply engrained in the mythology of American capitalism. The entire Busch family was involved with the company in some capacity, leading many business partners to assume that they had controlling share of the company. But most of the Busch family had gone into the cushier leg of the beer industry as distributors.

Such aggressive domestic growth also blinded execs to some fundamental changes in beer markets that took root during the 1980s. Postwar consolidation had been fueled in no small part by the popularity of light lagers among the baby boomer generation. Bud Light and Miller Lite were all about volume: cheap to make, cheap to buy, and profitable to boot. Both firms were able to respond to the bump in popularity of high-end super-premiums in the early 1980s by releasing Michelob and

Löwenbräu. But by the late 1980s, the star of the American macrobrewery was beginning to fall. Drinkers were demanding greater variety and pricier, higher-end beers. The market again began to fragment. The market share for imported beers—actually shipped over, not license-brewed in the US, as the Millerbräu fiasco forebode (see Chapter 13)—exploded from the 1990s onwards. On its heels was the less aggressive but increasingly significant growth of the craft sector. By the 1990s, in the American market for cheap domestic lagers there just wasn't anywhere for the Budweiser brand to go.

The Prescience of Interbrew

When we meet business journalist Wolfgang Riepl, he's impeccably dressed in a pinstripe suit and carrying a journalist notebook, even though we're the ones asking the questions. He's a man of few words but an encyclopedic knowledge of global trends in the beer market. The rise of Interbrew is documented in his book, *The Belgian Beer Barons*, which offers illuminating context on the beer multinational's creation and growth.

Scrutiny has been paid to AB InBev in the wake of the hostile takeover. A lead story exposé in *Bloomberg Business Week* told all regarding the multinational's cost-cutting practices. It was dutifully titled "The Plot to Destroy America's Beer." The focus was on the ruthless CEO Carlos Brito—darling of shareholders and scourge of employees of every rank who had grown used to the fat around the edges. Brito has earned AB InBev's nickname, the Walmart of beers. But coverage of the firm's origin story is scant. From whence did this cost-cutting monster come?

On paper, Interbrew was established in 1987. Unofficially, it dates back to the 1970s. Like in America, the introduction of lager to the Belgian beer market had prompted a shakeout of traditional breweries across its small landscape. By the mid-twentieth century, two competing brands fought for market dominance: Stella Artois and Jupiler. The Leuven-based Artois Brewery had superior facilities and an early lead, but domestic drinkers preferred Jupiler, brewed by the Piedboeuf Brewery in the south. Unbeknownst to the employees of both companies, Artois Brewery and Piedboeuf had been tacitly colluding to maximize profit since the early 1970s. Employees at Artois had no idea they were actually brewing Jupiler. In 1987, the two made their partnership official and their strategy explicit: market Jupiler to Belgians, while positioning Stella Artois as a premium export brand—Belgium's answer to the long-popular Heineken, brewed in nearby Amsterdam. But Interbrew did more than that. With craft brewers gaining market share in its home market in the late 1980s, it realized early on that it needed to complement its core lager beers with specialty beers.

Over the next two years, Interbrew acquired traditional lambic- and kriek-brewing Belle-Vue, white-beer-producing Brouwerij de Kluis in the small village of Hoegaarden, and Abbaye Notre-Dame de Leffe, a monastery producing traditional abbey-style ales (see Chapter 14 for more on Belgium's local beer styles). With these acquisitions, Interbrew was ready to supplement Stella's export strategy with three of Belgium's traditional styles. And this was just the beginning for Interbrew.

There's no one better than Riepl to reveal the deceptive simplicity of Interbrew's strategy. Every four or five years, Interbrew acquired a foreign brewery with the highest market share in a nation with a duopoly or triopoly. In 1991, they bought Hungarian Borsodi Sogyor; in 1995, Canadian Labatt; in 2000, British Bass and Boddingtons; in 2002, German Beck's and Spaten, and then in 2003, Löwenbräu. However, the biggest buys were yet to come. In 2004, they merged with Brazilian AmBev to form InBev; 2008 was, of course, Anheuser Busch; in 2012, Mexican Grupo Modelo; in 2013, Korean Oriental Brewery; and most recently, in 2016, SABMiller.

After every acquisition, Interbrew brought in a new CEO to skim the fat. No sentimentality was to be found: every time the story was the same. Costs were cut, staff laid off, and operating procedures streamlined for efficiency. Every time, conflicts arose. The acquisition of Labatt proved especially profitable. The reason? In Canada, alcohol is subject to legally mandated minimum prices far above the market price. It also had an effectively duopolistic structure, with Molson and Labatt dominating the domestic market. This, in conjunction with above-market prices, meant that Labatt could reap big profits. Employees at the firm had become accustomed to a luxurious lifestyle, corporate jets, and generous bonuses. Interbrew saw more than easy profits—they saw the possibility for even larger profits. With lower costs and the same prices, Interbrew was now enjoying a reliable stream of capital to continue the acquisition spree.

Still, the biggest prizes were yet to come. By 2004, tiny Belgian Interbrew had launched itself to become the world's third biggest beer firm, trailing Anheuser Busch and SABMiller, both brands bolstered by the sheer size of the American brewing industry. It was time for another game-changing maneuver: a merger with AmBev, then number five in the Brazilian market and riding the wave of ever-growing beer demand in Latin America. AmBev had an origin story similar to

Interbrew's: longtime competitors Antarctica and Brahma had merged to completely dominate Brazil's beer market share, and with an even stronger focus on cost-cutting.

The Interbrew–AmBev merger propelled newly formed InBev to the top, surpassing Anheuser Busch and Miller, both still reliant on the size of the American beer market. This was a beer multinational like nothing anyone had ever seen, with fingers in all of the fastest-growing beer markets. Soon after the merger, Stanford MBA Carlos Brito took hold of the reins, and the cost-cutting and fat-trimming became more heavy-handed than ever. Paradoxically, one of the first targets of his cost-cutting was the Leuven headquarters of InBev and the Stella Artois Brewery.

Just four short years later, like clockwork, InBev announced its intention to acquire Anheuser Busch, taking its mergers and acquisitions spree to the next level. The American beer industry was shocked. Many did not know who or what InBev was, and many assumed that the long-reigning Busch family together had a controlling share of the firm. But the financial crisis was full-fledged, InBev had the money, and the Busch family conflict had kept the company stagnating for three years. During this process, it was revealed that together they controlled less than 7 percent of their firm. When Warren Buffett agreed to sell his shares to InBev, other big shareholders followed.

Beer Monopoly

Ina Verstl has watched the industry she set out to cover invert before her eyes. A chain-smoking Brit living in the suburbs of Munich, she's the editor of the multilingual industry publication *Brauwelt (Brewing World)* and a professor of continental philosophy—which means she can wax Hegelian or Heineken depending on the occasion. Today, it's Heineken. Or more specifically, her book project *Beer Monopoly*. She's been covering the same story as Riepl and MacIntosh, but from a global perspective.

From time to time, her Hegelian views take over. Verstl calls the recent industry developments promiscuous. "They're all in bed with each other." It's a perpetual game of mergers and acquisitions and forced divestitures when competition authorities crack the whip.

In the past fifteen years, the global beer market has grown exponentially more concentrated by way of both foreign acquisitions and foreign direct investment (FDI) in countries with growing beer markets. In 2001, the top four firms claimed 21.7 percent of global market share. In 2005, this number was 35.8 percent. In 2014, AB InBev, SABMiller,

Heineken, and Carlsberg claimed a grand total of 45.7 percent of the market share for all beer in the world. And there's no sign of this process slowing down. In fact, the latest merger between AB InBev and SABMiller is accelerating this process.

AB InBev-type strategies have dramatically shifted the global beer marketplace. Historically, breweries have been family-run firms. Founded in 1864 by Adriaan Heineken, Heineken International grew under the leadership of the Heineken family. Its global growth flourished under the leadership of Freddy Heineken, Adriaan's direct descendent, who remained involved with the brewery until his death in 2002. Under Freddy's leadership, Heineken invested much time and energy establishing the Amsterdam-based beer as a global premium brand recognizable around the world. Later, this, coupled with an FDI-heavy acquisition strategy of investing in small local brands in emerging markets, has solidified Heineken's status as a major global player. Like Interbrew and SABMiller, Heineken poured funds into developing the Eastern European beer market following the fall of the Berlin Wall (see Chapter 7 for more on Heineken's post-communist investments).

Since the acquisition of Anheuser Busch, InBev's strategy has had a measurable influence on the actions of the other major players. Heineken made major InBev-esque acquisitions: Scottish & Newcastle in 2008 and Mexican FEMSA in 2012. SABMiller acquired Australian Foster's soon after the Anheuser Busch takeover. Following that acquisition, they released a statement explicitly stating the maneuver was designed to insulate them from takeover by AB InBev—unsuccessfully, as it turns out.

In 2016, AB InBev merged with SABMiller, which means one corporate entity earning half of the total global beer profits and producing one in every three pints of beer sold worldwide. The main difference between this acquisition and the landmark hostile takeover of Anheuser Busch? This time, no one was surprised.

7

Socialist Lubricant

Liberalization, Takeovers, and Restructuring the East European Brewing Industry

When Ján Pokrivčák matriculated as a freshman at the Slovakian University of Agriculture (SUA) in Nitra, Czechoslovakia, Principles of Economics was a very different course. As he explained:

> First you would learn the Marxist-Leninist ideology, and it would be backed by stupid statistics that our economy is improving and in the capitalist economy there's a high unemployment rate, poor people, homeless people, etcetera. Each textbook would start with an introduction about "The conclusions of the Communist Party Congress" which stated that we will increase production of steel by 5 percent, production of meat by 4 percent, production of whatever by 3 percent; and how it fitted into the central plan. The central plan was the most important—it was key to the functioning of society. And then you would learn basically how to organize central plans.

And, being in Czechoslovakia, a key part of communist planning concerned beer and brewing. The central plan identified how many hectares of barley would have to be sowed, on what farms, who would deliver the seeds, at what prices, which companies would turn the barley into malt, and ultimately which breweries would brew specific types of beer.

However, by the end of his first undergraduate semester, everything was different. It was the autumn of 1989, only a few months after a peaceful student protest in Tiananmen Square turned into a massacre. Discontent with the communist system was widespread, but dissidence was still dangerous. Thirty years earlier, popular protests in Prague to liberalize and democratize were met with Soviet occupation. The fall of the Berlin Wall on November 9 was followed by a wave of revolutions across the Eastern Bloc. Peaceful student protests in Bratislava and

Prague put pressure on the Communist Party of Czechoslovakia to consider democratic elections and, inevitably, market reforms. On December 29, 1989, Alexander Dubcek entered office as the first elected parliamentary leader since before World War II.

Academic life changed as well. "My schoolmates, the students of my age and slightly older, we actually brought about many changes at the university," Pokrivcák says proudly. Pokrivcák was among the first generation of economists to receive an education unthinkable just a few years prior: studying abroad, completing his masters in agricultural economics at Cornell University, and then further advancing his economics training at the University of Leuven in Belgium. When he returned home, the country had split in two, and he soon became a professor in Slovakia, teaching a new economics: one in which markets were analyzed rather than planned.

Not everybody was equally excited about the changes. While intellectuals like Pokrivcák fought for the reforms, the farmers and food companies he was studying were less enthusiastic. The centralized command economy had treated them well. Cheap and plentiful basic foods were a key priority of the Czechoslovakian Communist Party. "The West was the enemy: you and NATO," Pokrivcák jokes. "They were afraid that if something happened, we would run out of food and have to trade with the West. So a critical branch of the economy was the production of arms and agriculture." As part of that strategy, farms and food companies, including the barley, malt, and beer sector, were protected and subsidized.

Liberalization and privatization implied that farmers, food companies, and breweries would no longer be protected from competition and potential losses: they would have to compete and make production and technology decisions themselves. They would have to produce products that consumers wanted rather than serving the larger geopolitical goals of the Communist Party.

It turned out that planning the transition to a new economic system was as difficult as planning the economy under the communist regime. When production and markets were liberalized in the early 1990s, things fell apart throughout the economy. Barley and beer production was no different. Output collapsed and debts piled up.

But Western companies were eager to invest. They saw opportunities and long-run profits in neighboring countries in the center of Europe. Among the first were the brewing companies, who were very interested in a region with a long tradition of beer brewing and drinking. Within a few years, a large share of the Eastern European brewery industry was taken over by Western brewing multinationals. Their challenge was to upgrade the local breweries and get them back up and running. A crucial part of this was to upgrade their supply chains and make the farmers happy so that they were willing to produce quality barley for the market rather than for the communist central plan.

The Market Economy

In 1990, Peter Lelkes, the head of a cooperative farm, filled the barley order of a newly privatized food-processing firm. He then requested the agreed-upon payment of eight million crowns. The firm refused to pay. It hadn't occurred to him that this could happen. But his cooperative farm quickly learned they had few options for retrieving their money. There was no legal precedent—lawyers and judges were just as baffled as Lelkes with regard to how to deal with private contract disputes. Their previous familiarity was with one contract: the central plan, where personal profit was illegal.

"Today, eight million crowns could buy three tractors," he offers, still frustrated. It was two years until Lelkes retrieved the payment. But the farm had already taken a significant financial hit and inflation had reduced the real value of the payment.

Anecdotes like this were a dime a dozen in the years following the reforms. In the West, markets had co-evolved organically alongside basic regulatory institutions. Contract law, the means to enforce it, a socialized understanding of free market logic: none of these existed in post-communist countries immediately following the reforms.

Many farmers didn't understand how a market economy worked. The farmers at Lelkes' cooperative were accustomed to receiving an order passed down by the ministries from the Committee for Central Planning. "Planning and the economy were so simple then," he ruminates. Not only was there a guarantee he would sell his harvest, but the prices were fixed in advance. He also knew the price of all inputs: seeds, fertilizer, technology.

Farmers had no experience with making savvy market decisions when it came to their crops. "For years, some produced wheat nobody wanted to buy," explains Professor Pokrivcák. "They were shocked—they didn't understand why they weren't getting paid." The milk industry had the opposite problem. Dairy farmers started selling to international markets for a higher price, while milk-processing plants went broke when they had nothing to process.

The market was especially hostile to barley farmers in post-communist nations. In the ten years following the reforms, Slovakia's production of barley took a huge hit, dropping from 998 to 665 million tonnes per year. In the Czech Republic, Hungary, and Poland, barley production also fell by about a third. Bulgaria's drop was even more dramatic: from 1,487 to 662 million tonnes in 2000. There were many reasons why barley took an especially hard hit. The most obvious was that communist Czechoslovakia had overproduced barley under the central planning system with its subsidies and protected agricultural production system. The barley farms were not efficient enough to produce the same amounts in a competitive free market.

Another major reason was that farmers were reluctant to invest at all with no guarantee that processing plants would purchase their harvest. The communist supply chains that had guaranteed farmers a fair price were in disarray. Barley farms, malt-processing plants, and breweries comprise the supply chain for beer. In free market economies, coordination between firms in one supply chain is made possible by negotiated contracts between firms in the chain. Following the reforms, the legal infrastructure necessary to implement this type of coordination just did not exist.

Even when markets began to stabilize, early losses took a major toll on the agricultural sector. Agriculture operates on debt—firms need to buy inputs months before they receive payments for their products. Burned once, and a farm was devastated. As an industry in decline, credit channels were all but non-existent for farmers. No money, no seeds, no harvest, no beer.

The Takeover

Slovakia's ambassador beer brand Zlatý Bazant translates as "Golden Pheasant." It's an appropriate name for the brand that served as the career-launching pad for one up-and-coming Heineken executive Marc Bolland, nicknamed the "High-Flying Dutchman." Heineken acquired Zlatý Bazant, a brewery in Hurbanovo, Slovakia, in 1995. A young, ambitious Bolland jumped at the chance to reorganize the state-owned company. Ten years later, in an interview with Dutch-language publication *Elsevier*, he described his first impressions of the beer: "On the label is a golden pheasant, but the beast was mechanically constructed. My first thought was: how do I get life in there? Slovaks are poetic people. You can talk to them. I told designers the pheasant was alive and could be improved. No blind pheasant, he should look at you."

It's comical to imagine Bolland articulating this strategy to Imrich Alaxa. The former vice president of the communist-era Slovak Beer and Malt Association, Alaxa served as director of a newly privatized Zlatý Bazant for six years prior to Heineken's acquisition. Today, he greets us in a green flannel suit jacket and corduroys, firm handshake, thick accent, and a demeanor more frenzied mathematician than corporate smooth-talker. No waxing poetic à la Bolland, but his broken English comes with an unexpected clarity: "After the revolution, our problem was money. Capital, you know, yes?"

Capital was something Heineken could offer, and Zlatý Bazant was just the beginning for them. Between 1997 and 1999, Heineken acquired Corgon, Martiner, and Gemer, three other Slovakian brewery-maltings. Bolland was brought in to turn the bureaucratic operations into competitive enterprises. Production was consolidated, breweries became brands, and operations were restructured into three branches of subsidiary Heineken Slovensko: malting, brewing, and distribution. Following the 1999 acquisition of Gemer, Heineken claimed a 38 percent share of the Slovak beer market.

While Heineken focused on cornering the Slovak market, Interbrew, SABMiller, and Carlsberg raced to buy up breweries in other East European post-communist countries. The beer industry was one of the first to attract FDI following the market reforms. Tastes in beer tend to be regional and transport costs to export are high. If the big multinationals wanted a long-term cut of Eastern European beer markets, then capital investment in existing breweries was the most viable strategy. But as we know, fixed costs in beer production are high.

The top multinationals spent big to position themselves as early market leaders in different countries. It was like a game of Monopoly, with malt-processing plants, brewery kettles, and bottling lines rather than houses and hotels. Table 7.1 nicely illustrates the outcome of the strategic investments of the multinational brewing companies in the 1990s in Eastern Europe. Carlsberg had clearly concentrated on the Nordic countries (Estonia, Latvia, and Lithuania), close to its Scandinavian base, and the large former Soviet countries Russia and Ukraine. By 2000, it had a market share of between 23 percent and 50 percent in each of these countries. SAB Miller concentrated squarely on Central Eastern Europe: Hungary, Czech Republic, Slovakia, and Poland, while Interbrew invested in Ukraine, Hungary, and Bulgaria. Heineken's regional focus was in Central and South-Eastern Europe: it owned between 23 and 37 percent of the market in Bulgaria, Poland, Romania, and of course Slovakia.

Table 7.1 Market share (%) of multinational breweries in Eastern Europe in 2000*

	Carlsberg*	Heineken	Interbrew*	SABMiller
Estonia	50	0	1	0
Latvia	28	0	1	0
Lithuania	41	0	0	0
Russia	24	0	9	0
Ukraine	23	0	29	0
Hungary	0	9	25	25
Czech Republic	0	1	10	37
Bulgaria	0	23	37	0
Romania	4	36	13	12
Poland	8	33	0	22
Slovakia	0	37	0	24

* Carlsberg include Carlsberg and Baltic Beverages Holding AB.
Euromonitor. Market reports on beer, various countries <http://www.euromonitor.com/beer>.

The Restructuring

Alaxa recalls the change in numbers. He answers every question on the acquisition and restructuring with a series of statistics and measurements, animated with arrows, circles, and underlining. We tell him we don't need exact numbers, which he promptly ignores. But when he tosses the first scrap of paper aside, we realize he's not telling us numbers—he's telling a story. On brewing: "Before we produced beer forty to sixty days. Now fifty to seventy days. Then, the capacity was 550,000 hectoliters. This time, capacity it's two million hectoliters. We produce 1.7 million hectoliters." On employment: "We had fifteen brewery plants and thirty thousand employees before Heineken. Our country's unemployment 2 percent. This time, 850 employees and 14 percent unemployment. It is a reality." Alaxa makes no secret of his communist nostalgia, but it doesn't dampen his appreciation of Heineken's role post-reforms. "If Heineken didn't bought this company, these 850 employees—unemployees."

As a Westerner, these numbers scream "inefficiency," but it's eye-opening to hear him boast about the high employment of this firm. Alaxa lived the day-to-day of one institution's major philosophical shift in purpose. In communist Czechoslovakia, his job as vice president of the Slovak Beer and Malt Association was to make sure beer got made and people got paid. Maximizing employment always came before profit. Well, profit was illegal.

For decades, firms had been endlessly bureaucratic operations run by directors with no incentive to streamline operations. Heineken

Slovensko was established to turn a profit; its arrival could have been nothing but ambivalent. After all, Slovakia was still mired in an economic decline, domestic industries were still suffering from the post-reforms free-for-all. At one point during the *Elsevier* interview, Bolland ruminated on his three years in Slovakia: "I lived in the countryside, among the peasants, a conscious choice. If you need to lay off hundreds of people, you cannot do it from the capital, with a show car for driving."

During Bolland's three years orchestrating the restructure, he maintained one party line: "This is a long run game." It was an even longer run than he was anticipating. Bolland arrived in Slovakia armed with a sharp aesthetic sense and marketing savvy. He had big dreams for Zlatý Bazant as Slovakia's ambassador brand, similar to internationally renowned Czech exports Pilsner Urquell and Budweiser Budvar. But first, he would need to secure some high-quality barley.

The Supply Chain

Heineken never intended to get into the barley business, but they didn't really have a choice. The story is the same across the former Eastern Bloc: multinationals had jumped at the chance to acquire breweries in transitional markets, but they found that restructuring their new acquisitions to run as competitive enterprises was only the first of many challenges. Many didn't intend to enter the malting industry either, but breweries and malt houses were sold as package deals by post-communist governments. The bigger challenge was sourcing high-quality barley from local farms. Barley farmers were facing a credit vacuum—they needed capital upfront for seed, fertilizers, pesticides, and equipment, but banks were reluctant to lend to a sector in decline.

Heineken stepped up to the challenge early on. The newly established subsidiary Heineken Slovensko launched credit and farm assistance programs that advanced capital to farms to purchase inputs. "Farmers had two possibilities: from bank and from us," Alaxa says. "It's cheaper from us because three, five, ten percent," referencing to interest rates charged by banks as he counts on one hand. They also solicited the help of the university in co-sponsoring an agricultural consulting program. Farmers were educated on innovations in agriculture, including pesticides, fertilizer, and new technologies.

Similar ventures took place across Eastern Europe. Robert Persyn, a global expert in barley seed production and quality, sits in his renovated farmhouse in the outskirts of Hoegaarden, home to the famous Belgian white beer (see Chapter 8), reflecting on his own early naiveté about supply chain restructuring. He was hired in the early 1990s by Interbrew as a consultant to help them improve the quality of malt barley production in Bulgaria and Croatia. Interbrew came to him, frustrated that their attempts to import high-quality malt from the world market were blocked by the governments' reactionary increase of import tariffs on malt imports. They were forced to upgrade the entire domestic supply chain, bringing in foreign experts on malting and barley to improve quality, and working with local farmers and seed companies. Alaxa could not agree more: "Our farmers produce this barley. It is tradition, it is history." For Heineken in Slovakia it was also the only viable long-term strategy. Imported barley would be more expensive in the long run.

It took Persyn a few years to identify the problems in the local barley supply chains in the Balkans and to upgrade them, with financing from the multinational brewery. It takes time because there is only one growing season per year. But his efforts in Croatia and those of Heineken in Slovakia paid off. Data collected by Pokrivcák and his colleagues at the university in Nitra show that farms with Heineken contracts consistently had a higher yield than the national average following the implementation of credit programs. In 2000, the Slovakian average yield was 1.99 tonnes per hectare; for Heineken's farms, it was 2.77 tonnes per hectare. Similarly, in Russia, malting firms Soufflet and Champagne Cereals financed seeds and fertilizer programs for barley farmers through interlinked contracts. The programs were hugely successful in improving the quality of Russian barley. Prior to 2001, only 49 percent of Russian demand for barley was purchased locally. By 2007, that number was 85 percent.

Persyn also found himself upgrading barley quality in Russia and beyond. Encouraged by his success in Bulgaria and Croatia, a 15,000 hectare farm in Siberia hired Persyn to manage the production of barley for the local breweries. Since then he has worked for most brewing and malting multinationals, setting up improved barley production systems across the world wherever the companies are taking over breweries or malting plants, from India to the Egyptian desert.

Víťaz Víťaz

The Slovak phrase "víťaz víťaz" is translated to me twice as "winner-winner." Farmers from older generations have few kind words to say about the West, or open markets in general, but this sentiment evaporates at the mention of Heineken Slovensko. Heineken offered farmers the possibility of entering long-term fixed-price purchasing contracts, following years of post-reform market price volatility.

Barley farmer Pavel Raskovsky narrates why farmers always "win" with these contracts, "even when they sometimes lose." In 2012 he renewed his contract with Heineken for another three years. The terms stated that Heineken would pay a fixed price for the top 70 percent of his highest quality barley, with the option of purchasing the remaining 30 percent at market price. That summer, Slovakia received no rain until mid-July. Raskovsky's long-run average yield is 5.6 metric tonnes of barley per acre—that summer, it was 2.7 tonnes. Barley prices jumped up with the low supply. He sold 800 metric tonnes of his highest quality barley to Heineken for 200 euros per tonne, way below the market price. In fact, he was able to sell the remaining barley (which was not good enough for beer production) on the market for 250 euros per tonne. Raskovsky could have made more money without a contract in 2012, but the long-term security made the occasional loss worth it.

Vertical coordination introduced by fixed-price contracts by no means precludes competition. Rather, competition takes a different form: every time a contract is up for renewal, firms can renegotiate the contract condition. "They are mutually dependent on each other," explains Pokrivcák. "But there is an element of competition, there is bargaining for the surplus." Heineken will always bargain for a lower fixed price; barley farmers will try to keep the fixed price high. Whoever has more market power will have the upper hand in negotiations.

The Subsidies (Back to the Future)

In 2004, Slovakia joined the European Union (EU) and the circumstances of Heineken and its barley farmers changed yet again. Barley farmers became entitled to generous subsidies as part of the EU's Common Agricultural Policy (CAP). Government payments to farmers increased more than fivefold over the next five years. For the farmers, it was a return to a world of subsidies, fifteen years after the transition away from subsidies under the communist system to a free market economy.

Soon after EU accession, Heineken and the biggest malt processors in Slovakia dismantled their credit and advance payment programs to farmers. A study by the World Bank in 2003 had shown that most brewing and malting companies in Slovakia were providing credit programs for their suppliers. A revisit of the companies by Pokrivcák and his colleagues in 2008 found that these programs had been terminated and that the CAP payments were the main reason. With so much in subsidies coming to the farms, there was no longer a need for the breweries or malting companies to assist farms with credit programs. In fact, with guaranteed payments from the EU coming in at the end of the season, banks were happy to step in and pre-finance the farms. It was a highly secure loan system.

Heineken was able to take a backseat role as creditor, while the CAP payments actually directly added to the profit margin of Heineken Slovensko. The malt-processing branch had spent years establishing relationships with barley farms across Slovakia. After 2004, the EU's subsidies changed the financial circumstances of these farms. While they benefited directly from the extra income, it also changed their contract negotiations in unexpected ways. The extra subsidies changed the minimum fixed price they could sell barley for and continue to run their farm. And nobody realized this better than Heineken Slovensko. After many years of working with the barley farms, they had good insights into their suppliers' activities, profits, and bottom lines. Moreover, as a buyer with significant market power, Heineken Slovensko was perfectly positioned to renegotiate the contract terms and demand lower fixed prices from newly subsidized farms when contracts came up for renewal.

Bolland's marathon mentality had paid off in an unexpected way.

8

The Belgian White

Reincarnation of an Old World Brew

> When the young King of the Franks visited Hoegaarden, a monk
> sought out his advice about an abandoned orphan child left on his
> doorstep. Charlemagne, as the king would later be known, ordered
> the boy to be raised among the industrious brothers of the cloister
> and taught the ancient craft of brewing. Klaas (for Kluis, or "clois-
> ter") learned all the secrets of making and trading beer, growing up
> to be the town's iconic brewmaster. Crediting his long life and good
> health to the regular consumption of wheat beer, Klaas was buried
> in a beer barrel at the age of 100. A statue of Klaas stands in the
> courtyard of Brouwerij de Kluis to commemorate the legacy of
> Hoegaarden's ancient brewing tradition.
>
> The Legend of Klaas, orphan brewmaster of Hoegaarden

In April 2011, beer lover and journalist Roger Protz of *The Guardian* took
a moment to salute Pierre Celis, the enterprising Hoegaarden milkman
who pulled Belgian white ale from the brink of extinction. Celis will be
remembered for his dedication to brewing excellence and his single-
minded passion for the traditional Belgian white ale that drove him to
resurrect the ancient recipe after the last brewery closed in Hoegaarden,
his hometown in central Belgium, in the 1950s. Today Belgian and
Belgian-style white ales enjoy worldwide popularity in recognizable
brands like Hoegaarden, Blue Moon, and Shocktop.

Obituaries hail Celis as the "father of Hoegaarden beer," but the
famous white beer recipe predates Celis by at least 1,000 years. Belgian
white beer—*witbier* and *bière blanche* as it is known by the Flemish and
Walloons in its region of origin—is a top-fermented wheat and barley

ale spiced with hops, coriander, and bitter citrus. The recipe was refined by the brewers of Hoegaarden and exported across the Low Countries for centuries.

The Secret Gaarden

The Hoegaarden label shows two overlapping seals: on one, a hand holds a bishop's staff, on the other, a brewer's mash paddle. It is the original town seal, symbol of the shared power of the Holy Roman Empire and the Hoegaarden brewers' guild (which survives to this day as the Noble Order of the Mashing Paddle). The first record of Hoegaarden is in the tax rolls of 937, when it received a special tax exemption as part of its affiliation with the Prince-Bishopric of Liège, a vassal state of the Holy Roman Empire.

Sandwiched between the geographic power bases of Central Europe's Habsburgs and the French royal House of Valois in Burgundy, Liège served as a de facto buffer state and an intellectual and ecclesiastical center of Europe's Middle Ages. It traded on the premise that the two great empires preferred not to share a border. The town of Hoegaarden survived an early attempt by the expanding nearby city of Leuven to conquer it in 1185 during the Battle of Hoegaarden. It remained an enclave of the Prince-Bishopric of Liège and, as such, continued to enjoy tax-exempt status.

At the time, most cities in the Low Countries were autonomous political entities that controlled their own territories and public finance systems. They levied taxes to pay for public buildings, municipal services, and local militias. When the textile industry began to decline in the region, brewing took its place as a major source of tax revenue (see Chapter 2). In Leuven, tax levies from the brewing industry quadrupled between 1380 and 1560.

Hoegaarden, during this time, found itself in a uniquely advantageous position, as Liège's religious charter gave it a major tax advantage. By the late Middle Ages, Hoegaarden's breweries had become successful commercial enterprises. They became known for their good-quality white ale at a reasonable price (thanks to the tax exemption), which they sold in other cities in the region. Hoegaarden remained a major beer exporter for centuries, and continued to enjoy special tax status until the eve of the Napoleonic Wars. In 1758, Hoegaarden had a population of 2,000 and thirty-eight breweries: one brewery for every fifty-eight villagers.

However, science and the industrial revolutions would undermine this vibrant brewing economy in the next two centuries. And again a major threat came from the city of Leuven—this time not a military but a commercial attack. Among the casualties would be Tomsin Brewery, one of many small breweries in Hoegaarden, and the one where Pierre Celis worked as a boy.

A Rising Star

As we explained in Chapter 4, the late eighteenth and the nineteenth centuries were characterized by scientific breakthroughs that brought about a growing market for industrially produced lager beer. By the end of World War II, German-style lagers had come to dominate Belgium's beer market, a trend that began with Germany's occupation of Belgium during World War I.

The 1926 release of a clear, crisp seasonal lager originally called Stellamass—now known worldwide as Stella Artois—by the Artois Brewery of Leuven accelerated the popularity of German-style lager beers. The Artois Brewery seized on the success of its signature brand in 1920s Belgium and shifted production to lager beers. As other Belgian brewers followed suit, the consumption of lager rose. Lagers edged out the market for many of Belgium's traditional recipes, including the pale, spicy, unfiltered beer that was the pride of Hoegaarden.

In 1957, the last remaining brewery in Hoegaarden—the Tomsin Brewery where Pierre Celis first learned the brewer's craft—closed its doors upon its owner's death. For the first time in recorded history, the town of Hoegaarden was without a brewery.

The closing of the Tomsin Brewery so chagrined Pierre Celis, now a local milkman, that he resolved to rescue Hoegaarden's brewing legacy from oblivion. He started by brewing the traditional white beer in a tub, eventually raising funds from family and friends for the 1965 launch of the Brouwerij De Kluis (or "cloister," in homage to the beer's monastic roots). With Celis' local marketing—"Hoegaards Bier is Onsterfelijk" ("Hoegaarden Beer is forever!")—and growing reputation for brewing excellence, the beer grew steadily in popularity over the next twenty years. In an era of global consolidation for the brewing industry, Celis regained a pivotal foothold for the regional specialty through vigorous grassroots publicity, first among locals and then across Belgium. Hoegaarden beer grew quickly in popularity in Belgium, a sign of the emerging interest of consumers in craft beers.

Things were going increasingly well when fate struck and caused an unexpected turn in the Hoegaarden–Leuven relationship. In 1985, the Brouwerij De Kluis was suddenly destroyed by fire. The underinsured Celis was forced to turn to other brewers for rebuilding. Help came from an unexpected source—but it came at a high price. The Artois Brewery in nearby Leuven agreed to rebuild his brewery in exchange for 45 percent ownership equity. Artois had contributed to the demise of the original Hoegaarden breweries with its Stella lager. Now they were observing the unexpected popularity of Celis' new Hoegaarden threaten their profits.

The price was steeper than Celis had imagined. Unknown to him, Artois had been strategizing for years to dominate the beer markets of Belgium by colluding with the Piedboeuf Breweries of Jupille-sur-Meuse. When they merged in 1987 to create Interbrew, they gained a controlling share in Celis' company. Celis suddenly found himself overrun by outside managers, responding only to their shareholders. Moreover, they registered "Hoegaarden" as a trademark. Celis' beloved beer and his hometown's seal were now trademark property of his longtime Leuven-based rival. And they had plans to mass-market it on an unprecedented scale.

During the following decades, white beer production grew in this quiet, rural village and again employed a significant share of the population—as it had done for much of the previous millennium. But here the similarity stops. While before small breweries dominated the scene, now a single industrial brewery manufactured Belgian's traditional white beer on the outskirts of town and exported it to every corner of the world. When Interbrew and Brazil's AmBev merged in 2004 to create InBev and later merged with Anheuser Busch into AB InBev (see Chapter 6), Hoegaarden's white beer was produced by the world's largest multinational brewing company. The company owned the town's brewery, the rights to the Hoegaarden name, the town seal, and the beer recipe. Hoegaarden had become a global corporate brand.

Celis did not stay to watch this happen. He had long dreamed of the American market, so in 1985 he sold his remaining shares of De Kluis to Interbrew and moved to Austin, Texas, where the calcium-rich waters of the local aquifers promised good brewing and a new future for his beloved drink.

Branding the White in the Land of the Lite

The 1990s marked the early stages of the American love affair with imported and craft beers. The US market share for domestic lagers began falling in the early years of the decade as demand for imported beers increased. The beer-drinking public saw imports as a higher-end substitute for popular premium brands like Michelob. Pockets of adventurous consumers also began to seek out craft beers like San Francisco-based Anchor

Steam and Boston Beer Co.'s Sam Adams. And while domestic light lagers continued to dwarf the market share for imports and craft beers, it became increasingly clear to the big industrial brewers that investment in nascent beer markets was necessary. Number two and three brewers Miller and Coors began to explore tapping into the emerging markets for imported and craft beers.

But back to Celis. The father of Hoegaarden beer emigrated to Austin, convinced of the potential for craft beer in an American market dominated by industrial lagers. In 1992—the same year microbrewer New Belgium of Colorado released the amber ale Sunshine Wheat—the Celis Brewery brought its flagship brand, Celis White, to the local Austin market. Both beers used the traditional barley/wheat and spice recipe of the Hoegaarden white ale.

Though light lager was deeply entrenched in the Texan culture, Celis White attracted a small but enthusiastic following in Austin. He also received critical acclaim for his American-made white beer from the budding US craft movement. His Celis White brand garnered gold medals for several years running in the "herbs and spices" category at the Great American Beer Festival, the top tasting competition for the US craft brewing industry. The unfamiliar style of beer initially confused judges, but the organization would soon establish a separate judging category for the Belgian whites.

The Celis Brewery and its seasoned, Old World brewmaster attracted the interest of the Miller Brewing Co., which was exploring opportunities to enter the developing market for domestic and imported boutique beers. Pierre Celis accepted Miller's offer of state-of-the-art facilities and access to its US distribution network. Celis had been drawn in by the potential to expand the market for his beer, but his brewery lacked the capacity to meet even local demand. Problems of scale and transportation hampered operations. In 1995 America's number two brewer took a controlling stake in Celis Brewery of Austin, Texas.

However, it soon became clear to Miller that the beer's critical acclaim did not necessarily translate into profit. With Belgian white beer slow to catch on, Miller grew increasingly unhappy with its investment in the Austin brewery. Only a few months after the acquisition, Celis was once again confronted with a flock of corporate executives focused on the bottom line. The new cost-cutting strategies affected the quality of Celis White and dampened the local cult following that Celis had built in Austin. In 1997—only two years after its initial investments—Miller abandoned its quest for a white beer brand and auctioned Celis Brewery and its rights to the small craft brewer Michigan Brewing Company. Renowned beer writer Michael Jackson would later describe Celis' association with Miller as "a bruising encounter with the beer that should have made Milwaukee famous."

Miller was not the only American domestic brewery with its eye on the specialty beer market. Before merging with Miller in 2007, Coors had launched its own decade-long experiment in Belgian white beer. Coors followed a very different strategy to Miller. Coors hired home-brewing aficionado (and college student) Keith Villa in the early 1990s and sent him to Belgium, the birthplace of white beer, for formal training. He returned to Coors with a PhD in brewing biochemistry from the University of Brussels and the dream of developing an American-friendly recipe for the Belgian specialty. Villa teamed up with Coors marketing specialist Jim Sabia to create Blue Moon and moved their shoestring operation into Denver's Sandlot Brewery. The agreement with Coors gave Villa creative control but minimal investment capital. So Blue Moon took a cue from Sam Adams, another new entrant into the craft beer market, and started out small. Villa brewed his white beer by contracting breweries with excess capacity for the first four years.

Blue Moon's release drew neither the immediate following of Celis White nor any tangible boost to Coors' bottom line. And while the US craft beer movement was gaining momentum in the late 1990s, American consumers were unfamiliar with Belgian-style beer and its peculiar cloudy appearance. White beer was slow to catch on and the early years were financially challenging for white beer brewers, both large and small.

With Coors' limited oversight, the enterprising duo of Villa and Sabia were busy brainstorming marketing strategies to expose American lager drinkers to their Belgian-style beer. Villa altered the original white beer recipe to appeal to American tastes by replacing the bitter Curaçao orange peel with a sweeter Valencia variety. He also lightened the beer's color by supplementing the traditional wheat and barley recipe with oats. Meanwhile Sabia recognized that Blue Moon's small size could be leveraged to their advantage in the fledgling yet trendy market for craft beers. He promoted Blue Moon as a boutique brand with a grassroots advertising campaign and packaging that mimicked the craft beer look and feel, in spite of its corporate relationship to a large industrial brewery. In 1995—the same year Miller took a controlling stake in Celis' brewery—Coors brought Blue Moon's Belgian white to market.

Villa and Sabia criss-crossed the US in an on-the-ground marketing campaign to showcase Blue Moon's traditional European roots and Villa's own Belgian-based training and expertise. Inspired by the distinctive pairing of Corona and lime, they added an orange slice accessory that enhanced the beer's spicy citrus recipe. Villa personally lugged bags of oranges to every stop on the Blue Moon marketing campaign to encourage uptake of the trend.

But the Blue Moon campaign hit a major stumbling block shortly after it launched. The Belgian Brewers Association (BBA) insisted that Coors change its promotion of Blue Moon as "Belgian white ale." In 1997 the BBA appealed to the US Bureau of Alcohol, Tobacco, and Firearms, and successfully compelled Blue Moon to alter its labeling to read "Belgian-style white ale." Coors' half-hearted attempts at compliance led to the filing of a lawsuit by BBA in 1999. The trade association accused Coors of "falsely and deceptively" advertising its product as imported Belgian beer and sought to protect the interests of authentic Belgian brewers.

The BBA legal entanglement could not have come at a worse time for Villa and Sabia. The underfunded Blue Moon venture was still struggling for a market foothold in the late 1990s, and BBA's demands were daunting: a total shutdown in production and a Coors-sponsored broadcast television ad that notified the beer-drinking public that Blue Moon was made in the US. In a vulnerable position and sensing that Coors might jettison the brand rather than meet the demands of the BBA lawsuit if Blue Moon failed to be a market performer, Villa worked hard to convince Coors that the market was ripe for craft-style recipes. There was not only mounting evidence to support that view, but also emerging competitive forces from large and small brewers alike that persuaded Coors to stay in the Belgian-style white beer game. Coors and the BBA settled out of court and Blue Moon was rebranded as Belgian-style white ale in 2000.

Villa's belief was ultimately vindicated. In 2001, his Belgian-style beer found a critical mass of American consumers, and soon retailers were reporting rapid increases in consumption. By 2004 sales of Blue Moon were registering annual double-digit growth, becoming the fastest-growing brand in the Coors portfolio. The Great American Beer Festival added an additional award category for Belgian-style whites. Sales of actual Belgian imports like Hoegaarden were also surging. Consumption of Belgian and Belgian-style white beer went from fifteen million liters to 150 million liters between 2003 and 2009, tracking the growing popularity of microbrews. By 2010 the Hoegaarden recipe and its domestic counterparts were firmly established as a staple in America's expanding boutique beer market.

Looking back, it is clear that the cultivation of new tastes in the American beer market required patience and vision. Keith Villa's creative marketing and unswerving faith in the potential of Blue Moon kept his dream of Belgian-style white beer alive during the uncertain early years. Villa reports that Blue Moon owes some of its eventual success to years of corporate pleading and cajoling. But mostly, the shoestring operation of the Sandlot Brewery where Villa and Sabia created Bellyslide Belgian White—Blue Moon's original name—never lost Coors a dime, even in the leanest of times. In time, Blue Moon would become MillerCoors' fastest-growing brand.

The Battle at Hoegaarden: Twenty-First-Century Redux

Again, Pierre Celis did not stick around to watch all of this unfold. After his second unpleasant takeover by a large commercial brewer, this time on the other side of the Atlantic Ocean, Celis again left the brewery—and the country. He returned to Belgium in 2000 to find the market for white beer flourishing once again in his home country. His former Hoegaarden brand had saturated the Belgian market. With Interbrew's merger spree, soon-to-be AB InBev was prepared to take Hoegaarden global. Celis' objective to save his favorite beer from extinction had been achieved—and then some. Never before had the world consumed so much Hoegaarden-style white beer. Yet the incredible success was different to how he had envisioned it.

And the battle for Hoegaarden was not over yet. Soon after returning to Belgium, Celis witnessed another episode in the Leuven–Hoegaarden saga: an attempt to take the beer away from its roots. With growing Hoegaarden sales, InBev was looking to reduce the cost of production. In 2005, from its headquarters in Leuven, InBev announced plans to shut down the Hoegaarden brewery and move production to its larger facilities in Jupille-sur-Meuse, fifty kilometers down the road. The newly appointed CEO, Carlos Brito, the Brazilian businessman with an MBA from Stanford (see Chapter 6), had already developed a reputation as a take-no-prisoners executive with an unflinching focus on the bottom line. In 2004 he caused a stir in England with the decision to move production of Boddingtons beer from its 200-year-old brewery in Manchester to a new facility in Lancashire. While InBev shareholders favored Brito's unsentimental approach to corporate acquisition, many Belgian consumers were about to change their minds. Until that moment, despite the takeover of the Brazilian management team that came with the Interbrew merger with AmBev, many Belgians still thought of InBev as "their company." This sentiment died with the announcement that InBev would move production of Hoegaarden the white beer out of Hoegaarden the village.

Local protests were frequent and visible. Residents plastered signs all over town reading "Hoegaarden is brewed in Hoegaarden." InBev workers and Belgian residents joined in the cause. Following the announcement, 2,000 workers and residents took to the streets of Leuven to picket the firm's headquarters. A few months later, 2,500 employees from InBev subsidiaries all over Europe went on strike and traveled to Leuven to protest the decision. InBev went through with the move, but pressure from workers, citizens, and consumers continued. Following the move, Hoegaarden consumers all over complained that the beer had plummeted in quality. Notwithstanding all the formal tests and professional tasting panels that had told InBev that the quality was the same or even better, the public disagreed and revolted. Some cited the yeast, others the water, but sentiment all over Belgium was similar: Hoegaarden just wasn't the same.

When public pressure failed to subside, InBev's hand was eventually forced and production was moved back to Hoegaarden. InBev's reputation in Belgium never recovered but Hoegaarden white beer is again brewed in Hoegaarden.

The aging Celis lent his unflagging devotion and a legendary prowess for the craft of brewing to new recipes developed by small brewers until his death in 2011. The Michigan Brewing Company maintained the Celis Brewery brand until 2012, when the daughter of Pierre Celis, Christine, who learned the brewer's craft at her father's knee, bought the rights and reestablished the Celis Brewery in Austin. Christine Celis now collaborates with brewmasters from around the world to bring craft and limited-edition brews to the now-mature and ever-expanding craft beer market in the US.

9

The *Reinheitsgebot*

Protection against Competition or Contamination?

Munich, the capital of the southern German region of Bavaria, hosts two of the most important symbols of German beer culture. Each fall the city's world famous Oktoberfest attracts hundreds of thousands of beer lovers from Germany and all over the world for two and a half weeks of beer-drinking and dancing.

The second, much quieter, symbol stands tall in the center of Munich's *Viktualienmarkt*: a blue-and-white striped maypole depicting scenes of dancing, song, and conversation. The pole commemorates the medieval *Reinheitsgebot*, or "Purity Law"—a decree mandating that all beer be made from four ingredients: barley, water, hops, and yeast. Duke Wilhelm IV signed the *Reinheitsgebot* into law for Munich in 1487 and for all of Bavaria in 1516. It's the oldest food law still in effect and almost certainly the most celebrated. And according to Bavarian history professor Karl Gattinger, the celebrations were about to get a lot bigger when we met on the eve of half a millennium of *Reinheitsgebot*. "You can just imagine how big the celebration will be for five hundred years," the thick-accented and mild-mannered history professor said over a mass of beer at Munich's iconic Hofbräuhaus, a "beer palace" built at the end of the nineteenth century.

However, not everybody was celebrating the *Reinheitsgebot*. Critics argue that while it may at some point have served to protect beer consumers against the use of unhealthy ingredients in the production of beer (or against rising bread prices, with wheat prohibited in brewing), more recently the effect has been to stifle innovation in brewing and protect German brewers from competition.

Eventually the integration of Germany into the EU led to a challenge against the oldest existing beer regulation in the world. In 1987, exactly five centuries after Duke Wilhelm IV signed the initial *Reinheitsgebot*, the European Court of Justice ruled that it conflicted with European trade laws and ordered it to be removed for foreign beers. The *Reinheitsgebot* remained in effect for beers brewed within Germany.

Frank Van Tongeren, a senior trade and agricultural policy expert at the Organisation for Economic Co-operation and Development (OECD), became intrigued with how these regulations survived for five centuries despite numerous political changes. "That a rather simple and old law from our perspective—just a few lines of text written 500 years ago—still has influence today, it's just fascinating," says Van Tongeren. With such deep historic roots, the *Reinheitsgebot* presents a fascinating case study in how government regulations can persist, even as the impact of these measures shifts dramatically. In the case of the *Reinheitsgebot*, the shift was from consumer protection measure to protectionist tariff.

The *Reinheitsgebot* also offers a valuable case study for today's global trade discussions, where safety and quality regulations frequently serve as obstacles to international trade.

Origins of the *Reinheitsgebot*

It is generally argued that the *Reinheitsgebot* served first and foremost as a consumer protection policy—regulating the production of beer during earlier times to ensure the health and safety of the beer. Martin Zarnkow, a doctor of brewing science at TU Munich, argues that prior to the *Reinheitsgebot*, there were many incidents of brewers using additives that turned out to be toxic. During the Middle Ages, brewers experimented with rushes, roots, mushrooms, and animal products as beer additives. They were not always forthcoming about which ingredients they used.

The introduction of the *Reinheitsgebot* followed the spread of hops as a preservative. As we explained in Chapter 2, the northern German trade cities of Hamburg and Bremen began hopping beers to preserve them for export. It didn't take long for hopped lager to become culturally engrained and a central part of life in Bavaria. Bavaria's geographic advantages were twofold: proximity to the Alps offered consistently low-temperature caves where beer could be stored ("lagered") for weeks to ferment, and the region's climate was ideal for hop production.

Hop production is limited by geography. The plant must be a certain distance away from the equator to receive adequate extended light during the summer months, but close enough for moderate temperature. Bavaria and Bohemia, two of the biggest beer-drinking populations in the world to this day, are characterized by these ideal climatic conditions. Hallertau, a rural county an hour north of Munich where green hills are marked by long green vines climbing toward the sunlight, is one of the global powerhouses of hops.

The *Reinheitsgebot* may have served as a public health measure and insurance policy for consumers at a time when plagues and unknown diseases were commonplace, but this wasn't its only effect. The original *Reinheitsgebot* also set maximum prices for beer based on time of year. Beer sold between April 23 and September 29 could be sold for no more than one Munich pfennig, and twice that much the rest of the year. The price regulation and quality control was said to protect consumers from predatory practices by brewers, but regulations also protected the existing brewers. The requirements for beer licensing served as a form of guild protection by raising the cost of entry. Established brewers were advantaged compared to start-ups. The law thus reduced incentives for innovation and advantaged already big brewers that could brew at economies of scale. Lastly, the *Reinheitsgebot* also served as a form of trade protectionism, preventing brewers from other areas introducing their products to Bavaria.

The *Reinheitsgebot* and the German Nation

The domain covered by the *Reinheitsgebot* spread in the second half of the nineteenth century as part of the formation of Germany as a nation-state. Until then, Bavaria had been politically separated from the northern German regions. However in the nineteenth century, Bavaria's position, and the *Reinheitsgebot*, became a central piece of what became known as the "German Question." Nationalists saw the nation-state as a political entity with one language and culture binding peoples of a geographic area together. Otto Von Bismarck had united the northern Germanic regions into the German Confederation. Yet, the aristocratic and German-speaking Habsburgs still presided over the ancient Holy Roman Empire from the seat of power in Vienna. Bavarians were torn; they were Catholic like their southern neighbors in Austria, but the nationalist rhetoric resonated with the German-speaking population to the north. Bavaria at last joined their northern counterparts in 1871 to form the German Empire, under one condition: that the *Reinheitsgebot* law be applied to the entire German Confederation.

This was strongly contested in northern German regions that had developed different traditional brewing methods, including the use of sugar and spices. It took twenty-five years to come to an agreement. In 1906, an adjusted *Reinheitsgebot* distinguished between top-fermented and bottom-fermented beer. The barley, hops, and water limit would apply to traditional bottom-fermented lagers, while top-fermented beers that originated in north-western parts of Germany, including Alt and the Kölsch beers, were permitted to include malted wheat in their recipes. The law itself remained strict regarding the geographic extent to which these regulations applied.

However, the political constructions in Germany proved volatile in the twentieth century—and with it the regional spread of the *Reinheitsgebot*. Immediately after World War I, Bavaria demanded once again that the *Reinheitsgebot* be adopted and enforced nationwide as a condition for their entrance into the German Weimar Republic.

The conclusion of World War II brought about another division of Germany, this time between East and West. Eager to expand communist influence in Eastern Europe, the Soviet Union took control over East Germany. Many citizens tried to flee East Germany. This east–west migration came on top of earlier population moves with the upheavals of the war. As a result, 24 percent of West Germans reported that their place of residence in 1950 was different from that in 1938. One implication of these migration patterns was the production of a new beer called *süssbier*, or sweet beer, within Bavaria. *Süssbier* was permitted under the national *Reinheitsgebot*, but not under the stricter requirements of Bavaria.

The Bavarian Brewers Association was quick to respond, militating against the attempted production of *süssbier* with state policymakers and in the courts. Brewer associations in other states fought Bavarian brewers on the federal level. Skirmishes continued from 1949 to 1965. One brewer defied the Bavarian ban by shipping sweet beer from its facilities in Frankfurt. The German Federal Court of Justice settled the matter in 1965. Sweet beer could be sold in Bavaria, but not as "beer." By that point, the defiant brewery had begun marketing its sweet beer as a "nutritional beverage" within Bavarian state lines.

But the battle over the *Reinheitsgebot* continued as long as the borders of the country kept changing, caught in geopolitical crossfire. In 1989, the fall of the Berlin Wall liberated East Germans who had been forced to live under the communist regime, and the German nation reunited. Once again, the *Reinheitsgebot* complicated the unification. The East German brewery Klosterbrauerei Neuzelle had been brewing a traditional black beer recipe that dated back to 1410. The recipe was bottom-fermented beer with a sugar syrup as an additive that gave the beer its "black" color. Because it was not in accordance with the *Reinheitsgebot*, the beer had to be marketed as "Schwarzer Abt" (Black Abbott) instead of "beer." Klosterbrauerei Neuzelle was engaged in lengthy legal battles for several years. In 2005, the Federal Administrative Court ruled in favor of Klosterbrauerei Neuzelle, ruling that its beer could be legally marketed as "beer" on a technicality: the syrup was not a substitute for barley malt since it was added after the brewing and filtration process. Therefore, Schwarzer Abt was technically beer plus syrup, rather than the "nutritional beverage" it would be labeled if the syrup was added during the brewing process.

How Weissbier Survived the *Reinheitsgebot*

Before moving to the final battle, we want to reflect briefly on a remarkable observation: how is it possible that the region of Bavaria, which has defended the *Reinheitsgebot* with great vigor and force, is also associated with its world-renowned weissbier, a beer produced from wheat—which obviously violates the basic rules of the *Reinheitsgebot*? It turns out that the association of the center of the *Reinheitsgebot* with weissbier is the result of a loophole in the original regulation and its unintended (and unexpected) consequences.

Interestingly, the first centuries of the *Reinheitsgebot* coincide with major religious transformations splitting not just northern and southern German regions, but the whole of Europe. Just one year after Wilhelm IV signed the *Reinheitsgebot*, Martin Luther famously posted his ninety-five theses on the door of the All Saints' Church in Wittenberg, Saxony. Luther's criticisms served as a catalyst for the Protestant Reformation that divided Europe. The northern German trade cities—Hamburg, Bremen, and Dresden—turned Protestant, while wooded Bavaria geographically found itself the vanguard of Vienna, center of Catholic power and head of the Holy Roman Empire. Munich, long home to a monastic population (Munich literally translates to "where the monks are"), never wavered in its Catholic faith. Even today, Gattinger asserts with historic clarity, "The true Bavarians are all Catholics."

When Wilhelm IV signed the *Reinheitsgebot* mandating exclusive use of four ingredients to brew beer, he didn't think much about the choice of barley. Barley was the norm for brewing beer at that time. But Gattinger points to a record dating back to 1418 showing that a small enclave in lower Bavaria, near the Czech border, had begun to brew beer with wheat. The original *Reinheitsgebot* made a special exception for families in that region (Degenberg) who were given the exclusive privilege to brew weissbier. No one in northern Bavaria thought much of it at the time.

When Maximilian became the new ruler of Bavaria around 1600, with increasing expenditures to finance the Catholic Counter-Reformation against Luther's growing success, he set out to find ways to collect more tax revenue. He began eyeing the growing demand for beer as a potential source.

Under the *Reinheitsgebot*, lager beer was the drink of Bavaria. Brewers brewed from fall through spring, storing beer in caves in the Alps. In accordance with the *Reinheitsgebot*, they would brew the last beer in March, fermenting it to make it extra strong for consumption after the mandated April 23 cut-off. This was the origin of the *marzen* style.

But there was growing demand for beer, particular in the summer. Maximilian saw the opportunity for weissbier. Weissbier was a top-fermented beer, using a different yeast that did not require storage and so could easily be produced for the extra summer demand. It was brewed under special privilege in a small part of southern Bavaria near the Czech border. It is unclear whether Maximilian bought the brewing rights from the Degenbergs, or whether the privilege came back to the Duke of Bavaria as the Degenbergs died off. What is certain is that Maximilian now had a monopoly on weissbier brewing (*Weizenbierregal*) and used it effectively. Gattinger's historical analysis shows that weissbier indeed became the revenue stream the ruler had hoped for. In fact, according to Klaus Salhofer, professor in economics at TU Munich, it became the main budgetary income for the state of Bavaria and the monarch family during the eighteenth century, as the pubs were forced to serve the beer in order to keep their licenses.

Maximilian appeased the Bavarian brewers of lager beer by giving them a share of the pie. During the summer months, he allowed them to make extra profits by selling his weissbier to their customers. The Hofbräuhaus, the royal palace founded by his father, became the center for brewing weissbier during the summer months.

As demand for weissbier during summer months grew, more breweries were founded. Maximilian used the growing demand to raise more income as well as directly supporting the Counter-Reformation by selling the right to brew weissbier to those fighting the Protestants and to cities staying loyal to the Catholic Church. Building and maintaining Catholic cathedrals drained local coffers. Protestant simplicity was an appealing option for town politicians. Maximilian offered these cities a deal: the right to brew and sell weissbier if profits were used for the establishment and maintenance of Catholic churches.

Today weissbier brands as Paulaner or Erdinger are popular beers in Germany and abroad, and have been an inspiration for many craft brewers globally. For the travelers having a fresh weissbier in Frankfurt Airport it may be hard to imagine that the beer's roots lay in providing a few Bavarian villages an exception to a law in 1516, and its survival and growth to the need for government taxes to finance the war between Catholics and Protestants.

The *Reinheitsgebot* and European Integration

In 1957, Germany was one of the founding members of (what is now called) the European Union (EU). Since this date, the EU has expanded in size, from the original six members to the current twenty-eight. But, more importantly for the *Reinheitsgebot*, it has also deepened in terms of institutional and economic integration. When the EU was founded, the *Reinheitsgebot* applied to the sale of all beer within Germany. If a Belgian brewery wanted to sell its beers in German markets, they'd have to brew in accordance with the German laws of brewing. It was only a matter of time before this clause was challenged.

In 1987, the *Reinheitsgebot* faced its first attack from outside German borders. French brewery Brasserie du Pêcheur filed a lawsuit against Germany, arguing that the *Reinheitsgebot* constituted a non-tariff barrier to trade within the EU. The premise of economic integration in the EU is that free trade will increase the efficiency and wealth of all participating nations. Tariffs are illegal, but nations are allowed to retain other national laws providing they do not act as trade protectionism in disguise. If they do, they are considered "non-tariff barriers"—laws and regulations other than tariffs that limit trade between nations.

The question facing the European Court of Justice (ECJ) was this: did the *Reinheitsgebot* serve primarily as a protectionist measure to the domestic brewing industry? Or was it within the scope of the German government to uphold this historic law designed to protect consumers? The ECJ ruled that the *Reinheitsgebot* was an illegal non-tariff barrier to trade. The national government could regulate how beer was produced within Germany, but it couldn't extend this regulation to imported beer sold in Germany when there was no evidence of an imminent health threat.

The ECJ ruling came exactly five centuries after Duke Wilhelm IV signed the initial version of the *Reinheitsgebot* for Munich. Much had changed in the meantime. Even if the law was originally intended as a consumer protection measure in a time before people were aware of the dangers of bacteria and improper hygiene, by the twentieth century other ingredients used in beer outside Germany would not have a negative impact on the health of German citizens.

Most Germans still maintained a strong sense of pride in the law, but the ECJ and many trade economists think this was somewhat misleading. Frank Van Tongeren, the OECD trade and food policy expert, agrees: "[The *Reinheitsgebot*] is not just consumer protection, which is the part most people know in Germany. It was as much an industry policy, a protectionist policy protecting the interests of an industry group as anything else." Bavarian brewers had historically benefited from the protection of the *Reinheitsgebot* through Germany's transition to a nation-state. The law had favored Bavarian brewers and protected them from the competition presented by many other beers, and it was Bavarian brewers that were the driving force behind keeping the law in effect.

Non-tariff barriers hurt consumers by limiting supply, thus raising the price to consumers. Pre-1987, the German beer supply was limited to beer brewed in accordance with the *Reinheitsgebot*, thus depriving German consumers of other options and depriving other European brewers of the German market. Economists argue that the *Reinheitsgebot* actually hurts all consumers, even the welfare of those that would drink exclusively Bavarian beer with or without the law, because all prices would otherwise have been lower. Trade data seem to confirm these arguments. Germany had the lowest import penetration of beer in the EU.

So what happened after the ECJ ruling of 1987? If the *Reinheitsgebot* had been artificially repressing import penetration as the ECJ ruled it had, then its repeal should have increased the availability of imported beers in Germany. Data show that the market share for imported beers increased—slowly but significantly. Before the ECJ ruling, the market share for imported beer in Germany stood at just 1 percent. By 2000, a decade after the change in the rule, imported beers had increased to around 4 percent of the share of domestic consumption (Figure 9.1). Only after 2004, fifteen years after the ECJ ruling, was there a strong increase in imported beer. During the following four years Germany's import market share more than doubled, to 9 percent, although this is still substantially below the European average of 17 percent.

Competition or Contamination?

The long-lasting relevance of the *Reinheitsgebot* speaks to the deep-seated political power of regional Bavarian brewers. As a result of their continued

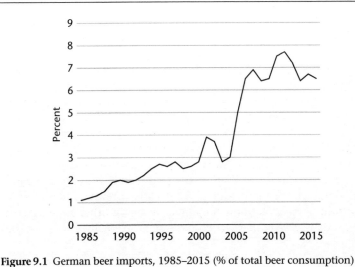

Figure 9.1 German beer imports, 1985–2015 (% of total beer consumption)

Van Tongeren, F. (2011). Standards and International Trade Integration: A Historical Review of the German "Reinheitsgebot." In J. Swinnen (ed.), *The Economics of Beer*. Oxford University Press; and Karrenbrock, J. (2016). The Internationalization of the Beer Brewing Industry. *Review* 72, Deutscher Brauer-Bund.

efforts, the *Reinheitsgebot* continued for five centuries, placing strict and burdensome red tape on the sale of beers beyond the traditional bottom-fermented pilsner style. The history of the *Reinheitsgebot* is a testament to the political influence of brewers' guilds and trade associations in southern Germany. Through legal and political arguments in state and national courts, it determined the beer style of Germany.

Van Tongeren explains that the taste component and consumer perception probably played a big role in the slow change after the ECJ ruling of 1987—"the adherence of Germans to what they think is quality beer." In fact, far from fading from relevancy, the *Reinheitsgebot* transitioned to function as a signal of quality. German breweries began advertising their adherence to the *Reinheitsgebot* prominently on bottles, and consumers responded.

The preference for tradition in beer is nowhere better on display than at Oktoberfest. Each fall, locals and tourists alike don traditional Bavarian garb, lederhosen for the men and cleavage-accentuating dirndls for the woman. Though the bright colors and synthetic fabrics seem out of place on postured mannequins, the antiquated cuts retain a timelessness once inside the tents, where the clash of thick liter glasses is drowned out by the sound of accented voices singing in unison.

10

From Land to Brand

How Nineteenth-Century Nationalist Politics Planted the Seeds for the Global Trademark Battle over "Budweiser"

The remnants of the communist period are still widespread in Europe's former Eastern Bloc: functional housing complexes—the egalitarian architecture of Le Corbusier—chipped paint, graffiti covered, and abandoned. But the city of České Budějovice tries its hardest to present itself as a picturesque tourist destination. Proximity to the castle in Ceský Krumlov doesn't hurt. The fourth largest city in the Czech Republic, Budějovice's pre-World War II architecture largely escaped destruction, the Habsburg-era ornamentation preserved under fresh coats of San Francisco pastels. It's a colorful city, decidedly divergent from the greyscale markings of its peers. But wander a few blocks beyond the designated city center and traces of its past are unmistakable. Even the old Europe architecture has a darker history—so much of the Czech Republic was preserved because Adolf Hitler invaded early, easily, and uncontested thanks to the appeasement policy of the League of Nations. The twentieth century has been rough for České Budějovice, formerly the multilingual Czech- and German-speaking city of Budweis under the Habsburg Empire. The city has a long history: in 1265, when the Kingdom of Bohemia was at the height of its power, King Přemysl Ottokar II first established the city as Budiwoj by giving 260 families the right to brew beer.

Culturally, České Budějovice is worlds away from the American city of St. Louis. And, yet, the two share a similar feeling of existing at crossroads of history. St. Louis' location along the Mississippi River turned it into a trade city, connecting Canada to New Orleans, while its eastern border to the wooded Missouri is known as gateway to the West—the cross-section of established American colonies and frontier first navigated by Lewis and Clark. Residents identify with the Midwestern culture of Chicago and Detroit, despite Missouri's complicated status as part of the American South. It was the only slave state to staunchly support the Union from the beginning of the Civil War. Even its famously unpredictable climate points to the city's ever-changing regional identity: the seasonal extremes from the landlocked Northwest intersect with tropical storms by way of Louisiana. And then there's the population: historically home to Southern belles and gentlemen, Mississippi merchants, and Western-bound working-class families looking for opportunity—just not looking hard enough to brave the wilderness, with many of these migrants coming from old Europe: Ashkenazi Jewish and German Catholic immigrants, demographically distinguishing the city from its staunchly Evangelical peers south of the Mason–Dixon line. One such German immigrant, Ebenhard Anheuser, established the city's most recognizable icon in 1860: Budweiser beer.

There's nothing Czech beer drinkers scorn more than American Budweiser. It's injurious, really, that the biggest brand in the world co-opted the German name of their city České Budějovice. The added insult: the perceived inferiority of America's favorite light lager. Central European loyalty rests squarely with Czech Budweiser Budvar, the "Budweiser" part of the name a German relic from its past as a city with two names. American beer drinkers, on the other hand, either don't know about the dispute or don't see why a Czech-speaking nation should have inherent trademark rights to the German word for their city. The difference in opinion highlights just how radically the political economy of beer has changed in a short period of time. Less than a century ago, in pre-World War I Europe, the idea that an American brewery might attempt to sell their beer as "Budweiser" to the Pilsner-loving Viennese royal courts would have just been confusing: American Budweiser wasn't a "brand," it was an oxymoron—a contradiction in terms. A century later, it's a billion-dollar question for an entirely new type of court.

Every couple of months, there seems to be some new ruling in the battle between Budweiser Budvar and Anheuser Busch over some iteration of all or part of the word "Budweiser." Myths and recycled facts cloud the issue of each new lawsuit: who registered the trademark first, which trademark laws are in violation of which international trademark laws, the extent to which Budweiser Budvar's tenuous claim to geographic origin applies. And when the fight over "Budweiser" is settled, the fight over "Bud" begins. Fifteen years ago, the firms were duking it out in a hundred separate legal battles all over the world, according to Budvar spokesperson Petr Samec. But the dispute has calmed down in recent years. These days there are only twenty cases still active. Budvar is definitely the "David" of this story, the small state-owned brewery heading up against "Goliath" Anheuser Busch, which was the biggest brewery in the world for most of the twentieth century and is today part of the biggest global multinational, AB InBev.

It's easily the oldest international trademark dispute, and the number of issues it forces courts to consider is mind-boggling. "Budweiser" was one of the earliest registered trademarks in America. But while Anheuser Busch cornered the politically stable US market with Budweiser, its counterpart in modern-day České Budějovice found itself in the crossfire of political and ideological tensions and military conflict. In one century, from the beginning of the twentieth to the beginning of the twenty-first century, the small city of České Budějovice went from being part of the Austro-Hungarian Empire, to independent Czechoslovak Republic, soon to be invaded and occupied by first Nazi Germany and then the Soviet Union. The fall of the Berlin Wall in 1989 sent the Soviets packing and brought back democratic elections in Czechoslovakia. This lasted for a few brief years, until the country split in two in 1993 with the Czech Republic separating from Slovakia. Ten years later both countries integrated into the EU. Phew.

All the while, Budweiser Budvar's reputation for quality beer was an asset serving different ends for political regimes that were directly at odds with one another. In short, this makes for a messy trademark dispute, one that forces every nation to call into question the validity of trading agreements established between entities that may or may not be politically relevant any longer. Should neighboring countries continue to honor their 1970s treaties with communist Czechoslovakia? But also, what right does a Czech-speaking country have to the German name after expelling German people from their borders after World War II?

For preceding the tale of two beers with one name is a tale of one city with two names: German Budweis and Czech České Budějovice. Beer has played an imperative role in the political economy of Budweis, one of many cities where Czech-speaking peasantry immigrated to German-speaking towns during the industrial revolution. Historian Jeremy King has analyzed archives and town political records kept since the mid-nineteenth century, documenting how the political economy of Budweis and České Budějovice serves as a microcosm of Europe as a whole. The depiction that emerges is of a period and a continent where emerging nationalist tensions ran so high and ideological conflicts so deep that they would cause near total destruction and a decade-long division of the European continent.

A Tale of Two City Names

Under the Habsburg Empire, České Budějovice was officially Budweis and Plzen was officially Pilsen. King Charles IV established the so-called "mile rule," giving German-speaking settlers in southern Bohemia monopolistic control of brewing activity for about nine kilometers around the city. In 1785, Bürgerliches Brauhaus Budweis was founded, and in 1876 the brewery officially trademarked "Budweiser Bier" in what was then the Kingdom of Bohemia.

The Bürgerliches Brauhaus was collectively owned by town property-holders and operated by a town hall committee, both of which were de facto German-speaking individuals. Representation for the town hall was decided on the same basis of property ownership in the town. The brewery was more than a public brewery—it was the means by which German speakers could maintain political power through control of the beer supply.

Almost a century later, the industrial revolution induced Czech-speaking peasants to migrate to towns, and a Czech-speaking middle class began to emerge. Led by Dr. August Zatka, Czech speakers founded a joint stock company, České Budějovický Akciovký Pivovar (or "Czech Budweis Joint Stock Brewery") in 1895 to compete with the publicly owned Brauhaus Budweis. Zatka's Budvar sold small, affordable shares that allowed non-property-holding Czech migrants to buy into the operation. The private corporation was not linked to town political power, but Zatka believed it was a means to the economic elevation of Czech people. They produced a beer called Budvar—a shortening of Budéjovický Pivovar (Budéjovický Brewery). But because German Budweiser was known and easier to pronounce, they marketed it abroad as Budweiser Budvar—distinguished from Budweiser Bier of the Bürgerliches Brauhaus Budweis. One advertisement shows the original Bürger brewery marketing their beer as "Budweiser Urquell," similar to the beer Pilsner Urquell in Pilsen (see Chapter 4).

Beer became the means by which town citizens declared their political allegiances and ethnic identity. Those who identified with the old German order drank Budweiser Bier, those who identified with the new Czech-led industrialism drank Budweiser Budvar. Soon, the Czech brewery began to turn a steady profit for its shareholders. Budvar grew wealthier and became more popular as an export as Budweiser Bier lagged behind, creating tensions in the town.

The Battle of the Budweisers

Meanwhile, unbeknownst to the Germans and Czechs fighting town politics, the German name of their city was being co-opted in the New World. Bavarian immigrant Ebenhard Anheuser founded the Bavarian Brewing Company in 1860 in St. Louis and began producing a "Budweiser" beer. When his son-in-law Adolphus Busch took over operations, he took the first steps to register "Budweiser" as a trademark. This was early in American history, when trademarks still didn't mean much. Busch's initial attempts failed, but he was persistent and in 1907 managed to secure "Budweiser" as one of the first exclusive trademarks to be registered with the American federal government. Busch claimed that he made up the name, but a letter to his grandson that was excavated decades later indicated that he named the beer "Budweiser" after "a respected brewery in Europe."

Early on, the distribution scope was local. Bürgerliches Brauhaus started exporting their "Budweiser Bier" to the US in 1875, but the two Budweisers didn't come face to face until the St. Louis World Fair in 1911. At this point, a casual agreement between the two companies was made: Anheuser Busch could exclusively market its "Budweiser" in America, while Bürgerliches Brauhaus had exclusive terrain in the old world. Note that this agreement was made with Bürgerliches Brauhaus and not with the Czech-speaking Budvar brewery involved in today's trademark disputes.

The Habsburg Empire had a tense relationship with America. Nicole Phelps, a historian who wrote her dissertation on communication between the Habsburgs and America, describes the nature of their relationship: "They didn't go to war with each other until World War I, but they did have a lot of disputes." In her archival research, Phelps dug up one document that illustrates the differing perspectives of the US and the Habsburgs on geographical indication. In 1911, the US Department of Agriculture communicated with the Austrian Interior Ministry about whether a beer had to be made in Pilsen to officially be called a pilsner. "Of course they [the Austrian Interior Ministry] said 'Yes, it does have to be made in Pilsen'." According to Phelps, the Habsburgs had the political stature to back up the exclusivity of their local monopolies on Pilsner and Budweiser until World War I changed the nature of the game.

The dissolution of the Habsburg Empire resulted in the establishment of the Czechoslovak Republic. With political independence came dependence on aid from the victors. "The Czechoslovak government really needed continued assistance," explains Phelps. "Central Europe had been blockaded by the Allies, so there had been all this economic devastation, and they still needed food imports which they're getting mostly from the US. It's not really a time when they can say 'Oh, by the way, we're going to insist on our exclusive right to Budweiser beer'."

Moreover, the recently formed nation was feeble. "The borders are hazy, there's still fighting going on, it's all kind of a big mess and it's in flux," says Phelps. In České Budějovice (now officially named), this big mess meant tension between the Germans and Czechs. Meanwhile, the bordering German Weimar Republic was crippled by inflation. By the mid-1930s, Adolf Hitler had risen to power and made his intentions to invade Czechoslovakia clear. In 1937, the weak Czechoslovak government was gathering resources to fight Hitler's announced invasion.

Back in America, CEO August Busch II spotted an opportunity to take advantage of the uncertain future of Czechoslovakia. Anheuser Busch proposed a meeting to discuss trademark issues surrounding "Budweiser." They paid a dividend of 127,000 dollars to the Czechoslovak government for the concession that Czechoslovak breweries not be allowed to call their beer "Budweiser" within America. A few months later, Czechoslovakia fell into German hands and the town was renamed Budweis.

The end of World War II brought about yet another paradigm shift in the great cross-global Budweiser rivalry. After 1945, the Soviet Union occupied Czechoslovakia. Leader Joseph Stalin exiled all traces of German-speaking history from the landscape. Budweis was officially renamed České Budějovice again. Bürgerliches Brauhaus and Budvar were integrated into the centralized command economy, but they remained two separate breweries. As part of the effort to eliminate all traces of their former connection to the German language and German-speaking peoples, Bürgerliches Brauhaus Budweis was renamed Meštanský Pivovar Budějovice. The former "Budweiser Bier" was rebranded as "Samson" and produced for domestic consumption.

The communist government was desperate for exports and Czech beer was one of their more reliably popular products. Despite being rebranded domestically with Czech names, Budweiser Budvar exported its beer under the German brand name. Since Budweiser Budvar and Samson were both communist state-owned breweries, the Communist

Party transferred the "Budweiser Beer" trademark from Samson to Budweiser Budvar for international export. Czechoslovakia also pursued some strategic trade agreements with Western European states to limit competition with American Budweiser, specifically with Austria and Germany, two nations that had long been reliable customers for Czech-style pilsner.

The Iron Curtain prevented a trademark war for decades during the Cold War. But the geopolitical context changed again in 1989 when a wave of revolutions brought about political and market reforms in the former Eastern Bloc. Following the Czechoslovak Velvet Revolution, the new government transitioned all companies into joint stock corporations and distributed stock among citizens, which could be traded on the free market. There were a few exceptions, including Budweiser Budvar, which stayed state-owned. The Czech government feared that if Budweiser Budvar became a publicly traded company, it would only be a matter of time until Anheuser Busch obtained a controlling share and shut it down.

During the early 1990s, Anheuser Busch tried to woo the citizens of České Budějovice. King describes how Anheuser Busch operated a giant red-, white-, and blue-adorned Czech–American friendship center in an effort to drum up local support for state sale of the brewery. "Anheuser Busch was very interested in buying the company twenty years ago," explains Petr Samec, representative of Budweiser Budvar. "The negotiations stopped because the conditions they provided were not acceptable to the Czech government because there were no guarantees that the brand Budweiser in the city would go on."

"It's possible to say the intellectual property is the most valuable part of the company," says Samec. But the Czech government thinks differently: "The most important part of the company are the trademark, and the know-how, and the tradition."

"Bud" as Geographical Indication

For two decades since then, trademark disputes between Anheuser Busch and state-owned Budějovický Meštanský Pivovar have been fought in courts all over the world, running the gamut on claims regarding which one could obtain exclusive marketing claims to three letters: "Bud".

It's easy to grasp the conceptual necessity of exclusive trademark rights to free market economies. Put simply, they give firms the incentive to maintain standards of quality and consistency by preventing a free-rider problem. They're a promise between firm and consumer, and consumers develop brand loyalty when they get consistent results from branded products. None of this can work without the ability to secure exclusive rights to a particular brand name. But before trademark law, there was terroir, the French notion that certain geographic regions produce food and drink a certain way. Under the guise of terroir, French regions such as Bordeaux and Burgundy maintain the exclusive right to market their respective styles of wine. To connoisseurs, terroir is about taste, but to economists it's about the trademark (see Chapter 13). Wine exports have historically been a major source of wealth for the French political economy. By retaining exclusive trademark rights to French regions, France is effectively ensuring that they can profit from perceived quality markers such as "Bordeaux" or "Champagne."

Does beer have a claim to terroir? Historically a low-value market compared to wine, beer production still maintains some basic factual similarities to vineyards. After all, it was the fresh spring water, local Saaz hops, and barley that famously allowed Josef Kroll to develop the first light lager, the Pilsner. Today, the Pilsner Urquell brand guarantees consumers a certain quality standard rooted in tradition, while the word "pilsner" has entered the beer lexicon as a style. Legally, the application of terroir to beer has few and unpromising precedents in favor of geographic association with style. The relevant ones have centered on the Budweiser trademark dispute.

In 2005, the World Trade Organization (WTO) ruled against Budéjovický Budvar's claim to "Budweiser," and later this precedent was extended to "Bud." The WTO ruling centered on the Agreement on Trade-Related Aspects of International Property Rights (TRIPS), signed by both America and EU member states. The US expressed concern that the EU legislation gave more protection to the geographical indications (GIs) of EU members that were denied the same protection for American equivalents. The WTO sided with the US, ruling that GIs shouldn't interfere with pre-existing product trademarks. This ruling included an additional blow to Budvar: GI protection does not extend to names in translation. While the GI registration of Budejovické pivo was fair and legitimate, this did not translate into the protection of Budweiser. The city of České Budějovice had effectively rescinded its claim to the German translation of its name when Czechoslovakia had erased all traces of its German past following World War II. Though the WTO ruling created some promising precedents for American Budweiser, there remained ambiguity. The WTO also ruled that individual member states of the EU could terminate Bud and Budweiser trademarks if they viewed them as infringing on the GI of České Budějovice. And so the disputes continued.

Justice Wears Beer Goggles

In the past fifteen years or so, the Budweiser trademark battle between Budweiser Budvar and Anheuser Busch has been fought in courts in countries all over the world, with diverse results. The fate of the two brands has diverged in each EU state contingent on national laws and historical context. The following two case studies, of Austria and the UK, offer a lens through which to view how different EU member states have approached the trademark dispute.

The linguistic, ethnic, and cultural differences between Austria and the Czech Republic today belie a deeply intertwined history, shared border, and taste for hoppy Pilsner. After all, the city of Budweis has had its fair share of hand-offs. Budweiser Budvar found itself exported from the Kingdom of Bohemia to the Czechoslovak Republic to Nazi occupation to Soviet occupation to communist Czechoslovakia to liberal Czechoslovakia to the Czech Republic. And then the Czech Republic joined the EU. The other big question that the Budweiser trademark dispute has brought to the forefront is: which of the treaties made by governments of the past carry over to regulatory organizations in the present?

In 1976, Austria signed a bilateral treaty with communist Czechoslovakia granting Budvar exclusive rights to market its beer as "Bud" in their neighboring nation. When the Czech Republic joined the EU in 2004, American Anheuser Busch seized the opportunity to contest this treaty. They began exporting American Budweiser to Austria under the brand names "Bud" and "American Bud." Budvar took the issue to court. The trademark dispute was decided in the Vienna Commercial Court with a simultaneous advisory hearing in the ECJ. The issue at stake: to what extent did the Austria-Czechoslovakia Treaty of 1974 apply to the post-EU Czech Republic?

The Vienna Commercial Court and the ECJ reached the same decision. The ECJ decided that the Czech Republic and Austria were both Member States of the European Union, and any pre-2004 agreements that contradicted EU community law were deemed void. EU community law includes the TRIPS agreement with America rescinding Budvar's claim to exclusivity of "Bud." It was still in Austria's power to decide the individual fate of "Bud" under its own appellate of origins laws. The Vienna Commercial Court was the one to make this decision. Yet another blow to Budvar. The court decided that "Bud" did not meet the standards for exclusive appellate of origin. It was fully within the rights of American Budweiser to export their beer to Austria under the "Bud" name.

A similar decision was made in Britain, to which both beers had been exported for over thirty years. Not only did both brands have an established product presence, but they viewed the island nation as a promising market for growth. Britain has no national lager, so the popularity of the style falls on Canadian Carling, Belgian Stella Artois, and both nations' iterations of Budweiser for their lighter beverages.

Budweiser Budvar had long been producing its lager within the UK through a domestic subsidiary. This alone rescinded claims to appellate of origin in export. But American Budweiser had also been exporting to the UK for some time. Both firms had tried and failed to register Budweiser and Bud for decades. In the latest suit, Anheuser Busch sued for the exclusive trademark rights to "Budweiser" within Britain. They argued that they had tried to register Budweiser before Budvar, and therefore had the right to the trademark. Courts had a vacuum of precedent, and little guidance from previous treaties.

The courts opted to allow both brands trademark rights. The ruling argued that based on over thirty years of exporting, different packaging and logos, and the general familiarity of British beer drinkers with brands and reputations, exclusive right to the trademark by one brand was not necessary.

The two breweries continue duking it out in courts around the world, establishing precedents for trademark case law as they go. In addition to being the world's first and longest trademark dispute, the "Battle of the Buds" exemplifies the inherent tension in formerly land-based commodities seeing their value derived from the rise of branding in an increasingly globalized world.

11

The Great Convergence

The Fall of the Beer-Drinking Nation and the Rise of the Beer-Drinking World

> You can't be a real country unless you have a beer and an airline. It helps if you have some kind of football team, or some nuclear weapons, but at the very least, you need a beer.
>
> Frank Zappa

Though beer predates the modern nation-state by several millennia, its production and distribution has long been tied to political power and influence—from the medieval role of monasteries to the crucial role of taxation of commercial brewing in funding British imperialist conquests. It's no surprise that nineteenth-century nationalist movements drew on regional beer-drinking customs to support their causes. The Irish republican cause spread through drinking songs over Guinness in rural pubs. Czech *pivovars* and German *brauhauses* in ethnically diverse Bohemia became the means through which citizens mediated ethnic tensions and alliances, as described in Chapter 10.

These popular histories still shape our perceptions of which nations are the biggest beer drinkers today. When we think of Germany, we imagine lederhosen-donning Bavarians toasting liters of heady pilsner every autumnal Oktoberfest. Britain conjures images of Londoners crowding into pubs after work to share pints of porter and pale ale. And then there's the café-centric Belgium, where beer connoisseurs travel to experience sweet abbey ales, perfect pours, and ornate glass goblets.

Beer plays such an integral role in the social life of these nations because of their historical geographic and material limitations. The most famous beer-drinking nations have temperate weather. The perpetually drizzling Britain and mild-seasoned Germany lack the warm

Mediterranean conditions necessary for vineyards. But they also don't experience the frigid winters that characterize the spirits-drinking cultures of Nordic and Eastern European countries. Geography has had an obvious historic influence on the production and consumption of alcohol, as has ancestry, culture, religion, and economic trends.

How do our stereotypes of which nations drink the most beer match up with reality today? How has economic development affected beer drinking? And what is the fate of the mythic beer-drinking nation in a globally integrated economy? These are questions only an economist can answer.

The Beer-Drinking Nation: Myth or Reality?

Forget lederhosen and lager pride: which nations actually consume the most beer? Global beer consumption has long been concentrated in three nations: the United States, Britain, and Germany (Figure 11.1). In 1960, these three accounted for more than half of worldwide beer consumption by volume. Fifty years later, in 2010, they claimed less than one quarter. What happened?

The simple answer is: China, Russia, and Brazil—and fast. Over the past decade, China surpassed the United States as the single largest beer market, Russia overtook Germany, and Brazil surpassed Britain (Table 11.1).

These simple observations suggest major changes in global beer markets but not what caused them. It may be that beer consumption

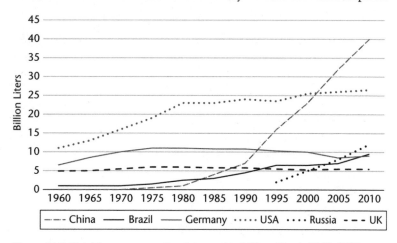

Figure 11.1 Total beer consumption by country (billion liters), 1960–2010
FAOstat

Table 11.1 Top five beer markets in the world, 1960–2010

1960	Billion liters	Share of world consumption
1. US	11.2	26.0
2. Germany	6.8	15.7
3. UK	4.7	10.9
4. Russia (USSR)	2.7	6.2
5. France	1.7	3.9

2010	Billion liters	Share of world consumption
1. China	45.5	25.8
2. US	25.6	14.5
3. Brazil	12.8	7.3
4. Russia	9.9	5.6
5. Germany	8.1	4.6

FAOstat

declined in the leading countries, or that beer drinking increased in the emerging economies or in countries which traditionally consumed mostly other alcoholic beverages such as spirits or wine. It turns out that all three are true. Markets in traditional beer-drinking nations are shrinking while beer markets in emerging economies and in traditional wine- and spirits-drinking countries are growing.

The size of these markets is highly dependent on population of course. While China is now the largest beer market in the world, the Chinese still don't drink anywhere near the volume of beer per capita that the Germans and Irish do. There are just far, far more Chinese. With an annual consumption of 25 liters per capita, China still does not touch the habitual consumption of citizens from beer-loving nations. Our stereotypes of these nations still dominate the list of highest per capita consumption: the Czechs earn the title of world-class beer drinkers, with an annual 143 liters per capita in 2013–14. Germany and Austria are close behind, both circling 110 liters.

But it's not just population growth driving China's race to the top. Germans may still drink way more beer, but the Chinese are drinking more and more beer every day. China's per capita beer consumption started at a feeble annual 1 liter per capita in the early 1980s, when their economic liberalization process started. But it has grown rapidly with the country's economic growth in the past three decades. Today's 25 liters of beer per capita thus means a twenty-fivefold increase over thirty years. In fact, there was a spectacular spike in beer consumption in the decade between 1995 and 2005. Similarly, Russian per capita beer consumption grew dramatically during its transition from a communist and vodka-drinking nation to a capitalist regime (see Chapter 12).

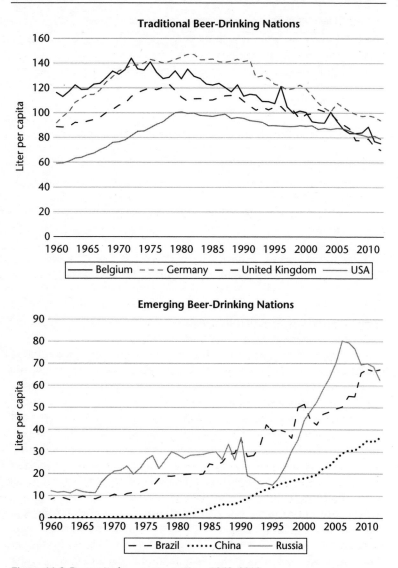

Figure 11.2 Per capita beer consumption, 1960–2010

FAOstat; and Colen, L. and Swinnen, J. (2016). Economic Growth, Globalization and Beer Consumption. *Journal of Agricultural Economics*, 67(1): 186–207.

While beer consumption has skyrocketed in emerging markets, the exact opposite trend has been at work in the historically largest beer markets. As Figure 11.2 illustrates, per capita consumption in countries like Belgium, the UK, the US, and Germany increased significantly after

World War II and through the 1960s and the 1970s. But beer consumption did not grow forever. It peaked sometime in the 1970s or 1980s, depending on the country. Since then, beer consumption has declined. This decline has been long (almost forty years in Belgium) and deep (from 145 to less than 100 liters per capita in Germany).

Total beer consumption in these nations has declined as a consequence. The exception is the US. Because immigration (and thus population growth) is much stronger in the US, total beer consumption has not fallen, despite the fact that per capita consumption has declined significantly.

What caused these changes? The fact that both China and Russia started consuming more beer when they switched from communism to capitalism may suggest that economic ideology (or the market) has something to do with it. Our research together with Liesbeth Colen, an economist formerly of the University of Leuven and now at the European Commission, suggests it may have, but indirectly so. We find two crucial factors: economic growth (income) and globalization.

Beer Consumption and Incomes

What happens when people have more or less money to spend? Economists and psychologists have argued about the impact of economic recessions on alcohol consumption patterns. Psychologists suggest that alcohol consumption, in particular alcohol abuse, increases during recessions as a response to the stresses of economic downturns. However, economists argue that as people's incomes fall during recessions they have less money to spend, and thus beer consumption will fall. Donald Freeman, an economist from the Sam Houston State University in Texas, who has carefully analyzed various datasets with different methodologies, concludes that, at least for the US, the data say that beer consumption does fall when incomes decline, and vice versa, but that the effect is modest.

But these studies typically focus on the short run—recessions typically last only a few years, after all. So what about the long run? Would we see the same reaction between income and consumption during, say, the Great Depression? Our research suggests probably not. The relationship between income and beer consumption is not fixed; it changes when countries get richer. In other words, the impact of increasing incomes in poor countries like China is different than increasing incomes in rich countries like the US. Look at the lines in Figure 11.2. For the "emerging countries" there is a clear increase in beer consumption over the past decades—a period of rapid income growth for most of these countries. Yet in the richer "beer-drinking nations," such as Germany, the US, and Belgium, where incomes have also increased, the evolution of beer consumption is very different. It looks like what economists call "an inverted U-shaped correlation." If people are poor and get wealthier, they can afford to spend more, and they consume more beer. But at some point this trend hits a turning point, and beer consumption begins to fall as incomes rise.

Why would beer consumption decline as incomes rise? The simplest explanation is that at some point people have had enough. There is likely an upper limit of how much consumers appreciate beer consumption. When a nation reaches this level of consumption, enjoyment does not increase with more beer. Another explanation is increased awareness and concerns about the potential negative health effects of alcohol consumption when income rises. Since the 1970s and 1980s, the health risks of alcohol consumption have become more apparent. Wealthier countries have demonstrated more concern regarding the health and social consequences of alcohol use. Governments have responded to increased health concerns by taxing alcohol, imposing limits on advertising and the sale of alcohol, and passing laws against drunk driving. Health concerns and regulations also work indirectly: studies find that the ban on smoking in bars has contributed to reduced beer consumption.

Using data from countries all over the world from the past fifty years, we calculated the turning point, i.e. the income level at which beer consumption starts declining with growing incomes. We found this turning point to be approximately US$21,000 per capita. This income level was reached by Belgium and the US in the 1970s, by Germany in the early 1980s, and by the UK in the mid-1980s.

These countries also demonstrate a tendency toward higher value beers. The trend away from pilsners in traditionally beer-drinking nations is reflected in a general attitude of "drink less, taste more." So while beer-drinking countries may be drinking less beer, they're also drinking more expensive beer.

The Global Convergence of Tastes

In James Joyce's *Ulysses*, Leopold Bloom speculates that "a good puzzle would be to cross Dublin without passing a pub." The venues are somewhat omnipresent along the twisty cobblestoned streets. Residents have go-tos, while newcomers learn that little distinguishes one darkened room and pint of mixed from the next. And the habitual after-work pint of Guinness is a given. Or is it?

Recently, Dublin has become somewhat of a magnet for foreign investors and headquarters of global companies thanks to low taxes on corporations. And as the big glass office buildings for multinationals have reshaped the horizon line, a crop of airy wine bars with international specialties, trendy décor, and tasting menus have found unexpected success among the old public houses of yore.

Dublin is not an exception. Trendy wine bars have opened up all over London and Brussels. As traditional beer-drinking nations get richer, they can afford to drink more exotic, imported beverages, such as wine and spirits. Inhabitants of traditional beer-drinking nations travel more as incomes increase, they are exposed to different tastes, and they're living in a more globalized world where the cost of imported wines and spirits has fallen. Declining prices for imported wines and cosmopolitan tastes may make the traditional pilsners of their grandparents seem old fashioned, as the next generation opts for something exotic: wine and spirits. Interestingly, this trend works the opposite way in countries where spirits and wine were the traditional drink. While Dubliners and Berliners now increasingly sip on wines, Parisians, Romans, and Russians now see an exotic quality to beer that they didn't before. As incomes increase in traditionally wine- and spirits-drinking nations, we observe an increase in beer consumption.

This change is dramatic, as Figure 11.3 illustrates. The graph shows the share of beer in total alcohol consumption for three traditional "beer-drinking nations" (Ireland, the UK, and Belgium) and three traditional "wine-drinking nations" (Spain, Italy, and Argentina). In the 1960s, the share of beer in the beer countries is around 80 percent and less than 10 percent in the wine countries. However, the gap has consistently narrowed since then. By now, there is little difference between beer and wine consumption in these categories. In fact, some of the traditional wine countries have even overtaken some of the traditional beer countries. The share of beer in total alcohol consumption has fallen from around 80 percent in the 1960s to less than 50 percent today in Ireland, the UK, and Belgium. Meanwhile, the opposite has occurred in countries like Spain, Italy, Greece, and Argentina. Beer is their new favorite drink, while wine is on its way out. In Spain, the share of wine in alcohol consumption fell from 65 to 38 percent between 1960 and 2010, and Greece experienced a similar fall in wine consumption from 86 to 50 percent. In all these countries, the share of beer increased sharply. A similar trend appears to be at work in traditional spirits-drinking nations. Russia and Poland have seen a sharp fall in vodka

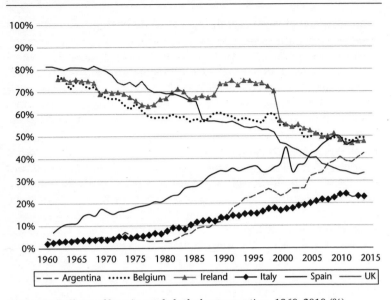

Figure 11.3 Share of beer in total alcohol consumption, 1960–2010 (%)

World Health Organization (WHO); and Colen, L. and Swinnen, J. (2016). Economic Growth, Globalization and Beer Consumption, *Journal of Agricultural Economics*, 67(1): 186–207.

consumption accompanying a rise in beer in recent years. In China, spirits consumption fell from 98.5 percent to 60 percent from 1961 to 2010. During the same period, beer consumption increased from 2 to 36 percent.

A Beer-Drinking World

The concept of beer-drinking nations (like Ireland and Belgium), wine-drinking nations (like Spain and Italy), and vodka-drinking nations (like Russia and Poland) is a thing of the past. Globalization has made the world's alcohol consumption patterns much more homogeneous than those of our ancestors. The impact on the breweries and the wineries is mixed. Those that have focused primarily on domestic consumers have seen their markets divide, and many have disappeared.

In contrast, those breweries that looked across the borders of their native countries saw their diminishing home market replaced by a much bigger global market. Today, Heineken, Guinness, Corona, and Stella Artois are available around the globe. Belgium is a good example of these dramatic changes. As Chapter 14 describes, Belgian breweries have adapted well to the changed market conditions. While domestic Belgian beer consumption has declined sharply, production has actually increased—much of it directed for export to so-called traditionally wine- and spirits-drinking countries.

A global "convergence of tastes" is changing alcohol consumption patterns. Nations that have long consumed a majority of their alcohol as one traditional drink are now consuming non-traditional forms in higher quantities. Today's drinkers are not taking their cues from geography or the traditions of their ancestors when determining their drink of choice. Nowhere was this more obvious than in Russia around the turn of the century.

12

From Vodka to Baltika

Deciphering Russia's Recent Love Affair with Beer

There is a famous scene in *Crime and Punishment* when Raskolnikov meets the town drunk at a bar. Despite his failure to support his family and his young daughters being sold into prostitution, it was he who suffered most miserably because, no matter how much he drank, he couldn't drink enough to forget this. Far from escapism, his alcoholism was slavery: he was powerless under the influence of vodka. The scene calls into question some truth about human nature for soon-to-be-murderer Raskolnikov to turn over in his mind: whether a man is in control or powerless in the face of an influence, whether the suffering imposed on himself and others is his own fault or a tragic situation. For as long as the Cyrillic alphabet has permitted Slavic writers to make permanent their sentiments, literature has presented the relationship of Russians to vodka as a tumultuous love affair, one inspired by diehard loyalty, mutual mistrust, and abuse.

However, future novelists may tell a different story. After centuries of a spirits-centric social fabric, in the 1990s the vodka-fueled nation unexpectedly switched to beer. The share of vodka as a percentage of total alcohol consumption fell from 40 to 15 percent, while beer consumption went through the roof. From 1995 to 2008, per capita beer consumption rose from 15 to 80 liters—a more than fivefold increase in consumption in less than a decade and a half before leveling off at around 80 liters per capita (Figure 12.1). This trend puts their per capita consumption at the same level as traditional beer-drinking countries like Belgium, in addition to positioning Russia as one of the most

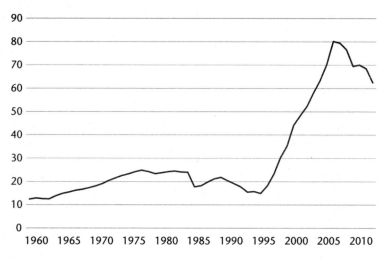

Figure 12.1 Beer consumption in Russia (liters per capita), 1960–2012
FAOstat

lucrative beer markets. In 2005, Russia's beer consumption surpassed Germany to become the third largest beer market in the world.

This dramatic change intrigued Koen Deconinck, an economist at the OECD and former PhD student at the University of Leuven. "When you look at the graph of beer consumption in Russia—it's like a hockey stick. It's almost flat until 1994, and then it just skyrockets," relates Deconinck. The most interesting question facing him: why did Russia suddenly switch to beer? Or, to take Russia as a choice case study: what, exactly, does it take for a spirits-drinking nation to transform to a nation of beer drinkers in such a short period of time? This is not just any spirits-drinking nation; this is Russia.

In his search for answers, Deconinck started doing what economists are trained to do: "I started with looking into the usual suspects: prices and incomes." It is true that after 1995, the price of vodka increased while the price of beer fell, but the changes were not anywhere close to significant enough to explain the change in consumption habits. Similarly, there were significant income changes but they did not relate easily to changes in beer consumption. After all, when incomes declined in Russia from 1990 to 1995, beer consumption still increased by 50 percent. In economic terms, Deconinck notes that "Neither prices nor incomes could explain the effects." He was trying to decipher a sustained, ten-year quintupling of consumption after all, launching Russia to the top league of beer-drinking nations. There must be different factors behind such a fundamental shift. So he turned to the history of vodka in Russia. Little did he know that the story was about to get a lot darker.

The Politics of Vodka

Historically, vodka consumption and mortality in Russia have been highly—and disturbingly—correlated. The Russian temperance movement of the early twentieth century represented the first attempt to curb intake of spirits at the dawn of the Bolshevik Revolution. Vodka was a major source of revenue for the oppressive czar, so communists teamed up with prohibitionists to encourage limited consumption. Following the Bolshevik triumph, the promised prohibition was short-lived—it was repealed only six years later in 1925. The stated reasoning was that alcoholism resulted from capitalist exploitation, and that a just society would bring about moderation on its own. Whether the promised society came to fruition is a value judgment, but high levels of alcohol consumption are a matter of fact. Vodka continued to be the drink of choice for the comrades during the height of the Soviet Union. And the mortality rate rose steadily during the decades of communist rule.

The tide turned in favor of moderation in more than one way when Mikhail Gorbachev became leader. A lifelong teetotaler and advocate for public health, Gorbachev recognized the corrosive role of excess vodka consumption on his nation. Under his rule, the Soviet Union implemented "Measures to Overcome Drunkenness and Alcoholism," a list of mandates as simple as forbidding the sale of vodka at work cafeterias. And they worked. In the four years following their implementation, the mortality rate dropped 24 percent in Russia—that's an estimated 1.6 million lives spared by stricter alcohol rules.

But the measures were unpopular and eventually Gorbachev's rules were no longer enforced—the campaign was repealed even before the Berlin Wall fell and the Soviet Union disbanded. The mortality rate spiked at 40 percent in the early 1990s. The institutional disruption and the end of the anti-alcohol campaign caused two million deaths. Among young men, life expectancy plummeted to fifty-seven years old—lower than the statistic for Haiti, North Korea, and Botswana.

In 1994, the new Russian government introduced a series of alcohol regulations similar to Gorbachev's efforts. They drew from Gorbachev's success, while including provisions designed for the new free market conditions.

Commercial Brewers and Commercial TV

The Russian government worried about the role that television might play in glorifying excess consumption, so alcohol was banned from TV commercials. But there was a loophole. Beverages with an alcohol content of under 10 percent weren't legally categorized as alcohol.

West of the former Iron Curtain it may sound like a joke, but the notion that beer is not alcoholic has deep roots in Russian culture. In fact, current beer market leader Baltika was founded with this conviction in mind. In 1978, the Gipropishcheprom-2 Institute submitted a plan to the Leningrad Association of Beer Brewing and Nonalcoholic Beverages Industry for a new brewery. Construction took a woeful twelve years, and by the time it was completed in 1990, the Soviet Union had disbanded, Leningrad was gone, and Baltika was located in St. Petersburg. They were also free to pursue profits.

The Soviet Union was a major producer of cheap cereals across its vast landscape, so when the markets opened, Russia was suddenly the world's leading producer of barley. However, this barley was usually grown for animal feed. Soviet-era breweries used low-quality barley to produce a watered down, subpar brew. But this was about to change.

Like in the rest of the former Eastern Bloc, the brewing and malting sector in Russia was one of the earliest to attract FDI from the West when the breweries were privatized and sold. In 1992 the Scandinavian joint venture Baltic Beverages Holding (later taken over by the Carlsberg Group) bought Baltika. Other multinational breweries such as Belgium's Interbrew, Turkish Efes, and Indian SUN breweries soon followed suit. French malting specialist Groupe Soufflet partnered with Baltika early on to build a malting subsidiary, Soufflet-St. Petersburg. The influx of foreign capital enabled major strides in stabilizing supply chains and investing in quality improvements to the barley malt and brewing sector.

These developments were well timed for Baltika's sudden strategic advantage over its competitors in the vodka industry: the ability to advertise on TV. Advertising was a new phenomenon in Russia. Never before did firms have the incentive to compete with each other, persuading customers into loyalty through memorable slogans and exaggerated claims of superiority. This was a population previously familiar only with Soviet propaganda at a time when loyalty to the state wasn't exactly "consumer choice." With the new possibility of drumming up sales through advertising, breweries found themselves poised to exploit their strategic advantage over high alcohol content competitors on broadcast television. When the regulations went into effect in 1994, several breweries rolled out ad campaigns introducing Russia to the new beer. The leading brewer, Baltika, put out a series of ads claiming that beer was originally invented in Russia. Beer consumption was framed as the reclamation of a lost (in reality false) history. And it worked. Sure enough, 1994 marks the origin of Russia's beer spike.

By 2008, the government corrected the advertising loophole, legally categorizing beer as alcohol and taking away the strategic advantage of breweries on TV. The impact was immediate. The growth in beer consumption halted and fell back in the following years to between 60 and 70 liters per capita (Figure 12.1). But the downturn is minor in the face of Russia's spectacular growth over the period from 1994 to 2008. By the end of this period, Russia had per capita beer consumption levels on a par with Belgium.

Drinking Age

They say you can't teach an old dog new tricks, but does this truism apply to the Russian beer market? Deconinck was interested in investigating how the changing demographics of Russia may have come into play in the beer spike. He approached the question with two hypotheses. It could be that a growing number of people began switching from vodka to beer, or that a small subset of society was driving the trend by drinking much more beer than vodka.

According to consumer surveys, the first hypothesis is more accurate. Rather than a small group of beer aficionados driving the trend, it appears that, across the board, Russians are drinking more beer and less vodka. The number of Russians drinking beer has been growing steadily since 1994 when the advertising started. And the changes indicated by these reports are significant: in 2003, 57 percent of the population reported drinking beer regularly, compared with 23 percent in 1995; the number of vodka drinkers decreased from 78 percent to 53 percent during this same time period.

Deconinck assumed that young people were driving the beer-drinking trend. Studies on consumption usually indicate that younger people shift habits more readily than older people. But when Deconinck broke the consumption surveys down by age group, he was surprised to find that beer drinking wasn't just a generational trend. More young people reported drinking beer, yes, but the increase in beer drinkers was fairly consistent across age groups. Even among the older generation (the fifty-plus age group), beer drinkers increased from 12 to 38 percent, while vodka fell slightly from 66 to 58 percent.

A Perfect Storm

So what does it take to turn a nation of diehard vodka drinkers (no dark pun intended) into beer lovers? Rather than point to any definitive factor, Deconinck prefers the "perfect storm" model to explain the long-lasting shift in habits. Quality improvements in barley, malt, and beer production after privatization and foreign investments changed what "beer" tasted like. While vodka advertising was banned, Baltika and Sun breweries launched major TV advertising campaigns of their new beers in the mid-1990s, around the time that vodka prices increased and incomes continued to fall.

Consumer survey data suggest that these initial changes in drinking behavior were propelled forward by peer pressure. Alcohol is social; people usually have what the rest of the group is having. After quality improvements, price changes, and television advertising convinced a critical mass of Russians to switch to beer in a short period of time, the rise in beer consumption was sustained by peer effects: once people started drinking beer, their friends did, establishing beer-drinking patterns in social groups and making permanent what might have been a temporary shift in habits. As Deconinck summarizes it: "People saw beer advertised, they saw that vodka was suddenly more expensive and beer cheaper, while their wages were falling, so they opted for beer and said, 'Hey, this isn't as bad as it was back in the Soviet days'."

And it appears that this perfect storm will have long-lasting effects. The younger the generation, the more likely they are to drink beer rather than vodka. Of the generation born after 1980, almost 80 percent drink beer, compared to around 40 percent of those born before 1960. This perfect storm may have changed the future of alcohol consumption, life expectancy, and eventually, Russian literature.

13

Trading Water or Terroir?

The Changing Nature of the Beer Trade

At some point in 2008, the American blogosphere got wind that Foster's, the imported lager heavily marketed for its Australian origins, was actually brewed by Molson and "imported" from Canada. Three years later, one Australian newspaper article made its rounds, revealing to customers that many of their favorite European brands—Peroni, Beck's, and Whitbread—were actually brewed under license by Foster's. The consumer reaction tended toward "How dare they?" After all, the "Australian for Beer" marketing campaign laid the Aussie accent on thick. But few people stepped back to point out one thing: how much sense does it make to ship beer to and from Australia, which is more than 7,000 miles from San Francisco and more than 10,000 miles from Europe?

Melbourne is no Champagne and claims to terroir are tenuous at best. Beer is mostly water and imported beers are packaged in heavy glassware, making them extremely expensive to ship. Unlike many of its alcoholic counterparts, most beers do not improve with age—they go bad. Despite these barriers, from 1990 to 2014, beer exports rose from 2 percent to 7 percent of the global beer market. Interestingly, this dramatic growth in beer trade is caused by two different processes. Multinational brewers are using takeovers of foreign brewers and their marketing infrastructure—and the associated scale economies—to sell their premium exports. On the other end of the beer market, the shift in consumer preferences toward craft beers has contributed to an increased demand for variety and for specialty beers, which are partially imported.

But even as globalization allows marketing export brands to be more seamless than ever, the beer trade still contains an inherent paradox. Export-oriented breweries may have more in common with elite Evian water than France's Burgundian vineyards. As far as the bottom line is concerned, the beer trade still relies on consumers' willingness to pay transportation costs for a product that is mostly water. And this is contingent on perhaps the most important ingredient in the export market: cachet.

American Import Market

Miller learned the hard way that people don't just want a foreign name—they want a foreign beer. In the 1970s, Heineken and the Munich pilsner Löwenbräu were America's two leading imports, together dominating the 1 percent total market share of non-domestic brews. Translating to "Lion's Brew," Löwenbräu's popularity was rooted in the reputation of Bavarian beer among Americans. With Anheuser Busch promoting its Michelob line of super-premium beers, Miller was looking for an entrance into the still-miniscule but promising high-end beer segment. Miller purchased licensing rights to the Löwenbräu brand name in 1974 and began brewing the recipe at their facilities in Milwaukee. Uninhibited by the German *Reinheitsgebot* (see Chapter 9), they added corn grits as an adjunct to lighten the recipe. But Anheuser Busch fought back by accusing Miller of falsely marketing Löwenbräu as an imported beer. In 1977, the Federal Trade Commission (FTC) ruled in Anheuser Busch's favor and Miller was forced to retract the "imported" label on its green bottles. The fiasco also brought quite a bit of bad press.

In the early 1980s, both Löwenbräu and Michelob benefited from the rising popularity of high-end beers. But the dominance of super-premiums was short-lived, and Löwenbräu sales peaked in 1983 as the imported beer market segment began what would be a long and steady rise. Löwenbräu could have been Miller's ticket to the top, but it had already lost its advantage as an "imported" brand. In an effort to recover, Miller launched a multimillion-dollar advertising campaign in 1986 emphasizing Löwenbräu's Bavarian roots. But nothing worked. Now nicknamed Millerbräu, the brand was unable to shake the FTC suit stigma. In ten years, sales fell from a 1983 peak of 1.4 million barrels to just 400,000 barrels. Meanwhile, former leading import competitor Heineken rode the rising import wave as number one for decades. Löwenbräu did leave America with one lasting legacy: the FTC precedent-setting ruling that foreign brands are not legally allowed to call their beer imported if it's brewed in the United States.

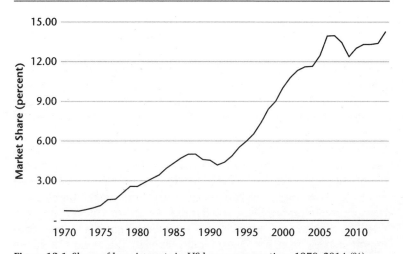

Figure 13.1 Share of beer imports in US beer consumption, 1970–2014 (%)

Elzinga K., Tremblay C., and Tremblay, V. (2017). Craft Beer in the United States: Strategic Connections to Macro and European Brewers. In C. Caravaglia and J. Swinnen, *The Craft Beer Revolution: An Economic Perspective*. Palgrave Macmillan.

Victor and Carol Tremblay, a husband and wife economist duo, have spent a significant part of their careers studying American beer markets. They contextualize the Millerbräu fiasco by identifying three subcategories of America's high-end sector: domestic super-premium beers produced by macrobreweries, imported beers, and craft beer produced by microbreweries. The market share of the high-end sector has risen since the late 1970s, closely corresponding with a rise in disposable income. While domestic super-premiums dominated the high-end sector for the initial rise, in 1985 they were surpassed by imports and never recovered. The market share of imported beers rose sharply throughout the 1990s and continued to rise steadily in the 2000s (Figure 13.1). When the 2008 financial crisis hit, the market share fell while that of super-premiums briefly recovered. The sort of reverse parallelism between imports and super-premiums suggests that the two subcategories act as substitutes: domestic super-premiums are inferior beers of the high-end sector, so consumption increases during recessions. The ascent of imported beers is certainly remarkable: from 1980 to 2014, the market share of imported beers rose from about 2 to 14 percent. But the interesting question as far as taste is concerned is why domestic super-premiums haven't been able to compete with imported beers.

Taste falls along demographic lines, complicating the story. Studies of consumer purchasing patterns suggest that imported and craft beers are luxury goods: the largest share of high-end beer drinkers earn more than $75,000 annually, while the largest share of Budweiser drinkers earn between $50,000 and $75,000. The story is not all about income, though. Lighter lagers are more popular than darker beers among women and in the southern regions, and regional differences can be pronounced. In 2009, the combined market share of imported and craft beer was approximately 17 percent in the US—though it was 33 percent in California and only 6 percent in Mississippi. There's little doubt that affluence has contributed to the popularity of imported beer. We know Americans can afford to pay more for the high cost of transporting imported beers. The question is: why are they willing to?

It's easy to jump to the conclusion that American beer is "worse" than imported beer, but that doesn't quite explain the trend. There are two ways that subcategories of a product can be differentiated. If they're differentiated vertically, consumers will universally choose one sub-category over another given a rise in income. We can then say one subcategory is "higher quality." For example, front-row tickets are the higher quality subcategory of tickets, while the nosebleed section is lower quality. But the Tremblays argue that beer is actually differentiated hori-zontally, so imported beers are not necessarily qualitatively better than domestic beers. Many consumers continue to choose Budweiser over Heineken even as they grow affluent. When subcategories are differenti-ated horizontally, an increase in income leads to an increase in demand for variety. People are willing to pay more for more options.

Branding the Premium Export

For most of the twentieth century, the beer trade was widely considered to be local. We can credit Alfred "Freddy" Heineken and Arthur Guin-ness with the modern-day global brand. Guinness had great branding. The "My Goodness My Guinness" campaign and the *Guinness Book of World Records*—created to settle bar fights—cemented the beer's iconic reputation. But Guinness's export market also made sense from an industrial organization perspective. There's only one Guinness because stout isn't in high enough demand for every nation to have their own stout macrobrewery.

The same is not true of lager beer. The idea of a "global brand" just didn't make sense: every nation had its own domestic macrobreweries and popular brands. Why would consumers pay extra for a lager brewed somewhere else?

Freddy Heineken was convinced they would. After thirty years of employment at his family's company, Freddy was appointed chairman of the board for Heineken in 1971. His directorship was shaped by his oft-cited conviction that "beer can travel," and he had big travel plans for Heineken. Freddy's formula was simple: a consistent product, marketed to young consumers, and sold in green bottles with a prominent "export" label. He added one final aesthetic touch when he trademarked a font for Heineken: Heineken sans and serif, characterized by "smiling e's." If you look closely, each of the three e's in "Heineken" is tilted diagonally to the left. Under Freddy's leadership, Heineken became the first truly global brand, proving that consumers will pay more for a lager brewed in Amsterdam with the right approach. At the same time, these early-comers—Heineken, Carlsberg, and Guinness—never lost sight of their domestic markets.

The same cannot be said for Stella Artois. Today, it's the sixth most valuable beer brand in the world. It's easily the most popular Belgian beer in every nation, with the exception of one: Belgium. At home, Stella is trumped by Jupiler, but this is part of the strategy. Stella and Jupiler were domestic competitors for decades, until they merged in 1987 to form Interbrew (see Chapter 6). Jupiler had been more successful in the domestic market, so Interbrew developed an alternate branding fate for Stella: a premium export brand with a global reach. Other newcomers to the global branding game tend to follow this model rather than the Heineken and Guinness models. Australia exports Foster's while Australians drink Victoria Bitter; Germany exports Beck's, which trails domestically as the fourth biggest lager.

Successfully marketing a global export brand is tricky because it has to justify the higher price resulting from transportation costs. Business journalist Wolfgang Riepl thinks the key to success is exclusivity. If a brand becomes too common in a domestic market, customers will lose their willingness to pay the extra cost of transport. But with the profitability of global brands comes the necessary tension between branding country-of-origin and actually brewing there. The most profitable option is to not import and say that you did. Or just heavily imply it, as was the strategy of Japanese Kirin and Australian Foster's.

Heineken and Stella Artois have made a point of brewing exclusively and importing from their respective countries-of-origin with only a few exceptions. Heineken has only established licensing agreements in Mexico, Vietnam, and Thailand apparently because those emerging beer markets place less of a premium on the country-of-origin authenticity. Stella Artois has kept production in Leuven, Belgium for all markets except the UK.

Why "The Most Interesting Man in the World" Will Not Always Buy the "Reassuringly Expensive"

"He speaks French … in Russian. He once had an awkward moment … just to see what it would feel like." The familiar voice of *Frontline* narrator Will Lyman announces the many feats of the Most Interesting Man in the World as a montage of adventure flashes before American viewers. The commercial ends with a mustachioed Jonathan Goldsmith leaning back in a booth next to a young woman. With a twinkle in his eye and a slight lift of his hand as if to toast, he addresses the viewer: "I don't always drink beer. But when I do, I prefer Dos Equis." The accent is mellifluous and the message crystal clear: imported beer is bourgeois, American lager, maybe not so much.

It may have started as playful hyperbole, but the campaign did make Dos Equis the most interesting beer brand on the internet. In 2011, the Facebook page of the Mexican lager became the first beer page to reach one million "likes." The success of the campaign has been remarkable. Sales for the Dos Equis brand rose 88.5 percent in the three years following the campaign launch, during a period when aggregate import sales rose only 1.2 percent. Analysts at *Beverage Industry* identified the campaign as the most recognizable in the beer industry in 2009.

The spectacular success of the Dos Equis campaign is just one of many in the American import sector. Riding on the success of the "Corona and lime" trope, Corona surpassed Heineken as the leading import in America. Imported brands benefit from economies of scale in advertising, the foundation of success for American macros. But successful ads take a different tactic than the balls and bros angle of domestic lagers past. Their angles prominently feature country-of-origin, cater to women and non-sports fans, and self-consciously diverge from the blue-collar-beverage reputation of domestic beer. Such advertising also doesn't come cheap. In America, Corona, Guinness, and Heineken have exceeded the industry average in advertising dollars spent per sale. When a campaign becomes a cultural trope, as has Dos Equis' Most Interesting Man, the dollars spent are well worth the widespread recognition and brand loyalty that ensues.

As Chapters 5 and 12 indicate, television is capable of playing a huge role in shaping consumer tastes. The Tremblays point to another potential factor in the continued triumph of imported beers over domestics: conspicuous consumption. Thorstein Veblen coined this term in 1899 in an attempt to explain the many times when a cost–benefit analysis couldn't make sense of a market outcome. People will pay more for a more expensive import because they want to show that they can. Or the price makes the beer taste better. If consumers are being misled about a product, correcting that assumption will lead to an increase in consumer welfare. But given the highly individualized taste in beer, it's more likely that the high prices of imported beer are serving consumer welfare by allowing drinkers to demonstrate their status. This explanation lends insight into why branding can go very wrong—a reality Stella Artois' UK marketing team is all too familiar with.

From its 1982 introduction, the beer has been advertised with the tagline: "Reassuringly Expensive." TV commercials for Stella toyed with the camerawork of European cinema, beginning with a play on 1986 French art house film Jean de Florette, followed by similar commercials in the style of cinematic war films, silent comedies, and even art house surrealism. From its introduction, Stella was positioned as the classy, high-end lager. And yet, somehow, it went from "Reassuringly Expensive" to "wife-beater."

For British pub-goers, Stella Artois became known as the beer of choice for rowdy football fans and referred to by an unfortunate slang term—"wife-beater." The slang is borrowed from the American slang for a certain type of ribbed tank top stereotypically worn by men who abuse their spouses. Their British counterparts, meanwhile, stereotypically drink Stella Artois, thus the slang. But it gets worse: the Stella stigma has morphed from drink of choice for so-called "lager louts" that also beat their spouses to the notion that Stella turns drinkers into especially violent drunks, prompting bar fights and spousal abuse. One 2007 *Daily Mail* article explored the phenomenon in depth, even citing a judge that condemned the beer based on how many times rabble-rousers and spousal abusers used it as an excuse for their behavior the day after in her courtroom. This has happened in spite of Stella's every branding effort to the contrary.

Pub owners have cited switching their lager on tap from Stella as a means of getting rowdy regulars to take their socializing elsewhere. Stella decreased the alcohol content of its recipe from 5.2 percent to 5 percent on the sly, but the stigma has proved impossible to shake. In 2012, it was revealed that AB InBev had hired a major lobbying firm to reduce internet references to the nickname. This only fanned the flames, and parody articles began circling such as that Stella would announce its support for gay marriage by introducing a "spouse-beater" recipe.

Growing Beer Trade in the Twenty-First Century

These fundamentals have determined global trade in beer for much of history, with beer exports mostly limited to a few global branding successes such as Heineken, Corona, Dos Equis, and Guinness, and otherwise to neighboring regions, such as Belgian exports to the Netherlands and Northern France and Canadian exports to the north of the US. Beer trade made up less than 2 percent of global beer consumption until late in the twentieth century.

However, since then trade has grown rapidly. The volume of beer exported more than doubled over the past two decades—from around six billion liters in 1990 to around fifteen billion liters in 2014 (see Figure 13.2). Moreover, the share of production that is exported has increased strongly as well: from less than 2 percent in 1990 to more than 7 percent most recently—a huge increase.

While advertising can play an important role in creating a brand name for imported beers for which consumers are willing to pay extra dollars, the Heineken and Dos Equis success stories in branding are not sufficient to explain the strong growth in trade that has taken place since 1990. International beer markets and trade have fundamentally changed in the twenty-first century.

Somewhat paradoxically, the increase in beer trade seems to have been caused by two very different, almost opposing developments: on the one hand the spread of multinational brewers who are using take-overs of foreign brewers (and their infrastructure) to launch and sell

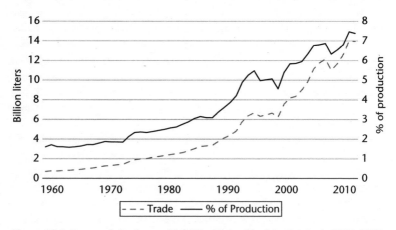

Figure 13.2 Beer trade in the world (billion liters, % of production), 1960–2013
FAOstat

their premium exports, and on the other hand the shift in consumer preferences toward more local and craft beers which has contributed to an increased demand for variety and specialty beers, which are partially imported. The rapid growth of beer multinationals through mergers and acquisitions in the 1990s and 2000s (see Chapters 6 and 7) has provided these multinationals with the local infrastructure and access to beer retailers, pubs, and consumers in many more countries. In this way they have been able to channel their export brands into many more markets and in areas where they were not able to go before, also realizing scale economies in marketing and shipping. These days, in many major cities in the world it is much harder to find a bar where they do not serve one of the prime export beers of the major beer multinationals, including Stella Artois, Heineken, and Guinness, than to find a bar where they do. Hence, these takeovers have made it cheaper to export "water" to other countries.

At the same time, it also has become more lucrative to capitalize on beer's claims to "terroir." The rapidly growing demand for craft beers in many countries in the world, and twenty-first-century consumers' willingness to pay extra for specialty beers, both local and imported, have created export opportunities for smaller brewers. With craft and specialty beers linking their quality more closely to their geographic roots and "terroir," the beer trade has fundamentally changed in recent years. Nowhere is this more obvious than in countries like Belgium.

14

Craft Nation

How Belgium's "Peasant Beers" Became the Best in the World

Seemingly overnight, AB InBev, the world's largest beer multinational, has tacked black, yellow, and red vertical stripes on to every urban sidewalk bar sign and supermarket beer display. The "Best of Belgium" campaign is promoting their holy trinity of high-end exports: Stella Artois, Hoegaarden, and Leffe. The cachet of imported beer is nothing new to American imbibers. It dates back to about when Heineken and Corona began chipping away at the long-standing dominance of domestic lagers in the early 1990s. In this regard, Stella Artois was a relative latecomer, only achieving comparable visibility in 2006 when InBev signed a distribution agreement with Anheuser Busch two years before taking over the firm. Hoegaarden was to follow, piggybacking on the popularity of Belgian-style white ale Blue Moon by marketing itself as the real deal. The "Best of Belgium" was designed to introduce American audiences to Leffe, their blonde abbey ale. Playing up the Belgian origin of these three brands is strategic—it's in the Leuven-based multinational's interest to both advertise its Belgian origin as a quality indicator and associate their products with the existing reputation of Belgian beer.

The growing number of craft beer enthusiasts aren't so easily wooed. "For real connoisseurs, if they say Belgian beers, they don't mean Stella or Leffe," says Stijn Vanormelingen, an economics professor at the University of Leuven. "They mean a huge variety of top-fermenting beers, the Trappist or abbey beers. And AB InBev is partially surfing on the same wave." Vanormelingen and his colleague, trade economist Damiaan Persyn, who now analyzes trade and industrial policies at the European Commission's research center in Seville,

Spain, both grew up in Belgium, giving them the sort of tacit expertise that comes with a lifetime of experience. Beer has long been an integral part of both Belgian culture and its political economy. It's no surprise that an emerging class of globally curious connoisseurs has taken to Belgium's diverse selection of unusual and highly localized brewing styles. But amid discussions of tripels and gueuzes, the economic factors contributing to Belgium's current reputation for great beer frequently go unexplored.

When did people start thinking that Belgian beer was so great, anyway? Americans may have first taken notice thanks to Michael Jackson—the Beer Hunter, not the King of Pop. In 1996, he published *Great Beers of Belgium*, a guide to diverse styles produced by smaller breweries around the small nation. As the market share for craft beer has grown in America, the reputation of Belgian imports seems to have taken on a life of its own.

Most prominently, attention has been paid to the nation's Trappist beers, specifically those produced by abbey Westvleteren, famous thanks to their notorious scarcity. In the past year, the *Economist*, *National Public Radio*, and the *New York Times* have all featured this brewery and its unusual decision to not brew to demand. Beer lovers must call and set an appointment for a given hour at a future date, at which point they can drive to Westvleteren and buy a crate of beer. Their schedule is booked more than a year in advance. But the Trappist monks wouldn't have it any other way, subscribing to the philosophy that "We're not monks that brew beer, we brew beer to be monks." The scarcity only makes Westvleteren more desirable. Meanwhile, those Trappist monasteries more generous with the fruits of their labor are more popular than ever both in Belgium and abroad. High-end restaurants like San Francisco's Monks Kettle pay tribute to the history of monastic brewing while pioneering the burgeoning art of beer gastronomy. Here, diners will shell out a whopping $17.50 for a third of a liter bottle of imported Rocheford 10. The prestige of Trappist beers is certainly their connection to history and tradition. It's a marketing appeal that breweries like AB InBev have attempted to capitalize on by producing abbey ales like Leffe, paying royalties to the monastery for the right to use its name.

But breweries capitalizing on the reputation of monastic beer is contrary to the function of such beer. "It is a temptation for other beer producers to use a name they do not deserve to use," explains François de Harenne, a spokesperson for the International Trappist Organization (ITO). "The Trappist producers wanted to protect their name and give an insurance to the consumers." In response to the proliferation of abbey

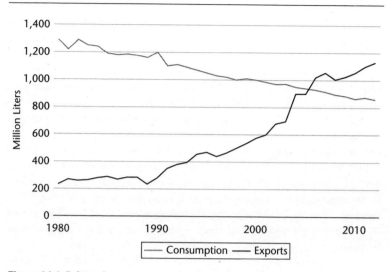

Figure 14.1 Belgian beer exports and domestic consumption (million liters)
Union of Belgian Brewers

ales in the market, the ITO rolled out the "Authentic Trappist Product" label, which is found on products that are actually produced in the monasteries. This assures consumers that if they pay for abbey ale, their money is actually going to the monasteries. Likewise, it protects the monasteries themselves from unfair competition. "From the rules of the order, they must live from the work of their hands," explains de Harenne. "They must produce what they need for living." The label has been a success, as Trappist-brewed beers enjoy a prestige above the abbey ales from major multinational corporations like Leffe. But the monasteries aren't the only Belgian breweries interested in securing a quality insurance label, nor are they the only ones that need to.

The recent media fascination with Belgian beer is matched by tremendous growth in Belgium's export market. The export boom started in 1990, and since 2005 Belgium exports more beer than it consumes domestically (see Figure 14.1). The export growth is driven both by the mergers and acquisitions which have culminated in AB InBev and the associated global spread in sales of Stella, Hoegaarden, and Leffe; and by the strong growth in exports by much smaller Belgian breweries, mostly selling specialty beers. From the perspective of trade economists Vanormelingen and Persyn, the sudden success of Belgian specialty brews as exports is unusual. "Next to that one big player [AB InBev], you have all these other small Belgian breweries that are able to sell their beers in the United States and faraway places like Japan and China," they describe. "To us as trade economists, this is a little surprising because normally we find that the largest firms are the biggest exporters." The popularity of specialty brews seems rooted in a mythic claim to craftsmanship, and the prevailing idea that Belgium has the best beer in the world. With medieval coats of arms and origin dates around the year Columbus sailed the ocean blue, Belgian brews are steeped in a history and tradition of small-scale brewing that the American craft beer movement lacks.

But what many self-styled beer aficionados don't know about "the best beer in the world" is that the success of these high-value specialty brews is a relatively recent phenomenon within Belgium as well. After German-style lager was introduced to the region in the late nineteenth century, all the unusual local styles that we revere today looked certain to die out.

The Shakeout

At the end of the nineteenth century, Belgium boasted more than 3,300 breweries. Every village had several brewers producing a regional style based on available ingredients. They didn't yet have access to tempera- ture- and time-measuring tools, so brewers were true craftsmen. They had to develop a sophisticated sense of smell, touch, and taste to brew the best beers they could. Many brewers were too poor to toss out ingredients if any step didn't go as planned, so damage control in the face of error was a necessary skill. If malting went wrong, they'd dilute the batch or add spices to disguise flavor. These spice combinations and technical tricks comprised the toolbox of the ancestors of today's diverse styles of Belgians.

Though German lager was first introduced in the 1870s, it really took hold during the World War I German occupation of Belgium. The bottom-fermented style could be brewed big and sold cheap, masking problems with standardization that plagued the efforts to scale up top- fermented brews. In Leuven, Artois Brewery was quick to catch on to the new style. In 1922, they released a Christmas edition lager, Stella Artois—"Stella because of a bright Christmas star," says Flemish brewing historian Raymond Van Uytven, a retired professor from the University of Antwerp. Van Uytven's father worked in the refrigerated cellars of Artois Brewery where beer was lagered for two weeks to ferment. Stella Artois was a mainstay of his childhood. He recalls his parents drinking the beer for breakfast, his mother adding it to every meal. "I have not thought on this for a long time. She used to make a soup with this lager beer, milk, and parsley," he recalls shaking his head.

One big selling point for Stella Artois was its bright, clear appearance—an aesthetic and quality improvement over the cloudy, inconsistent top-fermenting recipes of local brewers. The little guys couldn't compete. "There was a vogue about the clearness," says Uytven. "They were obsessed!" The numbers confirm this. For most of the twentieth century, the traditional beer-drinking nation underwent an extended shakeout and consolidation, transforming from a small, scattered network of breweries to a market dominated by several midsize and large lager breweries; the two early leaders were Artois Brewery with Stella and Piedboeuf with Jupiler. Vanormelingen and Persyn describe the transition to a dual market structure, where many very small breweries coexist with a few very large breweries (similar to the current market structure in the United States, following the entry of craft breweries). But the shakeout was extended and brutal for old-fashioned brewers. The number of breweries declined until 1980, when it finally stabilized around one hundred—less than 5 percent of the number at the beginning of the twentieth century (see Table 4.1).

The styles and the breweries that survived did so thanks to the efforts of a few men who couldn't imagine a world without them. One of them was Pierre Celis, the man who single-handedly saved the traditional white style of Hoegaarden (see Chapter 8). Another was Frank Boon, a longtime close friend of Celis: "We were called the revival guys," he laughs. Boon and Celis both began their careers against all the odds, driven by the impulse to preserve and the insight that this could only be achieved through forward-thinking innovation. "They thought of us like 'museum guys,' from the times that steam engines disappear from the railways. It was considered that gueuze and Hoegaarden—all these impossible local styles from our grandparents—they are going to disappear and that is OK because we want to drink lager beer. It is cheap, efficient, and easy to drink."

The Prescient Preservationist

Frank Boon speaks of his job today with a hint of self-satisfaction that most only dream of—the most elusive kind that only accompanies verifiable evidence that you were right all along, and that never fully fades. In Boon's case, he was right about gueuze. He runs Boon Brewery, a small but successful producer of traditional gueuze and kriek sour beers—a style of brewing dubbed "lambic" after its place of origin,

Lembeek, a village southwest of Brussels. They're distinguished by the process of spontaneous fermentation: rather than allowing beer to ferment in an enclosed container with an isolated strain of yeast, lambic beers are left out in the open to allow airborne wild yeast to spontaneously interact with sugars to produce alcohol. The beer is then aged for one to three years, giving it a sour taste—and an acquired one at that. In 1975, Boon took over the brewery from local brewer and character-about-town Rene De Vits during a time when price competition with industrial lager was next to impossible. But he had an idea to bring about a comeback for such unusual, costly-to-produce local styles: rather than brew cheaper, he'd brew more expensive. And he'd raise prices along with the costs. People thought he was insane.

"My parents were completely against it. They didn't accept my idea," he laughs. His great uncle, then-president of Artois Brewery, had good reason to be skeptical of his business plan. "At the time, there were about 270 breweries left in Belgium. He told me 'By the end of the century, the year 2000, there will be a place for one or two big lager breweries, maybe one Trappist, and the dortmunder pale ale style of beer. All other breweries are doomed to disappear.' That was the idea of the 1960s." There it is again, the smug smile between reminiscences. He earned it; when he was starting out, the future of gueuze looked dire indeed.

The competition posed by an industrial lager was a deathblow to so many local breweries partially because they didn't know how to compete. Lager stayed consistent and consistently inexpensive. Local brewers looked for ways to cut costs in order to compete with lager on the basis of price. Many began using lower quality ingredients and taking shortcuts to stay afloat. The quality of traditional local styles began to go downhill, further discouraging their purchase. Survival by no means meant success. The concept of value-added didn't occur to the mainly older brewers. Boon describes how many breweries that didn't shutter were "grandfather breweries," or "We keep this brewery open as long as granddad is alive." Families that owned these breweries had a clear disincentive to invest in new technologies that might've improved the quality of their products and frequently ran at a loss. It's no surprise that Boon's intended business direction looked like pure idiocy to his family.

Rather than the promise of success, Boon was driven by a nostalgic—maybe even quixotic—desire to preserve and protect this history. He keeps a memento of his own brewing familial heritage, a framed photograph of nineteenth-century Flemish men standing on a pick-up truck and toasting pints. They're his great grandfather, his uncle, and some friends, brewers from several generations back. He sprinkles our conversation with old myths and practices of Lembeek brewing. "When I took over, people still cleaned the barrels with chains," he says, with the incredulous look of a true history buff. Then he digs around in his drawer before pulling out an old metal tool. Brewers used these to scrape the yeast out of old gueuze barrels. "My friend gave this to me because he says, 'Frank, you are the only person still alive that knows what this is for.'"

We meet him at an opportune time—two weeks after the brewery's initial switch to a fully automated digital system in a new high-tech brewhouse. Before this, Boon still relied on the industrial-age mash-and-brew kettle from the days of De Vits. Boon built the new, streamlined system in a larger structure around the old stone brewhouse. The masher and brew kettle are obsolete here, but Boon still uses the same spontaneous fermentation chamber as before. This is part preservation, part practical. After all, spontaneous fermentation is impossible to standardize fully —there's a point at which you just don't know what's in the air. After describing the pipe system, he smiles and looks at us, "In the old days, you would not be allowed in here. It was a belief that women contaminate the wild yeast." Myths such as these were spread among the gueuze brewers of Lembeek, says Boon, where the practice was refined over centuries, designed to brew to the specific cocktail of wild yeasts found in the area around Brussels.

This built-in element of chance is one of a few reasons why traditional lambic brewing is necessarily a craft. Persyn puts it simply: "With top- or bottom-fermenting beers, your goal is to be as hygienic as possible. You only use one strain of yeast. But spontaneous fermentation, you let everything in," he says. Brewers like Boon who have dedicated their lives to refining and perfecting the process for their gueuze still don't understand it top-down. They couldn't brainstorm a new gueuze recipe for a new location. "You could try to make a pilsner beer in a different place and leave it out to spontaneously ferment. It would taste terrible! It's not the brew, it's not the yeast, the place, everything must match up," he explains. Many lambic connoisseurs believe that the area around Brussels has a unique combination of airborne yeast that is capable of producing great gueuze. "People hear sour beer and they say, 'Oh your goal is to make this beer as sour as possible.' That's not correct, the goal is to accept some sour so that it does not get more sour. With wine you accept some sour, but too much sour and it is vinegar," he explains. The barrel conditioning limits the extent to which Boon is able to scale up production in response to demand. The market is small for now because lambic and gueuze are an acquired taste, yet a small market may also mean higher prices if customers appreciate the nature of the product. Boon's continued success looks safe for now, but he didn't always brew with such confidence.

Boon began his career as a wholesaler in the 1960s. He traveled the Belgian countryside convincing local small brewers to let him sell their local styles in Brussels for higher prices. His proposition was met with frequent confusion. "This was the thinking of the brewers: why would you sell our beer in Brussels?" Sometimes they had logistical concerns, like a very small number of reusable bottles they couldn't afford to give up. Most didn't believe that anyone would actually buy beer at a higher price than the going price for lager. "The consumer idea in the 1960s was not that these were specialty beers. Brewers were local thirst-quenchers, like local bakers and other food suppliers. Beer was something that had to be sold at the basic price," he explains. Eventually, he curated a selection of 120 local styles that he sold at a small market in Brussels. This allowed him to save the start-up capital needed for his own brewery. When he had enough funds, he approached De Vits, the Lembeek gueuze brewer with an operation in dire need of a modern touch.

Boon's self-satisfaction melts into pure fondness when he recalls his predecessor. "He had a very good bottle of gueuze, but very small volume, and he was a crazy guy." De Vits ran the operation with his sister, both unmarried and in their late seventies. The only reason they hadn't gone out of business by 1975 when Boon was looking to buy was because they never modernized. "There was no electricity—they lived very nineteenth century," he says. The first time Boon visited, he witnessed De Vits' elderly sister elevating a cask of aged beer to the second floor by old-fashioned pulley and remarkable strength. With no electricity, they relied on coal, which they apparently supplemented with the leftover pits of cherries from the production of "kriek," a cherry beer which is another specialty of the Brussels region. "They worked day and night. And they survived because they used to find savings on everything." Even their café remained without electricity into the 1970s—locals drank in the dark when night began falling at 5.00 p.m. in the winter. Refills came from an open pitcher, which Boon describes, as the sister pouring with one hand while holding a petrol lamp in the other. In short, Boon's start-up capital was needed for an upgrade.

But his high hopes for marketing gueuze as a high-value beer would test his patience for many years. If he was going to charge higher prices, he had to strive for impeccable quality. "The quality we make today, it was impossible to make this quality twenty-five years ago because the equipment of breweries at that moment was so deficient," he says. Family breweries have been successful in Belgium because brewing is traditionally a labor-intensive activity that benefits from the additional labor that comes from having children. But Boon was on his own. He lived at the brewery and oversaw all operations daily. For the first decade, he still cleaned out all the barrels by hand—not with chains, but with soap and water. He stayed patient and diligent for fifteen years of uncertain future.

And then, in 1990, things took off. The number of small breweries started growing again as consumers started getting bored with the taste of ubiquitous lager and began appreciating the taste of Belgium's native brews again. Boon summarizes the remarkable turnaround: "We've grown every year since then. Today, we're selling thirty times what we did in 1990." The dawn of Belgian specialty beers had at last arrived, and decades of thankless dedication had given Boon Brewery a much-deserved early lead in the burgeoning high-value beer market.

Surviving the Shakeout on Dark Beer

The family-owned brewery Het Anker of the award-winning Gouden Carolus brand is a poster child for the type of high-value specialty beer that's captured the imagination of the new class of beer connoisseurs. It has history, quality, and doesn't make itself too available, which predictably intrigues self-styled aficionados. Fans that find themselves in the medieval city of Mechelen will discover a whole new side to the beer. The facility is likely the oldest continually operating brewery on the same site in Belgium, able to trace its roots back to a *begijnhof* in 1471. The *begijnhof* was a collective living community of religious women for centuries, which today has been turned into nicely renovated houses.

According to medieval history professor Erik Aerts, Mechelen's was the only recorded *begijnhof*–brewery–hospital, where sisters brewed beer to nourish the town's sick and elderly. We stand on the roof of Mechelen with Het Anker's export manager Hans Rubens, looking over the ancient city and its many cathedrals. His trained eye can point out ancient architectural clues to the brewery's past purpose—the uniform buildings, sporting a narrow architectural style, on the other side of Krankenstraat, meaning "sick street," were designed as patient housing. The brewery is lined by Nonnenstraat, or "nun street." It continued to be operated by the *begijnhof*-turned-convent until 1872, when the Van Breedam family took over operations. Five generations later, the brewery is still in the family, today run by nephew Charles Leclef. This is a brewery with history literally built into its walls. The old stone house where Leclef grew up and still lives is engraved with the family coat of arms and the brand namesake, the gold coins that Charles V, Holy Roman Emperor and native of the Low Countries, introduced to their economy.

Centuries of brewer craftsmanship have culminated in Gouden Carolus Classic, the brewery's flagship beer, which was named the world's best dark beer by the World Beer Awards in 2012. Much like Boon Brewery, Het Anker has experienced rising domestic demand for specialty beers coupled with attention from connoisseurs and new opportunities to export. Rubens' excitement about recent successes is tempered by an awareness of its exceptionality: "Young consumers, women also, are attracted to the world of specialty beers—local brews, Belgian brews, authentic products, true stories." Het Anker knows better than to take big sales for granted. After all, it was one of the few small breweries to weather the rising tide of industrial lager that culminated in AB InBev.

Rubens credits the brewery's survival to two pivotal decisions made by the third-generation Van Breedam, Charles, in 1962. The first was to stop brewing lager. Like Boon, people told him he was crazy. But he rightfully recognized that there would be no room for small and midsize breweries in the price-competitive lager market. Instead, Het Anker directed resources into producing its Gouden Carolus brown ale in small, quarter-liter bottles. Still, it might not have succeeded without his inspired second maneuver. Van Breedam approached Mechelen's other major brewery, Lamot, with a proposal: Het Anker would stop competing with them for the lager market, if they agreed to include one crate of Gouden Carolus brown ale in every shipment to the rest of Belgium to be sold at a higher price. The plan carried the brewery through the consolidation years and to date is the reason why the generation in their sixties and seventies recognize the Gouden Carolus brand. "From the seaside to the east of Belgium, the south of Netherlands to the north of France," waxes Rubens. "You still have people that remember their father took a crate of Carolus on a Sunday afternoon to have a drink with the local farmers or neighbors."

This history has instilled Het Anker with a cautious perspective on future growth. The right price, the right pour, the right temperature, and available information on the history of Gouden Carolus must all be impeccable. "If it's not done the right way, [the customers are] lost," opines Rubens. Opening customer channels is also the reasoning behind their on-site hotel and restaurant. The small brewery hosts tours three times per week and is currently curating a museum preserving old Belgian café life. "You can make a Carolus, it's not that difficult," says Rubens. "You can copy the beer, but not the soul of the beer." With impeccably curated décor and the brewery's diverse styles on tap, they're doing their part to share not just Gouden Carolus but the city of Mechelen, the legacy of the *begijnhof*, and the pride of the Van Breedam-Leclef family.

"What is now a big brand, in fifty years, can be forgotten," Rubens concludes. "It may be unimaginable today that such a beer can be lost, but then if you go into an old bar, you look at the walls, you see plates of beer that we don't even recall drinking. As brewers we shouldn't take it for granted—the success of Belgian beer and the positive image that Belgian beer has in the world."

Saved by the Devil

Duvel Moortgat's flagship strong blonde was launched as "Victory Ale" to celebrate triumph in the aftermath of World War I. The name was changed when its deceptive 8.5 percent alcohol content caught up with drinkers, who began referring to it as "nen echten duvel," Flemish for "a real devil." The recipe of Duvel hasn't changed since the early twentieth century, but Duvel Moortgat survived the shakeout by pioneering the value-added market in Belgium. Duvel Moortgat shares another similarity with Het Anker: it has stayed in the family, in this case the Moortgat family, for four generations since 1871.

The firm also envisioned what has become the beer's signature glassware: a short-stemmed goblet engraved with a "D" at the bottom, such that every correctly poured Duvel contains carbonation ribbons leading toward the top-center of the three-finger head. Many locales have great beer, but Belgium seems to retain exclusive claim to a sort of preeminent beer-drinking culture by elevating their beer with ornate stemware designed to enhance the specific characteristics of a specific brew. Goblets are more than just an afterthought in this nation.

For Belgian brewers it also involves a perennial struggle of the Belgian export market—how to export not just the beer but the Belgian smell, sip, savor approach that makes it all the better. Beer ambassador Nicolas Soenen describes the firm's self-imposed stakes: "It's no use brewing the best beer in the world if at the end, in the final step, the bartender ruins everything." Soenen's words may sound dramatic to the American ear, but the make-or-break perfectionism driving Duvel's international strategy may be what's needed for the Belgian approach to infiltrate target markets and actually justify the high prices of imported beers. The end goal is always that anywhere a customer sees Duvel on the menu, they can expect it to be poured with precision and care, in the correct glassware, and served with enough information to smell, sip, and savor. "It's not something that can be done overnight," says Chief Operations Officer Daniel Krug, but the midsize brewery is getting closer. To make it happen, Duvel Moortgat is currently paying hundreds of employees living and working abroad to get the pour right, every single time.

Prior to 2000, Duvel Moortgat relied on one product and one market—80 percent Duvel and 80 percent Belgium. However, in recent years the firm has expanded its portfolio of products and markets significantly. When Krug began working at Duvel in 2000, they had three employees working abroad. Thirteen years later, they have 400 employees working abroad. The company has grown three and a half times bigger, and their exports have grown sevenfold. From the beginning, Duvel was looking for a specific kind of customer in a specific market setting. "The main focus for Duvel is declining beer markets—beer markets where the consumers are drinking less, but they are drinking better," says Soenen. As a general trend, traditional beer-drinking nations are seeing volume consumption decline as the market share for inexpensive lagers is replaced by growth in higher-end segments. This had been going on in Duvel's four initial target markets: France, the UK, the Netherlands, and the US. The idea was to target customers that might drink three glasses of lager at a bar, and present the alternative of savoring one Duvel instead. Duvel frequently fills the role of Belgian specialty ambassador, giving drinkers in lager-dominated nations a taste of the world that could await them. Duvel has taken it upon itself to communicate the basics of a Belgian approach to beer: the correct glassware, the pour, the sip, and the savor necessary lest drinkers experience the hellish consequences of its namesake.

In recent years, they diversified their brand portfolio by acquiring well-respected small breweries: La Chouffe, the bitter blonde beer with a playful elf icon; Liefmans, a line of mixed fermentation fruit beers; Maredsous, a line of abbey ales; Vedett, a youthful brand with a sharp aesthetic; and De Koninck, an amber beer. Two international acquisitions added to their brand portfolio as well: in 2001, Czech pilsner brewery Bernard and in 2003, American craft brewery Ommegang. These brands all cater to high-value niche demographics, an important facet of Duvel's strategy. "We don't want to be the mass brewer, we want to be the best in certain segments," notes Soenen.

Will the Belgian Party Last?

Belgian beer is having its international moment. Returning to AB InBev's "Best of Belgium" campaign, featuring blonde abbey ale Leffe, white Hoegaarden, and premium lager export Stella Artois, the strategy is obvious when viewed in light of Belgium's increasing international acclaim as a beer mecca. AB InBev's success in marketing these brands has not gone unnoticed by the other major players. In 2000, Heineken purchased the rights to brew Affligem abbey ale. Brewing at Affligem abbey dates back to the Middle Ages. Like so many specialty brands, the brewery went bankrupt in the 1960s. Heineken purchased the rights to distribute the beer as an abbey ale with an official monastery branding. Likewise, Carlsberg purchased the rights to brew Grimbergen, another small Belgian brewery. Elevated by mass distribution networks, Affligem and Grimbergen are lurking behind Leffe and Hoegaarden as global specialty export brands. Only recently has Belgium joined Ireland, Denmark, and the Netherlands in the club of European countries that exports more than half its beer volume. But while these nations' export volume is dominated by one multinational brewery (Guinness, Carlsberg, and Heineken, respectively), Belgium is distinctive in that many small and midsize breweries have been able to find success exporting their beers alongside voluminous Stella Artois.

Frank Boon can easily laugh at the past chiding of his beloved gueuze as a "peasant beer." There's a sweet irony for him and his kind—the consistency, light color, and inoffensive flavor that once formed the basis for lager's superior status are now considered industrial qualities that relegate it to the lower end of the beer spectrum. Meanwhile, those obscure traditional styles, especially ones with built-in potential for inconsistency, are Belgium's most prized and priciest beers. The *New York Times* "Styles" section recently featured premiere gueuzes from in and around Brussels, breaking down the notes and tones of beers from top-end breweries with all the shameless specificity of a lifelong wine connoisseur. This is a style of beer that only a few short decades ago was served out of a pitcher to aging farmers who sat in the dark and sang Flemish drinking songs after a day's work. Today, there's a profitable export market to an elite customer base as far away as Brazil and Japan.

Sven Gatz, minister of culture in the Flemish government and former director of the Federation of Belgian Brewers, envisions that beer can be for Belgium what wine has been for France. And the Federation is taking steps to turn momentary recognition into a permanent legacy. Based on its proposal, UNESCO has just put Belgium's beer culture on its world heritage list. Gatz emphasizes that it's the only nation that continues to brew all four fermentation styles (top, bottom, spontaneous, and "mixed fermentation," in which an aged spontaneously fermented beer is mixed with top-fermented beer, then continues to ferment in bottle or cask). Diversity and a reputation for quality means that Belgian brewers are nicely poised to capitalize on the growing segment of high-value, specialty and craft beers in a number of international beer markets. And this is the plan. With a frenetic charisma, Gatz reveals his vision of Belgian beer as the "drink of choice for the new middle class in new urban areas."

The beautiful thing, from Gatz's perspective, is that multinational mammoth AB InBev is not actually in competition with the small family breweries and Trappist monasteries when it comes to achieving its international goals. The latter don't have the capital to create demand in foreign countries for Belgian beer, which AB InBev clearly does. Many small and midsize Belgian breweries have found great success in the export markets piggybacking on AB InBev and Duvel's strategy. Small breweries that can't afford to create demand in faraway export markets are actually pursued with invitations to enter these markets thanks to the global reputation of Belgian beer. Rubens lists off the inquiries for Gouden Carolus: "I have received this week—four inquiries from China, from different companies, people to work with our beers. We have a request from Paraguay, you can have a Carolus in Panama City since two weeks ago, Colombia is on the way, and you wonder . . . How would they even know of the existence of the beer Gouden Carolus?"

By advertising themselves as Belgian beers and advertising "Belgian beer" as a concept, breweries such as AB InBev and Duvel Moortgat have inadvertently laid the foundation for their domestic competitors to follow in their footsteps. Meanwhile, AB InBev's premium export trio of Stella-Leffe-Hoegaarden derives a good deal of name recognition and credibility from Belgium's reputation among connoisseurs—even if connoisseurs might not be talking about them. The end result: instead of competing for domestic consumers, advertising for the industrial exports of AB InBev and praise for the high-value specialty exports among connoisseurs are working synergistically to enhance the brand of Belgian beer all over the world, and inadvertently increasing the salability of both. It's a trade association director's dream. Branding Belgium as a beer mecca is key to ensuring that growth in the export market stays robust. "We will never be the volume market—never. And it's a small country so it's impossible," says Gatz. "But the added-value at the top of the pyramid, that's where we want to be. That's where we are, and that's where we want to stay."

But not everyone is as optimistic as Gatz, and some worry that the profitability of the Belgian beer brand might attract brewers to export without considering the long-term stakes they all share in maintaining a reputation of quality. Gouden Carolus' Rubens employs the pointedly non-European trope "cowboys" to describe "more aggressive [brewers] with less long-term vision." Duvel shares the same concern. Soenen speaks derisively of some of the rapidly growing number of new breweries, many of whom present their new brews at the annual Zythos Beer Festival in Leuven: "Some of the small brewers here, they make beer that is completely acidic. And then they sell it as a gueuze-style beer and they sell it as twice the price! If we make that beer, we throw it away. It's just a failure, you see?"

The resentment is not unwarranted or petty: the extinction of so many styles and breweries during the shakeout in the twentieth century goes hand in hand with the quality and commitment of those that survived. The quality of these breweries has shaped the international reputation of Belgian beer. They argue that it's not just unfair for free-riders to profit from this reputation without maintaining their quality standards. Breweries that fail to maintain a quality standard, and yet profit from the label of Belgian exports, will be working counterproductively to tarnish the good reputation of Belgian beer. "What happens if you are a customer who comes into contact with a Belgian beer which is a very poor, technically insufficient, discounted Belgian beer?" Rubens poses a hypothetical. "It takes a one-time incident to lose a customer, to have a completely different view of Belgian beer." Experts such as Theo Vervloet, long-time chairman and *éminence grise* of the Belgian Brewers Association, and Guido Aerts, brewing professor at the University of Leuven and organizer of the biannual Trends in Brewing conference, agree and further emphasize the logistical problems of guaranteeing the optimal quality with growing exports of small breweries. While large brewers have sufficient scale and capacity to organize their exports both in terms of (short) travel time and optimal travel conditions to reduce quality loss, small brewers often do not have this scale and capacity, particularly for long-distance exports, which may affect the beer's quality at the far away consumption site.

They all agree that amid the excitement about the international attention that Belgian beer is receiving, it's easy to forget that the stakes are very high. Many small and midsize breweries rely on international demand for Belgian beers to stay afloat. Domestic beer consumption has been steadily declining for decades, a trend which will likely continue. If the world suddenly decides Belgian beer is overrated, there will be another major shakeout because breweries have been relying heavily on growth in international markets.

In 2007, Het Anker and Duvel Moortgat were two of twenty-two breweries that banded together to form the Belgian Family Brewers Association. Membership in the association requires three qualifications: fifty years of continuous operation in the same site; family run and independently owned; and brewing traditional Belgian beers. A curved black, yellow, and red label acts as a quality indicator that consumers can reference instead of simply trusting the country-of-origin as being Belgium. "It shows craftsmanship and continuity," says Soenen. "It's not only Trappist or gueuze beers that have a tradition."

It's interesting to compare the values embodied by the Family Brewers Association with, say, the American Craft Brewers' Association, which serves a similar function. No American craft brewer (save Anchor Steam) could pass the fifty-year test, and few are family run. Part of this has to do with the history of American beer markets, but it also points to why Belgian brewers bring up the role of family frequently—the passing on of brewing traditions, but also the emotional ties and obligation to brewery and family as intertwined. While many Belgian brewers recognize—or perhaps concede—the formidable quality of American craft brews, they tend to place a higher premium on tradition and continuity than on the innovation and creativity of American craft brewers. Soenen thinks one of Duvel's strong points is the fact that it hasn't diverged from its original recipe since 1923—the innovation comes in improving quality standards in an attempt to make this one perfect recipe all the more perfect.

That said, the rapid growth of craft beers across the Atlantic, several of which have explicit links to Belgian recipes and traditions, has many Belgian brewers worried about growing competition in their export markets.

15

Hop Heads and Locaholics

Strategies of the American Craft Beer Movement

Northern California has long hosted many a tour of intoxicants: first, through the fertile Sonoma and Napa county vineyards famous for deep red Zinfandels, and then further along to California's "Emerald Triangle" of Humboldt, Mendocino, and Trinity counties, where agricultural yield provides relief for the state's bewilderingly high percentage of glaucoma patients and insomniacs. Microbreweries and brewpubs are relative newcomers on this terrain, though they've quickly established their niche among the mannered locavores' less coherent cousins—the locaholics.

As the story goes, India pale ale (IPA) was born of the imperial age, at the dawn of globalization, when English beer producers figured out that beer would last longer on boat rides if they increased the amount of hops and the alcohol content in their pale ales. How ironic, then, that what started as a preservation strategy has become a regional hallmark for many breweries in northern Californian, epicenter of "Michael Pollan America." It is in this region that "hop heads"—Sierra Nevada brewery's affectionate term for drinkers chasing ever-higher IBU (international bitterness unit) levels—get their back-of-the-tongue fix.

Picturesque coastal highways weave through vineyards while towns offer visitors the opportunity for a lineup of West Coast IPAs so strong they've become a style of their own. The trend is robust enough to warrant an informational directory, "Wine Country Beer." With recent growth and acquisition by Heineken, Lagunitas' IPA has gained national attention. Local visitors can enjoy increased access to smaller release batches of its IPA Maximus and Hop Stoopid brews. This is a brewery that considers their 47 IBU Dogtown brew to be the standalone pale ale. For comparison, Budweiser has an IBU of 7.

Forty minutes north, up-and-coming brewpub Russian River has gained industry attention with its Pliny the Elder, an ode to the Roman botanist who first documented the hop plant, and fifteen minutes past that, Bear Republic has capitalized on the regional success of its Racer 5 IPA by releasing the even more potent Hop Rod rye IPA and its seasonal Racer X with an IBU of over 100.

But kingpin of the region is undoubtedly Sierra Nevada, single-handedly making its hometown of Chico a tourist destination and leading the way nationally with its double IPA Torpedo—the top-selling IPA in the United States, and the product of founder Ken Grossman's wonkiness, utilizing a torpedo machine to double the bitter flavor. The national bestseller is sold locally alongside an experimental floral IPA with rose extract added to the aromatic hops, only slightly less bitter than the brewery's notorious Hoptimum.

These styles offer a visceral departure from the light lagers that American macrobreweries have been peddling in conjunction with the NFL for so long. These days, flagship brews are almost overwhelmingly top-fermented ales, and are frequently IPAs—diverse brews with dark, complex flavors and high alcohol content. And they're more expensive—a six-pack of Lagunitas costs about the same as a twelve-pack of Bud Light. And they've been a runaway success.

The American domestic market share for craft beer has been increasing steadily since the mid-1980s (Figure 15.1). But it took the Great Recession in 2008 to offer a first indication that California crafts were here to stay. Sales of the craft sector climbed from $5.7 million in 2007 to $12 million in 2012. This growth happened during a period when the beer market continued to shrink and sales for imported beers like Heineken and Stella Artois took a nosedive. During this span of time, sales of Sierra Nevada increased 23 percent and Lagunitas more than tripled their output.

But it wasn't always so easy for wine country breweries. The first brewer to envision scenic NorCal as a microbrewery mecca sadly did not see it come to fruition. Jack McAuliffe was a Silicon Valley optical engineer by day and illicit homebrewer by night. In 1976, he founded New Albion brewery, the name of Sir Francis Drake's claim to the California coastline not yet settled by Spanish conquistadors. It was an appropriate tribute given McAuliffe's goal of brewing traditional English porters, pale ales, and stouts among the winemaking practices passed down from Spanish-speaking Californios. Alas, New Albion, the brewery, met the same fate as Drake's control of the land. After six years of struggling financially to pay back loans for capital investment, McAuliffe declared bankruptcy in 1982.

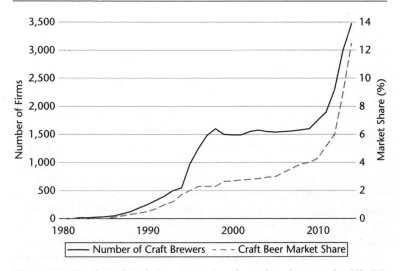

Figure 15.1 Number of craft brewers and craft market share in the US (%), 1980–2014

Elzinga K., Tremblay C., and Tremblay, V. (2017). Craft Beer in the United States: Strategic Connections to Macro and European Brewers. In C. Caravaglia and J. Swinnen, *The Craft Beer Revolution: An Economic Perspective*. Palgrave Macmillan.

The improbability of McAuliffe's story epitomizes the all-or-nothing nature of the American beer market: that a business model like brewing pale ales in California wine country could make the jump from pipe dream to profit strategy in just a few short decades. Now, the million dollar question surrounding the future of American beer is how, exactly, microbreweries will manage to turn their significant size constraints into their biggest competitive advantage.

First Wave Local, Second Wave Craft

Nestled at the bottom of Potrero Hill, positioned with a full view of the famous harbor for which the city is named, stands Anchor Brewery. This is one of six locations the brewery has occupied in recorded history, all as a San Francisco institution embodying the weight of its name. Founded in 1896, Anchor is the only brewery to continue brewing San Francisco's regional "steam beer." Though the exact origins of steam beer are somewhat a mystery, the style may refer to the nineteenth-century practice of lagering vats on roofs so the city's famous nighttime fog would cool them, creating a steam-like effect. The amber beer is brewed using lager yeast while fermenting in warmer ale-like temperatures. Anchor Brewery revived the steam beer for local consumption after prohibition. The brewery was shut down in 1959, sold and reopened in 1960, then sold again in 1965 because of struggles with finances. The third time was the charm: none other than Fritz Maytag, heir to the household appliance fortune, bought a 51 percent controlling share in the brewery within a few hours of visiting. A young Stanford graduate at the time, Maytag had the means to invest in Anchor, and he quickly developed a strategy: "Extremely traditional attitude towards materials and process, absolute basic old-fashioned brewing with purity and simplicity, but combined with modern food processing and equipment," he describes in an interview with Reason TV in 2010. Or, no more shortcuts. Maytag is something of a spiritual godfather to the craft beer movement, and Anchor is considered the "first craft brewery."

His vision was radical amid a culture resistant to change. The vanguard for small breweries at that time was the Brewers Association of America (BAA), founded during World War II by Bill O'Shea. In 1940, there were 684 breweries producing 54.9 million barrels of beer a year (see Table 4.1). When Maytag bought Anchor, the number of breweries had fallen to 197 producing double that amount of beer. By 1980, there were only 101 breweries but production had nearly doubled again, to 188.1 million barrels—the top five breweries produced more than three-quarters of that. Americans were drinking more beer than ever, but this beer was coming from a falling number of increasingly large-capacity macrobreweries.

The BAA was one of two institutional parents to the modern Brewers' Association (BA), the trade organization charged with protecting all things "craft beer." Recently, the BA hosted a night of reflection for the early-comers to the second-wave craft beer movement and small brewery survivors of the postwar shakeout. The forefathers of craft gathered, drinking and discussing the early days of the industry, Maytag, O'Shea, and their first BAA meetings. The recording of this conversation was made available on the BA Web site.

Nick Matt reminisced about his entry into the market, when he was asked to take over his family's Albany, NY-based brewery FX Matt Brewing Co. "When I joined our brewery, they [the macrobrewers] were selling beer at prices we couldn't make our beer for. That puts you in a pretty difficult competitive situation," Matt explains. "We are one of a handful of historic regional breweries in the United States." FX Matt, Anchor, and Philadelphia-based Yuengling were a few of the old class of American breweries that somehow managed to survive the great postwar shakeout and consolidation. But it was a struggle.

Jimmy Carter: Silent Hero of Craft Beer

The strategic mistake of these smaller regional breweries was trying to compete with the big macros on their playing field—through hype, publicity, and television advertising. The most memorable of these tactics may have been Billy Beer—the publicity stunt Louisville-based Falls City Brewing Company was sure could catapult them to the ranks of Anheuser Busch, Miller, and Pabst. Billy Carter had become network news' latest item of fascination—the beer-pounding, gas-station owning, verifiable redneck little brother of presidential Jimmy. Falls City approached fellow southerner Carter with a proposal: his very own namesake beer in exchange for continued publicity, complete with his Georgia charm. The tagline was flawless: "It's the best beer I've ever tasted. And I've tasted a lot," voiced over an image of a smiling bespectacled Billy against a Heartland backdrop in the highly publicized campaign of November 1978. But their fatal flaw was spending more attention on the marketing campaign than on the quality of the beer itself. Billy's public appearances became somewhat notorious as a familiar pattern emerged: too many Billy Beers pounded back and the truth that he still preferred Pabst for personal consumption would come out. America still preferred Pabst, too, it seemed. Falls City folded in October 1979, but Billy Beer lived on in advertising infamy the way all business Hail Marys seem to.

Meanwhile, his brother Jimmy became a silent hero of the microbrewery revival with two strokes of his pen. Carter signed two laws reducing the tax burden on small breweries. Paul Gatza, director of today's BA, admits that he is "the only nerd whose gone through all that stuff," upon receiving a folder of the BAA's political activities. Sure enough, Bill O'Shea had been working tirelessly to get a change in the excise tax through Congress since 1944. The bill had been revised a number of times: its final iteration would reduce the per barrel excise tax on breweries producing under 60,000 barrels per year from nine to seven dollars. In November of 1975, nobody believed that the bill would pass. In December, within a two-week period, some effective lobbying prevailed and the bill found its way through Congress. It was the first one Carter signed when he took office in 1976.

In 1979, Carter was responsible for penning another law important to the microbrewery movement, one redacting federal restrictions on homebrewing and brewpubs. In a carry-over limitation from the prohibition era, homebrewing was illegal under both federal and many state laws. Carter's law not only wiped away the federal limitation but also jump-started the process for legalization in many states.

In 1991, microbreweries like New Belgium were tossed another strategic competitive advantage by Congress. In order to generate more tax revenue, Congress doubled the excise tax on beer to eighteen dollars. The original tax cut pushed through by the BAA—seven dollars for breweries with an annual output of less than 60,000 barrels—remained the same. This gave microbreweries an additional competitive advantage over the biggest macrobreweries. In 2013, the final two states to outlaw homebrewing—Mississippi and Alabama—passed legislation to legalize homebrewing. So with some inspiration from the South, the seeds of the second wave were sown in California and Colorado.

Craft, California- and Colorado-Style

Touring Sierra Nevada's maze-like facilities feels akin to the home-brewer's Willy Wonka fantasy, a fact of which the trained tour guides are cognizant. "Now don't go searching for the river of beer here," smiles our guide Cindy as she lists off safety instructions before entering the hallway. Like the top hat-sporting chocolate producer, founder and owner Ken Grossman has a reputation for wonkiness but better labor practices. His pioneering torpedo machine is responsible for the potent back-of-the-tongue bitter fix that has made Torpedo the top-selling IPA in America. Black and white photographs of Grossman's early experimental equipment spot the hallways in the maze-like setup. According to legend, the 1979 production site utilized dairy tanks, a soft drink boiler, and salvaged equipment. By the early 1980s he had developed Sierra's golden ticket—their signature pale ale that today comprises 75 percent of production. The original founders have since become legends within the sequestered brewery, immortalized in a series of carefully shaded murals documenting the beer production process adorning the walls of a central room. The series is reminiscent of the stations of the cross, featuring 1970s dudes sporting Jesus-style haircuts, but aviator glasses belie the reverent feel.

Two other early brewing figures were Randolph Ware and David Hummer, physics professors at the University of Colorado, Boulder—one could say sunny Chico's mountainous kindred spirit—who opened Boulder Beer Co. in 1979. That Chico State and Boulder turned out to be early pioneers of the microbrewery movement shouldn't surprise us too much. Rolling gracefully from the cultural upset and migrations of the 1960s, the 1970s was a period of experimentation. Much of this experimentation was intoxicant-related. Luckily for future generations, some brave souls directed their own experimentation not just to the consumption but also to the production of said intoxicants.

Charlie Papazian was another Boulderite homebrewer prompted to action by the new law. In 1979, he founded the American Homebrewers Association (AHA) and later, the Association of Brewers (AOB), complete with bimonthly newsletter-turned-magazine *Zymurgy*. The surrounding Rocky Mountains provided a wealth of high-quality brewing water, which Papazian and his kin believed was wasted on the industrial lagers of Coors. Eventually, the AHA and AOB would merge with old guard BAA in a marriage that was messy, to say the least, and during the early 1980s the divergent cultures of the AOB and the BAA were immediately apparent to both parties. The Coloradoans and Californians leading the microbrewery movement were from the West: they sported hippie hair and aviators and were a far cry from the full-suited constituents of old brewing families at BAA conferences. Grossman and Papazian speak about the old days and Maytag's Anchor Brewery with a certain aspirational reverence, and the old BAA meetings as slowly fading figments of yesteryear's breweries.

Maytag took a young Grossman under his wing, inviting him to his first BAA conference in Fort Lauderdale. These were the O'Shea years, when times were looking dire for the regional brewing industry. Grossman describes feeling out of place: everyone was wearing a full suit and tie, feasting at banquets in hotel lobbies every night, reciting the pledge of allegiance, and singing Auld Lang Syne. It was a very different scene from the type of conventions that Papazian and his ilk would soon be hosting. "When we started having our conventions, people thought we were being disrespectful by not being in a tie and a jacket," says Papazian. "Boy has the industry changed a lot. Now we've got people wearing sandals to conferences."

At this point, Grossman didn't know his Sierra Nevada would be one of the best-selling craft beers in America. "I came back feeling very depressed because, during the evening, you talk about 'Oh, these guys closed last year, these guys aren't making it—they're going to close next month.' It was a very dismal time for the brewing industry—it was a survivors club—it was very negative, there wasn't a lot of excitement, except for Fritz." Maytag had been able to generate a following for his Anchor Steam beer by capitalizing on the high-end hippie chic reputation of San Francisco. Grossman was hoping he could do the same with Sierra Nevada, and he began soliciting Maytag for advice on how to run the operation.

Meanwhile, Papazian and his Colorado posse were at work expanding the activities of the newly founded AHA and AOB. First on their list of great ideas: a beer festival. They solicited the efforts of Tom Burns, brewer for Boulder Beer Co. and a thoroughly Western hop head who had somehow managed to win the hearts of the old fogeys at the BAA. Papazian marvels at how Burns' social prowess somehow enchanted the old guard. He was able to convince breweries to send a case of their beer for their new event: the Great American Beer Festival.

They didn't know it at the time, but these baby boomers were early to recognize the excitement that could be generated around creative and innovative beer recipes. But the shuttering of New Albion in 1982 served as a cautionary tale for these young businesses. Convincing the lager-chugging American masses to switch over from Bud, Miller, and Coors would require a persistent reworking of beer-drinking culture away from "what you do when the game's on." Cultural changes that last generally take a while to take hold.

Jim Koch was very aware of this. A departure from the free love and homemade beer mentality of his Western counterparts, Koch was an East Coast establishment man, a recent graduate from Harvard Business School with a family history in the brewing industry. Like Maytag, he recognized the untapped market for hand-crafted beers with quality ingredients. His business-savvy nature convinced him that rushing in heedlessly would be a mistake. He studied the failure of New Albion closely to figure out what not to do. The main struggle for small brew-eries early on was capital investment. So Koch employed a strategy that would be pivotal to the early success of many craft breweries: contract brewing. Koch's idea: build a customer base before you build a building.

He founded Boston Beer Co. in 1984, but he did not build facilities for the brewery until 1997. The American beer market was ripe for excess capacity to be contracted out to craft aspirants. During the late 1980s and 1990s, when many potential craft brewmasters were starting out, macrobreweries had extra capacity, making it mutually profitable for large breweries to contract space and workers to start-up brewers, freeing up funds for brand management and grassroots marketing.

However, contract brewers had to fight the stigma of contract brewing as not "authentic" craft beer, though many in the industry defend the practice. Bart Watson, spokesperson for the BA, disagrees with the stigma. "Brewing is very capital intensive and that made it difficult for breweries to get the start-up capital they needed," he explains. "Contract brewing helped fill a niche that people saw, this demand for full-flavored beer, [but] didn't necessarily have the resources or the infrastructure to produce it." By contracting space at already existing breweries, the high sunk costs associated with building extensive facil-ities could be avoided, reducing barriers to entry for many brewmaster hopefuls. Opportunities to contract-brew have decreased in recent years as excess capacity at macrobreweries has diminished. While over 22 percent of craft beer was brewed under contract in 2000, only 4 percent was produced in the same way in 2009. Though the practice is waning, its early role in jump-starting microbreweries like Boston Beer Co. was essential.

New Belgium: Culture of Ownership

Electrical engineer Jeff Lebesch and social worker Kim Jordan were a Colorado couple with a love of bikes and the great outdoors. During the late 1980s, they embarked on a cycling expedition around Belgium that would change their lives. After tasting the diverse array of sweet and spiced top-fermented ales that the small nation had to offer, Lebesch and Jordan had their calling: bring Belgian flavors back home to Colorado. In 1991, they founded New Belgium Brewery in Fort Collins, Colorado. Fort Collins could be called the poor man's Boulder. Also the site of a university, and about an hour outside metropolitan Denver, the city has a history as a brewing center, hosting both Anheuser Busch and Coors facilities. But today, it's New Belgium that dominates the conversation. With smooth jazz playing in the background and a folksy décor consisting of mutilated bike parts for tables, chairs, and everything in between, the bar and restaurant are designed to emphasize the spaciousness typical of the American West. One may even mistake it for an actual workplace. The open kitchen feels more like a living room than a break room, while a white board lists the birthdays and workplace anniversaries of employees for the upcoming month. It's no secret that New Belgium workers love their jobs. Quality of life is so high here that spokesperson Bryan Simpson reports the brewery boasts a 97 percent retention rate among workers. Additional job security is also facilitated by the brewery's steady and likely-to-continue success. Jordan and Lebesch's flagship ale, Fat Tire Amber Ale, took off soon after opening and has since shown no signs of slowing down. Today, their brewery is the third biggest in the craft segment, trailing Sierra Nevada and Boston Beer Co. Like the two other market leaders, New Belgium had the benefit of an early start in the market. But their timing was by no means a guarantor of their later success.

During the early 1990s, the main contenders in the craft beer segment were Sierra Nevada, Boston Beer Co., and two Seattle-based breweries, Pyramid and Redhook. Between 1992 and 1998, the number of craft brewers suddenly quadrupled. Then, for almost a decade between 1998 and 2008, the number of craft brewers somewhat stabilized. There is some evidence that the shakeout affected smaller breweries during this period. Though most craft breweries are independent and thus do not report profit margins, an examination of three publicly traded breweries—Boston Beer Co., Pyramid, and Redhook—shows tumultuous fluctuations in their per barrel profit during this period.

With its flagship Fat Tire Amber Ale, New Belgium not only survived this initial shakeout, but joined the ranks of craft beer's big dogs, Sierra Nevada and Boston Beer Co., which were both comfortably coasting ahead on the popularity of their signature Sierra Nevada Pale Ale and Samuel Adams Boston Lager. Meanwhile, early market leaders Pyramid and Redhook fell behind during this period. Don Chartier, spokesperson for Lagunitas, attributes the decreased market share of these two to their decision to go public. "They're still selling their product but the craft beer market is pretty educated," he says. "Whether or not the beer is better, worse, different, people see that and they know that."

In addition to size, the BA designates that breweries must be independent to be officially considered "craft." First off, independent breweries are not responsible to shareholders, thus removing the incentive to cut back on quality to increase profit margins. The BA also feels a responsibility to protect independent brewers because they do not have the advantage of capital influx that can be brought about by public investors looking to turn a profit, and nor do they have access to the distribution networks that macrobreweries can offer. As a result, they must be more strategic in their expansion. Though Boston Beer Co. is publicly traded, it is not owned by any multinational corporation, and therefore still falling under the guidelines of the BA. The focus on independence raises questions about the utility of different corporate organization structures in the craft beer segment. Do independent brewers have more incentive to produce higher quality beer than publicly traded brewers?

New Belgium offers a compelling case study for an alternative to selling out to shareholders. Though CEO Kim Jordan is still a major part of the brewery, a few years back she began considering how it would be possible to scale back her role and sell off her shares while still maintaining the integrity of the organization she had built from the ground up. Simpson describes why the options available weren't appealing to Jordan and her family, who held a controlling share: "We looked at it: partnerships and private investors and IPO [initial public offering], in all of those, you lose a great deal of control over who you are and what you do. Generally what you have is when you have an investor come in, and they're looking to flip it. So they're going to come in and cut costs and turn it over in four or five years—that's what they want to get out of it." Influenced by her background as a social worker, she opted for an alternative corporate structure model: reorganize New Belgium using an employee stock ownership plan (ESOP). Rather than sell shares of the company to highest bidders looking to quickly turn a profit, Jordan sold shares of the brewery to employees of the company—the workers invested in the brewery's long-term health and growth and in their fellow employees, who were more interested in their craft than their portfolio. With this model, workers at New Belgium take pride in and ownership of their role in the company because they actually do have a stake in its success.

Simpson glows when he discusses the ESOP model. It's responsible for not only making New Belgium more of a home than a workplace, but it actually facilitates an entrepreneurial culture that has led to some key changes in efficiency and improved operations. "This is the kind of culture where you can float an idea, if your proposal's got weight and you've done your research, you can make some big changes." People can get immediately involved in upper-level decision-making committees if they want to. He notes the success of one proposal to scratch an extraneous cardboard insert which was being used to package bottles. "We've got guys on the line making proposals that save us millions of dollars a year and tons of cardboard," he says. "When you are really literally an owner of a thing, you've got the power to say this." It's also something Simpson has experienced firsthand. As a long-time journalist, Simpson was looking for a communications-type job during the 1990s when New Belgium was just starting up. He could tell the brewery was a new type of workplace, so he opted for a temporary position just to get in: working on the bottling line. Soon enough, he had basically created his own job description as marketing and public relations director at the fledging brewery. From what he's observed, the branches of operations have grown more specialized as the brewery has expanded. However, Jordan's ethos of bottom-up cross-pollination perpetuates itself at this point. It's an integral part of the brewery as an institution, and it's not going away any time soon.

There's a reason people at New Belgium love their jobs. After their first year working, the brewery provides veterans with both a high-end bike and a customized key-holder braided by Jordan herself. Simpson describes how even the most masculine members of the team find themselves tearing up at the hand-off ceremony. At the five-year mark, workers get an all-expenses-paid trip around Belgium similar to the one that inspired the brewery. And at ten years, workers themselves exercise their ESOP power to bring about a much-coveted, rarely offered benefit: a paid six-month sabbatical from work to do whatever they so desire. "It's certainly rejuvenating," says Simpson. It's also not hard to see the benefits Jordan's innovative ESOP model have had on New Belgium's long-term success. One must only subscribe to an old truism: happy brewers make good beer. And that certainly seems to be the case.

Advertising Authenticity

Nestled in the Marin foothills, led by fearless leader Tony Magee and his gang of hop heads, Lagunitas has successfully capitalized on an outsider image that's made it a national hit. In fact, their resistance to federal authority remains as silently subversive as California's drug laws. The name for their innovative ale, internally called "Kronik" with a backward "k," was approved by state regulatory laws but nixed at the federal level. The interstate commerce-approved label instead reads "Censored," though every year they chip away at the size of the stamp relative to the text underneath. Their tagline of "Beer speaks, people mumble," might as well come with an addendum that labels insinuate. Daily tappings at 4:20 aside, Lagunitas is more interested in dealing NorCal's cannabinoid cousin: hops.

Such innuendo adds to an off-beat aesthetic that has fueled Lagunitas' success in new markets. "The biggest compliment you can get is, people come out here and say 'I drank your beer in New York, in Florida, I had an idea of what you guys would be,' and to come up here and say, 'Yea this is exactly you'," says spokesperson Don Chartier. Lagunitas hosts a tasting tour distributing free and generous portions of seven select brews—the Sonoma County model meets *That '70s Show*. Fuzzy chairs, vintage comic book posters, and bumper stickers alongside a series of beer bottles labeled with cover art from Frank Zappa's complete discography, a gigantic "Duff Beer" flag, and a foosball table serve to decorate this manchild cave. Here, drinking on the job is not only encouraged— drinking is the job.

In this setting, the placement of these relics hints at the divergent marketing strategies of craft brewers. In the early days of craft beer's emergence, capital constraints prevented small breweries from relying on the large-scale print and television advertising campaigns common among macrobreweries. The one exception is Boston Beer Co., which spent $14.11 per barrel advertising Sam Adams in 2009, far above the industry average of $4.88 per barrel. Though the market dominance of

Boston Beer has grown significantly with its advertising efforts, small microbreweries have been holding their own without billboards and commercials.

Rather, the low-budget and grassroots marketing tactics of craft breweries seem to have played an important role in their early success and appeal. Simpson describes one of his early maneuvers to increase the exposure of New Belgium. He points to an old junker van, apparently called an Airstream trailer—thoroughly a relic of the 1950s. It was in this van he took his self-created job as marketing director on the road to set up beer schools educating Denver's bartenders on the joys of Belgian beer. "We'd drive that into an account, bring all the front-line servers out, then we'd do a slide show—an old-school slide show, it was really anti-technology," he jokes. "We'd put on the music, we'd talk about 'Here's the brewhouse,' pour the beers, and then talk about the beers."

Market research suggests that small craft breweries may benefit from the absence of advertising efforts because craft beer tends to appeal to a demographic that frowns on large-scale campaigns. Simpson would be inclined to agree: "A lot of the intuitive things we did early on were fun and quirky and weird, and I think craft beer drinkers want to see that— they want to see the personality behind the brands and the people making them. That's part of the allure and the appeal of the category." This is the philosophy behind Lagunitas' "Beer speaks, people mumble" tagline: they want their beer to advertise itself. "More than getting the word out, it's getting the liquid out," Chartier explains. Lagunitas' primary strategy is to donate its beer to local nonprofit organizations to sell at fundraisers. "It's a win–win for us. It helps get our beer into your hands, and it helps nonprofits," Chartier says.

New Belgium has similarly taken the philanthropy-as-advertisement route with its much-anticipated annual Tour De Fat. Simpson describes it as "basically a critical mass, without all the anarchy." Many have questioned what bikes have to do with beer, to which Simpson simply replies, "Bikes and beer: where's the connection? Well, where's not a connection?" The Tour De Fat is hosted in a different city each year with a chosen nonprofit to which all proceeds are donated. It starts as a legally sanctioned critical mass ride: streets are shut down so cyclist beer lovers can ride together. The race is followed by music and festivities in a park where one person vows to give up his car for a year in exchange for a high-tech cruiser bike. Simpson describes the goal of Tour De Fat as both philanthropic and empowering in the face of the "gloom and doom preachy thing," he says. "We're very pro-bike, less anti-car." And it seems to be working so far. But for New Belgium, Lagunitas, and Sierra Nevada, the days of shoestring budgets are behind them. These days, a process of craft consolidation is on the horizon.

In 2000, the four largest craft brewers produced around 40 percent of US craft beer, a number that has changed very little in the past decade. The primary problem that growing breweries are now facing is how to increase production capacity to meet rapidly growing demand. The most recent trend is Western breweries looking to expand out East. In order to save costs on transportation, they need new facilities. Well, they need new facilities anyway, as the biggies are currently operating at max capacity. The state of choice is North Carolina. Simpson explains: "They are very pro-business down there, and they definitely incentivize that. They also have excellent brewing water, and they have a deep beer culture." Currently, both New Belgium and Sierra Nevada are building facilities in Asheville, while Coloradan Oskar Blues opts for the nearby suburb of Brevard. Lagunitas is also expanding, currently at work constructing a facility in Chicago as a foothold into the Midwestern market. The spectacular success of these craft breweries raises concerns that their size will jeopardize the special connection they have with their local fans.

For example, the buddy-buddy atmosphere facilitates a culture of innovation at these breweries, and their recent success is the product of increased demand for variety. In this regard, their small size works as an advantage—it allows them to adapt operations quickly in response to local demand. Chartier offers a metaphor: "with a bigger ship it takes longer to turn."

The growing popularity of growlers has also benefited craft breweries' small-size advantage of offering variety. In addition, it allows them to accommodate a new trend: "As the market is shifting, people are not drinking at bars anymore, they're drinking at home," says Chartier. While on-premise distribution tends to benefit breweries that can offer variety, growlers offer a middle ground by allowing people to take fresh, new beer home with them. New Belgium similarly displays a dedication to continuously fueling creativity and innovation to develop new and exciting beer brands. One recent exciting prospect: a collaboration with Belgian Boon Brewery (see Chapter 14) to brew a Transatlantic Kriek. Simpson describes the two-step process of creating the aged, sour beer, "He starts a brew there, does spontaneous fermentation, ships it here, and we do a blend." Similarly, Boston Brewing Co. teamed up with renowned German Weihenstephan to brew innovative Infinium, a sixteen-dollar bottle of beer with a recipe patented by Dr. Martin Zarnkow. As they grow in size, craft breweries may no longer have the strategic advantage of specifically responding to local demand, but the new stature of the American craft brewing world has also opened up the potential for mutually beneficial international collaborations. As always, small brewers hold true to another part of their core ethos: collaboration—rather than competition—with each other.

"Look at how many brands Sam Adams or Sierra Nevada or New Belgium have, and they frequently have one-offs or seasonal beers, or collaborations that they do at a much smaller scale than their flagship brands," lists off Watson. He's defending the segment against criticisms of these breweries' newfound size. "Yes, it's an industrial process, but you're seeing people within the craft push the limits, explore, take the beer back to its roots and meld that with modern methods."

In 2015, Heineken announced that it was purchasing a 50 percent stake in Lagunitas. For a company like Lagunitas where authenticity is central to its brand, this caused uproar among many folks, who decried the brewer as selling out. "The fact is, what we emulate is what we put out there," Chartier explained to me prior to the announcement of Heineken's acquisition. "We're being sincere—this is not a marketing campaign, this is just what we do." Announcing the joint venture with Heineken, founder Tony Magee inexplicably quoted Nietzsche and pondered whether history was ready for this new model of brewing.

Though the Heineken acquisition made waves due to the immense popularity and authentic feel of Lagunitas, it exemplified macrobreweries' interest in capitalizing on the growing market share of craft beer. AB InBev has similarly acquired Goose Island, Bluepoint, and Elysian in an attempt to claim their piece of the lucrative value-added craft beer market pie. Whether the highly publicized acquisition by Heineken will affect Lagunitas fans' loyalty to their favorite Marin brew remains to be seen. Chartier did point to formerly dominant breweries Pyramid and Widmer's decision to go public as a reason for their decreasing market share in the early 2000s. At the same time, the partnershi!p with Heineken will offer Lagunitas access to markets at a much faster rate than relying on organic growth. It's a risky move for a brand that credits so much of its success to perceived authenticity. But as Frank Boon can attest, taste in beer has bucked surefire market predictions before, and it certainly will again.

The recent developments have not deterred new entrants in the US craft beer markets, in fact they may have stimulated them, with access to finance and small-scale brewing technology and know-how more available than ever. Since 2008 a second wave of explosive growth in craft breweries has occurred. Since then one new craft brewery a day on average has opened in America.

Conclusion

How Beer Explains the World

On September 8, 2016, after seven generations of brewing Belgium's Bosteels family decided to sell their brewery, locally famous for its Tripel Karmeliet and dark Kwak beer, to AB InBev, the world's leading multinational beer company, to be integrated into its "craft and specialty network." The news was startling to Belgians in particular, where Tripel Karmeliet is all but revered and the brewery is older than the nation of Belgium itself. But in light of the story of our book it should not be surprising. Only a year prior to this, iconic American craft brewery Lagunitas shocked the US beer world when it announced a 50 percent sale to multinational Heineken.

In the past two decades, craft beers have re-emerged and rapidly grown, frequently out-competing the mainstream lager macrobreweries. In the same era, the lager macrobreweries have become globally integrated multinationals, ushering in an era of unprecedented market concentration. Now, on the eve of the merger of SABMiller and AB InBev, the two primary players in what has become a global oligopoly, we are observing a rush to acquire and capitalize on the growing popularity of these small craft breweries. It was the prescience of milkman Pierre Celis to save white beer from extinction in rural Belgium. But it was the reach and market power of what was then Artois Brewery, now AB InBev—to which Hoegaarden was a reluctant sellout—which brought Hoegaarden beer to every corner of the globe. The small craft breweries offer passion, preservation, and innovation; the macrobreweries offer global distribution networks.

Beeronomics is the story of civilization filtered through the prism of an ancient brew. It's a story about global empires and war—both commercial and military, religion and science, innovation, market, and political power, globalization and its discontents. It traces beer's 10,000-year odyssey as vital nourishment in early societies to the world's most consumed alcoholic drink today. Beer propelled the shift from our hunter-gatherer way of life to agrarianism. It bankrolled British imperialism, and eased post-communist Eastern Europe into a market economy.

Taxes, Religion, and Power

The power of the British Royal Navy, the success of the Counter-Reformation in southern Germany: what do they have in common? They can all thank beer for their position in the annals of European history. Or, more accurately, beer taxes. Beer has shaped the trajectory of Western civilization more than most political philosophers might like to admit. And in fact, an archival glance back reveals that beer taxes underwrote events that shape our modern world. The introduction of hops, the growth of commercial brewing, and changes in tax policies are among the many innovations that have shaped Western civilization at pivotal moments. Beer taxes became a major source of revenue for the ruling classes, strategically employed to consolidate political power, spur or hinder innovation, and finance wars.

At some point around 700 AD, one medieval spice thought to promote fertility, and associated with mystical powers, was added to beer. Five centuries later, hops would revolutionize the global brewing industry. But not just yet. A curious aspect of this story is why the most ubiquitous ingredient in beer took so long to become a widespread practice—and when it did, it did so completely. So why didn't monasteries employ hops' preservational powers in their own brewing? It all began when brewers in the trade cities of Hamburg and Bremen found a way to monetize hops' unique function as a preservative. When imported barrels of hopped beer arrived in England and the Low Countries, the new style undermined a major source for local tax revenue: *gruit*, the additive blend that municipal governments taxed and distributed to local breweries. For hundreds of years this side-effect of the use of hops led to its prohibition in some of the major beer-producing countries. It was only when commercial brewing developed, and with it a shift to a new tax model, that hopped beer was permitted. The slow dissemination of hops exemplifies the struggle that innovations faced in overcoming political obstacles before entering ubiquity.

After a century and a half of non-stop warring, the Great Britain of the nineteenth century was truly remarkable: imperialist superpower abroad, industrial powerhouse at home. But how did such a small island nation with so few natural resources manage to win so many wars against its continental rival France? And how did it do so without taxing its population into submission and inhibiting commercial development? Britain's rise to military power is intrinsically linked to bureaucracy and the industrial revolution in brewing. As we explained in Chapter 3, the British Parliament passed the tax burden on to the new urban proletariat by levying high excise taxes on cheap beer: porter. But Britain was not the first country to discover the power of beer as a tax resource. A recent study by Koen Deconinck and Eline Poelmans of the University of Leuven shows that the successful uprising of Dutch cities against the Spanish Empire, which ultimately lead to the split of the Low Countries into the Netherlands and Belgium, was financed largely by beer taxes.

And it wasn't just the Protestants who used beer taxes to finance wars. Devoutly Catholic Bavarian King Maximilian I needed to find a way to atone for his father's debts. Munich was the center of the Catholic Counter-Reformation, collapsing upon itself thanks to the constant barrage of attacks from Protestant forces. If nothing else, northern Germans had an edge over the Catholics when it came to money. But Bavarians drank more beer. Maximilian I brilliantly concocted a scheme to monetize the existing German beer law, the *Reinheitsgebot*, into social policy by leveraging a royal power to instill the right to brew weissbier— the top-fermented wheat beer that stood as an exception to the state-wide ban on summer brewing. The Bavarian crown used its monopoly on weissbier production both to pay back debts associated with hosting the Counter-Reformation and as a form of Catholic social policy.

Science, Technology, and Industrial Restructuring

After the fall of Rome, European monasteries dominated the brewing world for nearly 1,000 years. In fact, they were the only places beer was manufactured on something close to commercial scale. But that changed in the thirteenth century when scientific innovation, increased trade and taxes, and economic expansion acted together to turn beer into a commodity. The decline of monastic brewing continued through the Reformation, when many monasteries were destroyed, and was completed during the reign of Napoleon, who destroyed Europe's remaining monasteries—and their breweries.

The scientific discoveries of the eighteenth and nineteenth centuries caused a dramatic transformation of economic activities in the Western world: the industrial revolution. Some important discoveries happened in and around beer, and contributed to the lager beer style which was so conducive to profitable large-scale brewing. Scientists were fascinated by the process of beer (and wine) fermentation and made major contributions to biology and chemistry. Even basic elements of statistics were developed in brewing. In his fascinating research on "Guinnessometrics," Steve Ziliak of Roosevelt University in Chicago traces the origins of the ubiquitous t-test to the nineteenth-century Guinness brewery in Dublin where new statistic techniques were developed to calculate what was the optimal quantity and quality of hops to maximize the Guinness brewery's profits.

Early refrigeration technology joins pasteurization and inferential statistics as nineteenth-century scientific developments produced by the brewing industry. In the Czech Republic, almost every brewery is located near a pond. This may seem surprising, as water for brewing did not come from ponds but from rivers. The purpose was different. Before refrigeration technology, brewers would cut ice from the pond every winter and shovel it into underground cellars for the refrigeration, or lagering, process. The bottom-fermentation method allowed brewers to scrape out the yeast easily and made for a more consistent, reliable style of beer. It had originally been co-opted by Bavarian brewers who took up the practice of storing beer in caves in the Alps during the summertime. Brewers in Munich, Plzen, and České Budějovice recognized the potential for profit this style of beer offered in newly urbanizing cities. This started the search for a technology that could keep beer cool without relying on extracting ice blocks in January.

The reason behind beer's role in the scientific revolution is that, as urbanization brought large populations of rural migrants together in condensed cities, the possibility of brewing on a large scale presented lucrative opportunities to profit—for whoever could figure out the technology necessary for success.

While brewers contributed to the emerging canon of applied scientific research, these new technologies in turn revolutionized the brewing industry. Steam engines, refrigeration, and commercialized yeast made it possible to manage the production process closely and produce new types of beer, paving the way for low-cost, large-scale brewing of consistent quality. The industrial revolution thus changed the nature of the beer market (from top to bottom fermentation) and the structure of the brewery sector. Small, local breweries shuttered en masse throughout the twentieth century while a few, large-scale industrial operations cornered domestic markets. The UK entered the twentieth century with more than 6,000 breweries. By 1980, there were less than 150. By 1990, three American breweries produced more than 95 percent of domestic beer.

However, change not only came from within the sector but also from outside. In fact, the spread of television advertising served as an unlikely culprit in the decline of small local breweries. In America this force of brewery consolidation started in the 1950s as commercial TV swept the country. In Europe, where TV stations were publicly owned, this process did not start until the end of the twentieth century as commercial TV took off.

Globalization after the Fall of the Wall

When Ronald Reagan requested Gorbachev to "tear down this wall" in the late 1980s, he meant both literally and figuratively—economic reforms in the former Eastern Bloc opened up a long-sequestered part of the world to free trade and flow of foreign capital. In conjunction with changing tastes, these new possibilities lead to foreign direct investment (FDI) in emerging markets like Poland, Russia, and China, speeding up the rate of global integration. As an ancient and politically charged commodity, beer offers a unique lens through which we can understand how local rituals and regulations are both succumbing to and resisting the forces of globalization.

Across the former Eastern Bloc, previously subsidized barley farmers found themselves in a credit vacuum and their crop prices in a tailspin. But by the mid-1990s an unlikely hero came out of the woodwork: while banks were less than reluctant to lend to a sector in decline, the brewing industry was among the first to attract FDI. When multinational brewers invested in formerly state-owned breweries and malt houses, they learned that first they'd have to repair the supply chains all the way up to the farms if they wanted eventually to become profitable operations—a process that is repeated today in growing African economies.

Russia, a nation with vodka so integral to its historic national identity, suddenly saw a generation of drinkers opt for beer. For as long as Cyrillic has permitted Siberians to make permanent their literary philosophies, Russian writers have been in an abusive relationship with vodka. But in the late 1990s, the nation had a sudden and passionate fling with beer. In less than a decade, the Russian beer market quintupled. It was a perfect storm. Foreign takeovers brought in capital and better brewing techniques—and, at least as important, new advertising strategies. New regulations limiting the advertisement and sale of alcohol were designed to curb the rising mortality rate, but there was a loophole: in Russian law, beer wasn't officially categorized as "alcohol." The combination of advertising targeted to young people, better quality, and income growth soon made beer the most popular drink in Russia, especially among the young generation.

Globalization has integrated billions of consumers into a single market. Smartphones from Apple or Samsung are used by consumers across the globe. Starbucks coffee shops now attract customers in places with a proud tradition of their own coffee, such as Vienna and Milan. The story is similar in the beer and alcohol industries, but in a way that is even more spectacular. When you ask people about the drink of choice of countries, they will typically associate Russia with vodka, Spain and France with wine, Germany with beer, etc. But this association is based on historical stories, not on today's consumption.

Beer consumption has declined in the traditional beer markets as each new generation of drinkers in Germany, Britain, and Belgium shift toward wine and mixed beverages. The opposite is happening in countries like Spain, France, and Argentina, where consumers are foregoing their traditional wine for more beer. The concept of Spanish preferences for Rioja or the French preferring Bordeaux or Champagne no longer fits their actual consumption patterns: most people there drink beer, not wine, in the twenty-first century. This global convergence of tastes has effects far beyond the cafés and pubs where it is manifest. These changing consumer patterns have brewing companies setting their sights on countries with little beer tradition but growing incomes.

Multinationals and Trade

While beer trade contributed to the spread of hop technology in the Middle Ages, and today's IPAs have their roots in British colonial trade, these were exceptions. Until quite recently, beer trade made up a small share of production. And, with some exceptions, most exported beer was shipped just across the border. It was just too expensive to ship beer (which, effectively, is mostly water) over long distances. With beer prices going up and high-end consumers considering beer as a valuable alternative to wine—and being prepared to pay good dollars for specialty beers—trade in beer has grown exponentially.

The globalization of markets and convergence of taste is not only reflected in changing consumption patterns across the globe, but also in trade and global company structures. The removal of international restrictions on trade and investments has allowed the process of consolidation that started in the early twentieth century to go global at the end of the twentieth century.

Beer trade and global integration has also triggered a series of trade disputes. Since the early modern period in Europe, political rulers have secured income by claiming control of the land, its fruits, and its beers. Today, extracting profits from beers happens in court battles over trademarks and copyrights. The "Battle of the Buds" is a frequently cited case study in international trademark dispute. The fight over "Budweiser" can be traced back to the nineteenth century, linking the history of the city Budweis, immigration in early industrialist America and feudalist Bohemia in the Holy Roman Empire, to communist Czechoslovakia and beyond. There's no clear answer: American Budweiser is the first registered brand name, but the historic German name of the Czech city České Budějovice is "Budweis." In the past decade the two firms have seen over one hundred decisions issued by various judges and international trade panels, with several dozen lawsuits currently in progress in eleven nations.

Beer trade has grown further, with brewing companies extending beyond their borders, a process which started in the 1980s as brewers in countries such as Belgium and Holland searched for foreign growth with domestic consumption declining rapidly. These brewers went on a buying spree in the 1990s and 2000s, culminating in a few companies dominating the global beer industry.

There's no better example than AB InBev claiming one-third of the world's beer to illustrate just how dramatically a globalizing world has impacted the brewing industry. The creation of this huge beer company is a story of the mouse eating the elephant: in the throes of the 2008 financial crisis, at some point the hostile takeover of Anheuser Busch by Belgian-Brazilian multinational InBev caught America by surprise. Twenty years earlier, Anheuser Busch was twenty times the size of Belgian firm Interbrew and the largest brand in the world. Popular books *Dethroning the King* and *Bitter Brew* have documented the fall of an American icon. While American firms grew organically through expansion of their brands in the world's largest beer market, the era of global integration had been marked by mergers, acquisitions, and forced divestitures in nations with previously concentrated beer markets. When these merged companies set their eyes in the biggest price, the US breweries were unaware and unprepared.

The Craft Counterrevolution

Industrialization, consolidation, global integration ... For a century, consumers switched to the cheap and consistent offerings of large-scale breweries. But sometime around the late 1970s, a change of current began to take hold: increased patronage of small, local breweries, a willingness to spend more money for less beer, and an interest in traditional brewing techniques and styles with stronger flavors than the industrial light lager. In the United States, this has manifested itself through the popularity of hoppy IPAs, while in Belgium the fastest-growing domestic sector has been abbey and Trappist ales during the past two decades. From San Francisco to Beijing, abbey ales shipped from Belgium's Trappist breweries can sell for US$18 in upscale restaurants. Beers are paired with dishes as part of the new art of "beer gastronomy." Traditional, authentic abbey ales have become the face of a global counterrevolution in brewcraft, challenging the dominance of multinational mass producers of lager beer. In the US, the most consolidated brewing industry in the world is giving way to a fast-growing craft beer sector as consumers reject industrial, mass-produced beer.

Does this trend reflect a return to medieval beer markets that had been swept away by the twin tides of industrialization and consumerism, or is our obsession with craft beer built on mere romantic nostalgia? The truth, as it turns out, lies somewhere in the middle: the craft beer boom claims a relationship with tradition, but it is also a distinctly twenty-first century phenomenon—a reaction to mass-produced, industrial beer, but one that makes effective use of tools from the scientific revolution in brewing, twenty-first-century marketing techniques, and, increasingly, global trade.

The craft beer movement has been framed as a counterrevolution to industrial brewing, a triumph of locavorism. And the recent popularity of the craft sector is truly remarkable, posting double-digit growth despite much higher prices than industrial competitors Bud, Miller, and Coors. But what, really, is the reason that small local brewing suddenly became a viable business model when it did? In the US, the story begins with a change in tax law passed by Jimmy Carter in 1979, and continues with the strategic business models of early leaders: contract brewing to counter high fixed costs and the success of grassroots marketing campaigns. But now the underdogs are facing a paradox: what happens when David becomes Goliath? It has caused heated discussions surrounding the definition of "craft," and the controversy surrounding "faux craft."

Belgian beers have received their fair share of hype in recent years. Following the publication of Beer Hunter Michael Jackson's *Great Beers of Belgium*, connoisseurs from as far as Japan and South America have been flocking to the tiny nation for beer tours of its oldest breweries. Indeed, the historical diversity of styles in Belgium is indisputable, from the sour gueuzes and cherry beers to the sweet abbey ales. But what connoisseurs may not realize is that these beers were not great or even considered good as recently as the 1970s and 1980s. The regional styles so adored today were called "peasant beers" by fans of industrially produced, cheap, and consistent lagers like Stella Artois.

Interestingly their current success is as much due to the multinational brewers than to the local small-scale craft brewers—some who have remained independent, and some not. Arguably the most remarkable case is that of Hoegaarden. Hoegaarden's story is full of surprising twists. On every bottle of Hoegaarden white beer are two intertwined symbols: one of a bishop's staff, the other of a brewer's paddle. It's the seal of the tiny Brabantian village of Hoegaarden, but it's also the trademarked property of multinational giant AB InBev, owner of the village's name-sake white beer. Hoegaarden's history as a brewing center dates back to the fifteenth century. Upon the closure of the brewery in the 1970s, unable to compete with industrial lager beer, the brewery was restarted as a small craft brewery fighting to preserve its rich wheat taste. Just imagine the outrage when AB InBev bought it. Yet they introduced and now sell Hoegaarden all over the world. It also inspired brewers world-wide to produce Belgian-style white beer, and led to the success of brands such as Blue Moon and Shock Top in the United States.

And now it appears that Tripel Karmeliet will go the same direction as Hoegaarden. The abbey-style beer produced by Bosteels Brewery was named after a nearby historic monastery, though it was developed by Bosteels only in 1996. In the two decades since, Tripel Karmeliet has accumulated status as a craft icon, a beacon of quality in a market saturated by mass-produced industrial lagers. As the global beer market has grown more consolidated than ever, breweries like Bosteels—which struggled to survive during the years of consolidation—have been able to charge higher prices for what is now considered a high-value product. The story came full circle when Bosteels announced its sale to AB InBev—the inevitable drumbeat of innovation, integration, and mass distribution marches on.

Selected Bibliography

Adams, W. (2006). Markets: Beer in Germany and the United States. *Journal of Economic Perspectives*, 20(1): 189–205.

Bamforth, C. (2008). *Grape vs. Grain: A Historical, Technological, and Social Comparison of Wine and Beer*. Cambridge University Press.

Baron, S.W. (1962). *Brewed in America: The History of Beer and Ale in the United States*. Little, Brown.

Billen, R. (2005). *Pierre Celis: My Life*. Media Marketing Communications MV.

Brewer, J. (1990). *Sinews of War: War, Money and the English State, 1688–1783*. Harvard University Press.

Cabras, I., Higgins, D., and Preece, D. (eds.) (2016). *Brewing, Beer and Pubs: A Global Perspective*. Palgrave Macmillan.

Caravaglia, C. and Swinnen, J. (2017). *The Craft Beer Revolution: An Economic Perspective*. Palgrave Macmillan.

Clark, P. (1983). *The English Alehouse: A Social History, 1200–1830*. Longman.

Colen, L. and Swinnen, J. (2016). Economic Growth, Globalization and Beer Consumption. *Journal of Agricultural Economics*, 67(1): 186–207.

Deconinck, K., Poelmans, E., and Swinnen, J. (2016). How Beer Created Belgium (and the Netherlands): The Contribution of Beer Taxes to War Finance during the Dutch Revolt. *Business History*, 58(5): 694–724.

Deconinck, K. and Swinnen, J. (2015). Peer Effects and the Rise of Beer in Russia. *Food Policy*, 51: 83–96.

Elzinga, K. (2009). The Beer Industry. In J. Brock (ed.), *The Structure of American Industry*, 12th edition. Waveland Press.

Esslinger, H.M. (ed.) (2009). *Handbook of Brewing: Processes, Technology, Markets*. Wiley-VCH Verlag GmbH & Co. KGaA.

Freeman, D. (2011). Beer in Good Times and Bad: A US State-level Analysis of Economic Conditions and Alcohol Consumption. *Journal of Wine Economics*, 6(2): 231–51.

Gammelgaard, J. and Dörrenbächer, C. (2013). *The Global Brewery Industry: Markets, Strategies, and Rivalries*. Edward Elgar.

George, L.M. (2009). National Television and the Market for Local Products: The Case of Beer. *Journal of Industrial Economics*, 57(1): 85–111.

Holt, M.P. (2006). *Alcohol: A Social and Cultural History*. Berg.

Hornsey, I. (2003). *A History of Beer and Brewing*. The Royal Society of Chemistry.

Jackson, M. (1996). *Great Beers of Belgium*. Brewers Publications.

King, J. (2005). *Budweiser into Czechs and Germans: A Local History of Bohemian Politics, 1848–1948*. Princeton University Press.

Selected Bibliography

Knoedelseder, W. (2014). *Bitter Brew: The Rise and Fall of Anheuser-Busch and America's Kings of Beer*. HarperBusiness.

MacIntosh, J. (2011). *Dethroning the King: The Hostile Takeover of Anheuser-Busch, an American Icon*. John Wiley & Sons.

Mathias, P. (1959). *The Brewing Industry in England 1700–1830*. Cambridge University Press.

Nelson, M. (2005). *The Barbarian's Beverage: A History of Beer in Ancient Europe*. Routledge.

Nye, J. (2007). *War, Wine and Taxes: The Political Economy of Anglo-French Trade, 1689–1900*. Princeton University Press.

Persyn, D., Swinnen, J., and Vanormelingen, S. (2011). Belgian Beers: Where History Meets Globalization. In J. Swinnen (ed.), *The Economics of Beer*. Oxford University Press.

Poelmans, E. and Swinnen, J. (2011). A Brief Economic History of Beer. In J. Swinnen (ed.), *The Economics of Beer*. Oxford University Press.

Rabin, D. and Forget, C. (eds.) (1998). *The Dictionary of Beer and Brewing*, 2nd edition. Fitzroy Dearborn.

Riepl, W. (2009). *The Belgian Beer Barons: The Story Behind Anheuser-Busch InBev*. Roularta Media Group.

Stack, M. (2003). A Concise History of America's Brewing Industry. In R. Whaples (ed.), *Economic History Net Encyclopedia of Economic and Business History* <https://eh.net/encyclopedia/a-concise-history-of-americas-brewing-industry/>.

Swinnen, J. (ed.) (2011). *The Economics of Beer*. Oxford University Press.

Swinnen, J. (2017). Why Belgian Beer is the Best in the World. An Economic Explanation. *Choices Magazine*.

Tremblay, V. and Tremblay, C. (2005). *The U.S. Brewing Industry: Data and Economic Analysis*. MIT Press.

Unger, R.W. (2001). *A History of Brewing in Holland, 900–1900: Economy, Technology, and the State*. Brill Academic.

Unger, R.W. (2004). *Beer in the Middle Ages and the Renaissance*. University of Pennsylvania Press.

Van Tongeren, F. (2011). Standards and International Trade Integration: A Historical Review of the German "Reinheitsgebot." In J. Swinnen (ed.), *The Economics of Beer*. Oxford University Press.

Verstl, I. and Faltermeier, E. (2016). *Beer Monopoly: How Brewers Bought and Built for World Domination*. Brauwelt International.

Wilson, R. and Gourvish, T. (eds.) (1998). *The Dynamics of the International Brewing Industry since 1800*. Routledge.

Ziliak, S.T. (2008). Guinnessometrics: The Economic Foundation of 'Student's' *t*. *Journal of Economic Perspectives*, 22(4): 199–216.

Index

Note: Italic *f* and *t* after page numbers denote Figures and Tables respectively

AB InBev 4, 55, 58, 60, 76, 80, 95, 125, 167
  abbey ales 130
  advertising for industrial exports of 142
  "Best of Belgium" campaign 129, 140–1
  international goals 142
  mergers and acquisitions 61, 131, 159, 161
  rising tide of industrial lager that
    culminated in 138
  trademarked property of 169
  see also Anheuser Busch
Abbaye Notre-Dame de Leffe 59, 129–31,
  140–2
abbey ales 5, 130, 131, 141
  blonde 59, 129, 140
  market share of 1
  popularity of 2
  sweet 103, 169
  traditional, authentic 168
additives 13, 16, 87, 162
  animal products as 84
  regulation and taxation of 17
  ubiquitous 15
Adorno, Theodor 49
Aerts, Erik 137
Aerts, Guido 143
Affligem abbey ale 141
African economies 165
African Americans 47
AHA (American Homebrewers
  Association) 151
Alabama 150
Alaxa, Imrich 67, 68, 69, 70
alcohol 10, 25, 28, 40, 119, 134
  female deities assigned specifically to
    production of 9
  government legally categorizing beer
    as 117
  lives spared by stricter rules 115
  loosened license restrictions 35
  nationwide prohibition of (1919–33) 45
  protectionist policy 26

  regulations limiting advertisement and
    sale of 166
  subject to legally mandated minimum
    prices 59
  taxing 26, 108
  television advertising banned 5
alcohol abuse 107
alcohol consumption 105, 162
  changing patterns 111
  effect of economic growth and
    globalization on traditional habits 4
  excess 116
  future of 118
  high levels of 115
  historic influence on production and
    104
  monopolistic hold of porter brewers
    on 34
  potential negative health effects of 108
  recessions and 107
  share of beer in (1960–2010) 109, 110*f*
  UK adept at deriving tax revenue from
    imperialist conquests 35
  vodka share in 113
  wine share in 109
  working class burdened by way of 34
alcohol content 13, 39, 46
  deceptive 139
  decreased 125
  high 116, 146
  increased 145
  lower 45
alcoholism 113, 115
amber ale/beer 140, 148
  see also De Koninck, Fat Tire, Sunshine
    Wheat
AmBev 59–60, 76, 80
America 25, 45, 119, 129, 139, 165
  closure of breweries 46
  earliest registered trademarks in 95
  early industrialist, immigration in 167

America (*cont.*)
  Habsburg Empire's tense relationship
    with 97
  import market 120–2, 124
  pils-style beer popular in 42
  shakeout in the brewing industry 6
  television and breweries 47–54
  top-selling IPA in 146, 150
  see also North America, South America, US
American Budweiser 99–102, 167
  scorned by Czech beer drinkers 94
American craft beers 76, 77, 78, 130,
    132, 140
  fast-growing sector 168
  formidable quality of 144
  four largest brewers 158
  iconic 161
  market share 122, 147*f*
  new entrants in 159
  now-mature and ever-expanding
    market 81
  number of brewers quadrupled/
    stabilized 153–4
  strategies of 145–59
American Craft Brewers' Association 144
American Revolution (1765–83) 33
American South *see* Alabama, Florida,
    Georgia, Louisiana, Mississippi,
    Missouri, North Carolina, Texas
Amsterdam 21, 59, 61, 123
Anchor Brewery (London) 29, 30, 31
Anchor Steam Brewery (San
    Francisco) 76–7, 144, 147–8, 151
Anglo-French Treaty (1860) 25, 35
Anheuser, Ebenhard 42, 94, 97
Anheuser Busch 59, 97–9, 120, 129, 153
  battle between Budweiser Budvar and 94,
    95, 101, 102
  hostile takeover/acquisition of 3, 55, 56,
    60, 61, 167
  predecessor to 42
  sports fans divided along branded
    lines 48
  tight hold of August Busch III on 57
  see also Budweiser, Michelob, Shock Top
Antarctica beer 60
Anti-Corn Law League 24
AOB (Association of Brewers) 151
Argentina 109, 110*f*, 166
Aristotle 11
Artois Brewery *see* Stella Artois
Asheville 158
Ashkenazi Jewish immigrants 94
Athenians 10, 11
Austin 77, 81

Australia 41
  see also Foster's, Melbourne, Victoria Bitter
Austria 32, 41, 97, 99, 105
  see also Habsburgs, Vienna
Austria-Czechoslovakia Treaty (1974) 101
Austro-Hungarian Empire 95

BAA (Brewers Association of America) 148,
    149, 150, 151, 152
baby boomers 49, 57, 152
Babylon 10
Baltic 18
  see also Estonia, Latvia, Lithuania
Baltic Beverages Holding 116
Baltika 116–18
Baltimore 50
Barclay, John 29
barley 4, 8, 12, 13, 15, 17, 40, 46, 63, 77, 78,
    83, 86, 87, 100
  coke-malted 30, 41
  imported 70
  mashed 38
  overproduced under central planning 66
  protected and subsidized 64
  quality 65, 69, 70, 71, 118
  subsidies for 71, 72, 165
  technology that allowed toasting without
    burning 38
  top-fermented 73
  wood-malted 30
barley production 69–70
  drop in 65–6
  world's leading producer 116
baseball 47, 50, 51
Bass 59
Bavaria:
  bottom-fermentation method 164
  geographic advantages 84
  lagering practice 38, 40
  Reinheitsgebot 4, 83–91, 120, 163
  see also Groll, Maximilian, Munich,
    Wilhelm IV
Bavarian Brewing Company 42, 97
Beach, James C. 47
Beck's 59, 119, 123
beer:
  acidic 143
  best in the world 132
  cheap 163
  considered as valuable alternative to
    wine 166
  elite prefer wine over 9
  expensive 108
  full-flavored 152
  future of 40

global consumption of 5*f*
high-value 136
imported 58, 77, 120, 124, 129, 130
innovative 158
pils-style introduced for first time 44
political economy of 94
priciest 141
primary advantages of 44
primitive 10
prized 141
Protestantism, constitutional government
    and 26–9
Russia's recent love affair with 113–18
science of 40
share in total alcohol consumption
    (1960–2010) 110*f*
strategic regulation and taxation of 28
subpar 20
see also abbey ales, American craft beers,
    bock, brown ale, cherry beer, dark beer,
    fruit beers, gueuze, kriek, lager, lambic,
    marzen, pale ale, peasant beers, quality
    beer, sour beer, specialty beers, stout,
    sweet beer, Trappist ales, white beer *also
    under following headings prefixed* 'beer'
Beer Act (UK 1761) 32, 35
beer barons 43, 55–61
    burgeoning oligopoly of 26
    wealthy 31
beer cartels 32–4
    government-tolerated 36
beer consumption 2, 3, 106*f*, 110*f*, 114,
    121*f*, 166
    global 104
    incomes and 107–8
    total, by country 104*f*
beer-drinking nations 4, 11, 46, 76, 79
    biggest populations in the world 85
    emerging 106*f*
    fall of 103–11
    mythic 104
    patterns in social groups 118
    savvy macrobreweries in 2
    top league of 114
    younger people 117
    see also traditional beer-drinking nations
beer festivals *see* Great American Beer
    Festival, Oktoberfest, Zythos
beer industry 44, 57, 67, 124
    consolidation of 46, 48
    emerging international 18
    global 42, 167
    shocked 60
beer markets 2, 117, 144
    all-or-nothing nature of 147

boutique 79
changed dramatically 48
concentration of 53, 167
consolidation in 53, 57
cornered 57
craft 78, 81, 147*f*, 152, 154, 159
cultivation of new tastes in 79
current leader in 116
declining 140
domination of 76
dramatically changed 48
Eastern European 61, 67
emerging 105
encyclopedic knowledge of global trends
    in 58
fastest-growing 60
global 3, 4, 60, 104, 119, 169
high-value 137
import 120–2
industrial revolution changed the nature
    of 164
international 126, 143
lager in 58, 75
largest 3, 4, 43, 56, 57, 104, 105, 106,
    114, 167
less-developed 18
lucrative 18–19, 113–14, 159
medieval 168
nascent 77
one of the most lucrative 113–14
primary regulating and marketing
    device in 4
quintupled 165
radical shift in 6
shrinking 146
size of 57, 60
specialty 78
top five in the world 105*t*
traditional 166
turbulence in 43–6
value-added 159
beer monopoly 55–61
beer production 3, 38, 45*f*, 64, 71, 76, 87,
    100, 121
abbey-style 169
decline in 45, 53
decreased 45
fixed costs in 67
fundamentally changed 30
illegal 45–6
increased fourfold 44
murals documenting the process 150
quality improvements after
    privatization 118
recovered strongly 44

beer production (*cont.*)
   scale economies in 36
   side-effect of hops in some major
      countries 162
   strong and continuous growth in 43
beer trade 166
   changing nature of 119–27
   global integration and 167
   growing 5, 126–7, 167
   international 126
   jump-started 39
begijnhof 137, 138
Belgian Brewers Association 143
Belgium 113, 126, 163
   beer barons 55–61
   beer consumption 106*f*, 108, 166
   number of breweries 43*t*
   peasant beers 129–44
   white beer 69–70, 73–81
   World War I German occupation of 132
   see also Brabant, Flanders, Gaul, InBev,
      Leffe, Lembeek, Liège, Mechelen, Stella,
      Walloons
Belle-Vue 59
Bellyslide Belgian White *see* Blue Moon
Benedictine monks 39–40
Berlin Wall (fall of) 4, 61, 86, 95, 115
   Eastern Bloc revolutions following 63
Bernard (Czech pilsner brewery) 140
bière blanche *see* white beer
bitterness unit levels *see* IBU
black beer 86–7
Bloomberg Business Week 58
Blue Moon 73, 78–80, 129, 169
Blues, Oskar 158
bock 19
   see also doppelbock
Boddingtons 59, 80
Boerhaave, Hermann 40
Bohemia 37–8, 42, 85, 101, 103, 167
   see also Charles IV, Pilsen, Přemsyl
      Ottokar II, Wenceslaus II
Bolland, Marc 66–7, 69, 72
Bolshevik Revolution (1917) 115
Boon Brewery 133, 137, 138, 158
Boon, Frank 133–8, 141, 159
Bordeaux 26, 29, 100
Borsodi Sörgyár 59
Bosteels family 161
Boston Beer Co. 77, 152–4, 156–8
   see also Samuel Adams
Boston Red Sox 50
Botswana 115
bottom fermentation 3, 37–46, 87, 91,
      141, 164

brewed big and sold cheap 132
   hygiene in 135
   regulations concerning 86
Boulder 151, 153
Boulder Beer Co. 150, 152
Brabant 21
   see also Brussels, Hoegaarden, Leuven
Brahma beer 60
brand loyalty 100, 124
brand management 152
brands 3, 4, 48, 59, 67, 81, 99,
      101, 125
   ambassador 66, 69
   authenticity central to 159
   award-winning 137
   big 139
   biggest/largest in the world 94, 167
   boutique 78
   competing 58
   corporate 76
   diversified portfolio 140
   expansion of 167
   export 58, 119, 123, 127, 141
   fastest-growing 79, 80
   favorite 119
   first registered name 167
   flagship 77, 159
   foreign 120
   high-value 140
   holy trinity of 46, 57
   imported 5, 120, 124, 126
   interesting 124
   local 57, 61
   marketing 119, 141
   national 49, 51, 53, 57
   new and exciting 158
   niche 140
   personality behind 157
   playing up the origin of 129
   popular 89, 123
   premium 58, 61, 76, 122–4
   profitability of 123, 142
   recognizable 73, 138
   regional 57
   signature 75
   specialty 141
   success of 141, 169
   trademark rights 102
   valuable 123
   youthful 140
   see also global brands, rebranding
Brasserie du Pêcheur 89
Bratislava 63–4
Brazil 3, 4, 59–60, 76, 80,
      141, 167

beer consumption 104*f*, 105*t*, 106*f*
  see also AmBev, Antarctica, Brahma,
    InBev
Bremen 18, 21, 84, 87, 162
  see also Beck's
Brevard 158
brew-mistresses 10
breweries/brewing 6, 47–54, 148
  cradle of civilization 7–13
  East European 63–72
  family 136, 142–4
  formerly dominant 159
  see also commercial brewing, common
    brewers, homebrewing,
    macrobreweries, microbreweries,
    multinational breweries, porter
    brewers, small brewers; *also under*
    various names, e.g. AB InBev, Budweiser,
    Carlsberg, Coors, Corona, Guinness,
    Heineken, Interbrew, Miller, Stella
brewpubs 145, 149
  up-and-coming 146
Britain *see* UK
British pale ale 41
Brito, Carlos 58, 60, 80
Brooklyn Dodgers 47, 50
brothels *see* tavern-brothels
Brouwerij de Kluis 59, 73, 75–6
brown ale 138
  highly-hopped 30
Bruges 20
Brussels 20, 55, 134–6, 141
  trendy wine bars 109
  see also University of Brussels
Budweiser 6, 42, 56, 57, 122, 145,
  152, 168
  light lager style popularized by 46
  market share 3
  trademark battle over 4, 93–102, 167
  see also American Budweiser
Budweiser Budvar 4, 69, 94–102
Budweiser Urquell 96
Buffett, Warren 60
Bulgaria 66, 67, 68*t*
  malt barley production 70
Bürgerliches Brauhaus Budweis 96, 97, 98
  see also Meštanský
Burgundy 21, 74, 120
Burns, Tom 152
Busch, Adolphus 97
Busch, August (II) 98
Busch, August (III) 55–6, 57
Busch, August (IV) 55–6
Busch family 55, 56, 57, 60
  see also Anheuser Busch

California 122, 147, 151
  counties: Humboldt 145; Mendocino 145;
    Napa 145; Sonoma 145, 156; Trinity 145
  see also Chico, Marin, San Francisco
Canada 5, 94
  alcohol subject to legally mandated
    minimum prices 59
  beer exported to 41
  exports to the north of US 126
  see also Carling, Labatt, Molson
Canadian Ace (brewery) 50
CAP (EU Common Agricultural Policy) 71, 72
Caribbean 32
Carling 102
Carlsberg 67, 116, 123, 141
  market share 61, 68*t*
Carlsberg Laboratories 41
Carter, Billy 149
Carter, Jimmy 149, 168
Carthaginians 10
Catholics 12, 17, 26, 28, 85
  center of power 87
  Counter-Reformation 88, 163
  immigrants in St Louis 94
  war between Protestants and 89
cause and effect 48, 51–3
Celis, Christine 81
Celis, Pierre 73, 75–8, 80, 81, 133, 161
Celts 10, 11
Central/Eastern Europe 62, 63–72, 94,
  98, 104
  funds poured into developing the beer
    market 61
  investments by Western breweries in 4
  post-communist, eased into market
    economy 162
  Soviet Union eager to expand communist
    influence in 86
České Budějovice 4, 93, 95, 99, 164, 167
  see also Bürgerliches Brauhaus Budweis
Champagne 100, 166
Champagne Cereals (malting firm) 70
Charlemagne, Holy Roman Emperor 2,
  11–12, 16, 17, 73
Charles IV, King of Bohemia 96
Charles V, Holy Roman Emperor 137
Chartier, Don 154, 156, 157, 158, 159
cherry beer 136, 169
Chicago 50, 52, 94, 158, 164
Chico 146, 150
  see also Sierra Nevada brewery
China 4, 104, 132, 142
  beer consumption 104*f*, 105*t*, 106*f*,
    107, 110
  FDI in 165

claret 26, 29
Clark, William 94
Coca Cola 44, 49
Code of Hammurabi (legal document) 10
Cold War 49, 99
Colen, Liesbeth 107
Colombia 142
Colorado 151, 153
  see also Boulder, Denver, Fort Collins
commercial brewing/brewers 80
  commercial TV and 116–17
  growth of 162
  medieval Europe 15–22
  taxation of 103
Committee of Porter Brewers 33
common brewers 29, 30, 31
communism 63–9, 71, 95, 98–9, 101, 167
  demise of 4
  mortality rate during 115
  remnants still widespread in former
    Eastern Bloc 93
  Soviet Union eager to expand
    influence 86
  transition to capitalist regime 105, 107
comparative advantage 23
competition 60, 71, 77, 142, 144, 159
  consolidation and 42
  fierce 19
  foreign 4, 24
  looming threat of 34
  New World 43
  price 48, 134
  prime 20
  protection from 4, 64, 83–91
  strategic trade agreements to limit 99
  unfair 131
competitive advantage 147, 150
constitutional government 28
Coors 6, 57, 152, 153, 168
  Belgian white beer experiment 78–9
  light lager style popularized by 46
  sports fans divided along branded
    lines 48
  tapping into emerging markets for
    imported and craft beers 77
  see also MillerCoors
Copenhagen 41
Corgon 67
Corn Laws (UK) 24, 25, 34
Corona 78, 110, 124, 126, 129
Costa Rica 1
craft beer *see* American craft beers
craftsmanship 30, 138, 144
  mythic claim to 132
Crime and Punishment (Dostoevsky) 113

Croatia 70
Czech Republic 67, 68t, 93, 95
  barley production 66
  see also Bohemia, České; Budějovice,
    Prague
Czechoslovakia 66, 68, 95, 100–1, 167
  Committee for Central Planning 65
  Communist Party of 63, 64, 98–9
  see also Czech Republic, Slovakia

Daily Mail 125
dark beer 122, 137, 139, 161
  world's best 138
  see also black beer
David Copperfield (Dickens) 34
De Koninck 140
De Vits, René 134, 136
Deconinck, Koen 114, 117, 118, 163
Denmark 141
  see also Carlsberg
Denver 153, 157
  see also Sandlot Brewery
Detroit 94
Detroit Tigers 50
Dickens, Charles 34
doppelbock 39
Dos Equis 124, 126
Drake, Sir Francis 146
Dreher, Anton 41
Dresden 87
drinking age 117
drinking songs 28, 103, 141
Dubcek, Alexander 64
Dublin 108–9, 164
Dutch Republic 26
Duvel Moortgat 139–40, 142, 143, 144

East Germany 86–7
Eastern Europe *see* Central/Eastern Europe
Ebbets Field 47
ECJ (European Court of Justice) 4, 84,
  89–91, 101
economic growth 4, 105, 107
economies of scale 3, 21, 36, 85, 119, 164
  advertising 51, 57, 124
  benefits of 30
  enabled by scientific innovations 29
  marketing and shipping 127
Economist, The 130
Efes 116
Egypt 8–9, 11, 70
Einbeck 19
Eleanor of Aquitaine 26
Elsevier (Dutch-language publication) 66, 69
Engels, Friedrich 34

England 41
    imported barrels of hopped beer 162
    see also Glorious Revolution, Henry II,
        Leeds, London, Manchester
Enkidu 7–8, 9
Epic of Gilgamesh 7, 8
Erdinger 89
ESOP (employee stock ownership
    plan) 155, 156
Estonia 67, 68*t*
EU (European Union) 71–2, 95, 101
    TRIPS signed by America and 100
    see also ECJ, European Commission
Euphrates River 8
European Commission 107, 129
excise tax 17, 149
    doubled 150
    general 21
    high, on cheap beer 163
    unprecedented rise in revenue from 31

Falls City Brewing Company 149
Family Brewers Association 143, 144
Fat Tire Amber Ale 153, 154
FCC (US Federal Communications
    Commission) 47, 52–3
FDI (foreign direct investment) 4, 60, 61
    attracting 67, 116, 165
fermentation 8, 10, 15, 84, 148
    extended 38
    mixed 140, 141
    spontaneous 134, 135, 141, 158
    theories on how yeast facilitated 40
    see also bottom fermentation, top
        fermentation
Flanders/Flemish people/places 21, 73,
    134, 139
    drinking songs 141
    Trends (industry paper) 55
    see also Bruges, Brussels, Gatz, Ghent,
        Hoegaarden, Riepl, Van Uytven
Florette, Jean de 125
Florida 156
    see also Fort Lauderdale
Fort Collins *see* New Belgium
Fort Lauderdale 151
Foster's 5, 61, 119, 123
France 11, 12, 24–6, 126, 138, 140,
    141, 163
    beer market 105*t*
    beer production 44
    see also Brasserie du Pêcheur, Florette,
        French wine, Gaul, House of Bourbon,
        Napoleonic Wars, terroir, Valois
free-rider problem 100

Freising 39
    see also Weihenstephan
French wine 25, 141
    pamphlets on alternatives to 28
    tariffs/customs duties on 23, 28, 35
    see also Bordeaux, Burgundy, Champagne
fruit beers 140
FTC (US Federal Trade Commission) 120
FX Matt Brewing Co. 148

Garrick, David 32
Gattinger, Karl 83, 87, 88
Gatz, Sven 141–2
Gatza, Paul 149
Gaul 11, 12
Gemer 67
George III, King of UK 32
George, Lisa 47, 48–53
Georgia 149
German-style lager 132
    dominance of 6, 75
    introduced 132
    popularity of 75
Germanic tribes 7, 11, 12
Germany 16, 37, 44, 46, 48, 94, 99, 100, 167
    beer stats: consumption 104*f*, 106*f*, 107,
        108, 114, 166; markets 43, 105*t*;
        production 45*f*
    Brewers' advertising budgets 54
    Federal Courts 86, 87
    integration into EU 84
    monastic brewing 12
    top four firms and market share 53
    see also Bavaria, Berlin Wall, Bürgerliches
        Brauhaus Budweis, East Germany,
        Einbeck, Hannover, Hanseatic League,
        Nazi Germany, Saxony, Weimar
Ghent 20
global brands 5, 61, 76, 126
    modern-day 122
    profitability of 123
    specialty 141
globalization 4, 16, 17, 56, 102, 107, 109,
    110, 119, 162, 167
    after the fall of the Berlin Wall 165–6
    dawn of 145
Glorious Revolution (England 1688) 26,
    28, 35
Goebel Brewing Company 50
Goldsmith, Jonathan 124
Gorbachev, Mikhail S. 115, 165
Gouden Carolus 137, 138, 142
Great American Beer Festival 77, 79, 152
Great Recession (2008) 146
Greece 109

Index

Greeks 10, 11
Grimbergen 141
Groll, Josef 38
Grossman, Ken 146, 150, 151
Groupe Soufflet 70
  see also Soufflet-St Petersburg
gueuze 141, 143, 144, 169
Guinness 103, 109, 110, 122–4, 126, 127,
    141, 164
Guinnessometrics 164

Haarlem 21
Habsburgs 37, 74, 85, 93, 96, 98
  tense relationship with America 97
Haiti 115
Hallertau 85
Halsey, Edmund 29
Hamburg 17–19, 21, 84, 87, 162
Hannover 18
Hanseatic League 17–20
  see also Bremen, Hamburg, Wismar
Hansen, Emil Christian 41
Harenne, François de 130–1
Harvard Business School 152
Hathor (goddess) 9
Hegelian views 60
Heineken 5, 60, 66–7, 70, 110, 120, 122,
    123–4, 126, 127, 129, 146, 165
  acquisition of Lagunitas 159, 161
  market share 61, 68t
  popularity of 59
  purchase of rights to brew Affligem abbey
    ale 141
Heineken, Adriaan 61
Heineken, Alfred (Freddy) 61, 123
Heineken Slovensko 67, 68–9, 71
  profit margin 72
Henry II, King of England 26
Het Anker 137, 138, 139, 143
Hitler, Adolf 93, 98
Hoegaarden 4, 69–70, 73–7, 79, 80–1, 129,
    133, 140–2, 161, 169
  global spread in sales 131
  see also Brouwerij de Kluis, Tomsin Brewery
Holy Roman Empire 74, 85, 87, 167
  see also Charlemagne, Charles V
homebrewing 19, 78, 149, 151
  final two states to outlaw 150
  illicit 146
  see also AHA
Hop Rod rye IPA 146
hops 4, 30, 31, 38, 39, 74, 83–6, 100, 101,
    156, 168
  commercial brewing in medieval
    Europe 3, 15–22

increased amount in pale ales 145
  plant first documented 146
  rose extract added to 146
  side-effect of the use of 162
hostile takeovers 3, 55, 56, 58, 60, 167
  landmark 61
House of Bourbon 27, 28, 32
Hume, David 23, 24
Hungary 44, 66, 67, 68t
  see also Austro-Hungarian Empire,
    BorsodiSörgyár
Hurbanovo 66

Iberians 10
IBU (international bitterness unit)
  levels 145, 146
InBev 56, 59, 61, 76, 129, 167
  looking to reduce cost of production 80
  strike of employees from subsidiaries 81
  takeover of Anheuser Busch 3, 55,
    60, 129
  see also AB InBev
India 32, 33, 35, 70
  see also IPA, SUN
Indo-European tribes 11
industrial lager 75, 138, 141, 168
  brewing center unable to compete
    with 169
  high-quality brewing water wasted
    on 151
  market dominated by 77
  mass-produced 169
  price competition with 134
industrial revolutions 21, 26, 29, 30–1,
    34, 37–46, 54, 57, 74, 95, 96,
    163, 164
Infinium (innovative beer) 158
Interbrew 61, 67, 70, 76, 116, 167
  alternate branding fate for
    Stella 123
  book on the family behind 55
  market share in Eastern Europe
    (2000) 68t
  mergers and acquisitions spree 56, 80
  prescience of 58–60
investment see FDI
IPA (India Pale Ale) 145, 166
  double 146
  hoppy 168
  top-selling 146, 150
Ireland 35, 109, 110f, 141
  see also Dublin, Guinness
Irish republican cause 103
Iron Curtain 99, 116
Ishtar (goddess) 8, 9

Italy 11, 12, 109, 110*f*
   see also Milan, Peroni, Rome
ITO (International Trappist
   Organization) 130–1

Jackson, Michael 130, 168–9
Japan 1, 25, 132, 141, 169
   see also Kirin
Jedlik, Ánios 44
Jordan, Kim 153, 154, 155, 156
Julius Caesar 7
Jupiler 2, 56, 58, 123, 133
Jupille-sur-Meuse 76, 80

Keely (brewery) 50
Kirin 123
Klaas *see* Brouwerij de Kluis
Klosterbrauerei Neuzelle 86–7
Koch, Jim 152
Korbinian 39
Korea (Oriental Brewery) 59
   see also North Korea
Krankenstraat 137
kriek 59, 133–4, 136, 158
Kristallweiss 39
Kronik (innovative ale) 156
Krug, Daniel 139–40
Kwak beer 159

La Chouffe 140
Labatt 59
lager 59, 78, 86, 88, 104, 124, 148
   canned 57
   cheap 57, 58, 133, 169
   classy 125
   conducive to profitable large-scale
     brewing 164
   consistent 169
   craft beers out-competing mainstream
     macrobreweries 161
   dominance of 3, 129, 140, 168
   going price for 136
   high-end 125
   hopped 84
   imported 76, 119
   inexpensive 140
   introduction to the beer market 58
   light-colored 38, 41
   market share for 76, 140
   national 102
   premium 140
   price-competitive market 138
   savvy macrobreweries producing 2
   seasonal 75
   taste of 137

   see also German-style lager, industrial
     lager, light lager; *also under various lager*
     brewers e.g. Beck's, Budweiser, Carling,
     Carlsberg, Coors, Foster's, Heineken,
     Labatt, Miller, Pabst, Stella
lager louts 125
lagering practice 38, 40, 41, 84, 132,
   147, 164
Lagunitas 145, 146, 154, 156–9, 161
lambic 59, 133–4, 135
Lancashire 80
Latin America 59
   see also Costa Rica, Panama City, South
     America
Latvia 67, 68*t*
Lavoisier, Antoine Laurent 40
Le Corbusier 93
Lebesch, Jeff 153
Leclef, Charles 137
Leclef family 138
Leeds 44
Leffe *see* Abbaye Notre-Dame de Leffe
Lelkes, Peter 65
Lembeek 134–6
   see also lambic
Leningrad 116
Leuven 20, 21, 74–5, 80–1
   Zythos Beer Festival 143
   see also Stella Artois, University of
     Leuven
Levittown 49–50
Lewis, Meriwether 94
liberalization 63–4, 105
Liefmans 140
Liège 74
light lager 46, 57, 77, 122
   first 100
   industrial 168
   perceived inferiority of America's
     favorite 84
   styles that offer visceral departure
     from 146
Linde, Carl von 41
Lithuania 67, 68*t*
London 33, 34
   common brewers 29, 31
   porter brewers/drinkers 3, 26, 30–2,
     35*f*, 103
   trendy wine bars 109
   see also Anchor Brewery
London and Country Brewer, The 30
Louisiana *see* New Orleans
Louisville 149
Low Countries 18, 162
   beer consumption 13

Low Countries (*cont.*)
  gruit 17, 20–2
  see also Belgium, Netherlands
Löwenbräu 58, 59
  Miller accused of falsely marketing 120
Luther, Martin 87, 88

MacIntosh, Julie 55, 60
macrobreweries 2, 56, 58, 122, 146, 154
  biggest, microbreweries' advantage
    over 150
  capacity of 148, 152, 153
  capitalizing on growing market share of
    craft beer 159
  craft beers out-competing 161
  global distribution networks 161
  large-scale advertising campaigns
    common among 156
  super-premium beers produced by 121
Magee, Tony 156, 159
Manchester 24
  see also Boddingtons
Maredsous 140
Marin 156, 159
market economy 65–6, 71, 99
  post-communist Eastern Europe eased
    into 162
market share 67
  abbey ales 1
  all beer in the world 61
  craft beer 59, 77, 122, 130, 146, 147*f*,
    154, 159
  four largest brewers 48
  high-end sector 121
  imported beers 58, 77, 90, 120–2
  lager 76, 140
  largest beer market in the world 3
  multinational breweries in Eastern
    Europe 68*t*
  top four firms 53, 60
Martiner 67
Marxist-Leninist ideology 63
marzen style 88
Mason-Dixon line 94
Mathias, Peter 28, 33
Matt, Nick 148
Maximilian I, Duke/King of Bavaria
  88, 163
Maytag, Fritz 148, 151, 152
McAuliffe, Jack 146–7
McDonald's 49
Mechelen 137, 138
Melbourne 119
Mesopotamia 2, 3
  see also Enkidu

Meštanský Pivovar Budějovice 98, 99
Methuen Treaty (Portugal–England 1703) 23
Mexico 123
  FEMSA 61
  Grupo Modelo 59
  see also Corona, Dos Equis
Michelob 57, 76, 120
Michigan Brewing Company 77, 81
  see also Detroit, University of Michigan
microbreweries 145, 146, 151, 157
  competitive advantage of 147, 150
  craft beer produced by 121
  growing popularity of 79
  jump-starting 153
  law important to 149
  revival of 149
  see also New Belgium
Midwestern market 158
Milan 166
Miller 6, 57, 60, 77–8, 149, 152, 168
  light lager style popularized by 46
  multimillion-dollar Löwenbräu
    advertising campaign 120
  sports fans divided along branded
    lines 48
  tapping into emerging markets for
    imported and craft beers 77
  see also SABMiller
Millerbräu fiasco 58, 120, 121
MillerCoors 80
  see also Blue Moon
Milwaukee 78, 120
Mississippi 94, 122, 150
Mississippi River 93
Missouri *see* St Louis
Molson 59, 119
monks 12–13, 17, 39–40, 73, 87
  see also Trappist ales
More, Sir Thomas 28
multinational breweries 2, 64, 70, 109, 154
  biggest global 95
  challenging the dominance of 168
  cost-cutting practices 58
  export volume dominated by 141
  major 131
  market share in Eastern Europe
    (2000) 68*t*
  rapid growth of 127
  spread of 126
  takeovers of foreign brewers 119
  world's largest/leading 76, 129, 161
  see also Carlsberg, Guinness, Heineken,
    InBev, Leffe, SABMiller
Munich 60, 85, 87, 120, 163, 164
  Hofbräuhaus 83, 88

Viktualienmarkt 83
see also Löwenbräu, Oktoberfest, Paulaner, Spaten, TU Munich

Napoleonic Wars 27, 33, 34, 74
Narragansett 50
National Bohemian Beer 50
National Public Radio 130
nationalist politics 93–102
Nazi Germany 49, 95, 101
see also Hitler
Neolithic Revolution 8
Netherlands 2, 12, 138, 140, 141, 163
Belgian exports to 126
Dutch lexicon 16
see also Amsterdam, Dutch Republic, *Elsevier*, Haarlem, Heineken, William of Orange
New Albion brewery 146, 152
New Belgium (microbrewery) 77, 150, 153–9
New Orleans 94
New York 47, 52, 156
Albany 148
Schenectady 52
see also Brooklyn Dodgers
New York Times 130, 141
Nietzsche, Friedrich 159
Ninkasi (goddess) 9–10
Nitra 63, 70
Noble Order of the Mashing Paddle 74
Nordic countries 67, 104
see also Scandinavia
North America 32
see also Canada, US
North Carolina *see* Asheville
North Sea 18
Nye, John 23, 24–8

OECD (Organisation for Economic Co-operation and Development) 84, 90, 114
Oktoberfest 83, 103
sponsor tents at 42
tradition in beer on display at 91
oligopoly 3, 31, 32
global 161
Ommegang 140
O'Shea, Bill 148, 149, 151

Pabst 57, 149
pale ale 41, 103, 146, 147, 154
dortmunder 134
increased amount of hops and alcohol content 145

popularity of 30
signature 150
see also IPA
Panama City 142
Papazian, Charlie 151, 152
Paraguay 142
Pasteur, Louis 40
pasteurization 3, 40, 164
Paulaner 41, 89
"Pax Britannica" 34
peasant beers 129–44, 169
Pemberton, John S. 44
Pennsylvania 50
see also Philadelphia
Pepin the Short 16
Perkins, David 29
Peroni 119
Persians 10
Persyn, Damiaan 129–30, 131, 133, 135
Persyn, Robert 69–70
Peter Fox (brewery) 50
Philadelphia 52, 148
Philip the Good, Duke of Burgundy and King of France 21
Piedboeuf Brewery 58, 76, 133
Pilsen 37–8, 96, 97
see also Plzen
Pilsner 39, 46, 91, 94, 99–101, 103, 108, 109, 120, 135, 140
Pilsner Urquell 37, 38, 41, 42, 69, 96, 97, 100
Plato 10–11
Pliny the Elder 11, 15, 146
Plzen 37, 42, 96, 164
Po River 11
Poelmans, Eline 163
Pokrivčák, Ján 63, 64, 65, 70, 71–2
Poland 67, 68*t*, 165
barley production 66
sharp fall in vodka consumption 109–10
Pollan, Michael 145
porter 23–36, 41, 103, 146, 163
porter brewers 34, 36
major 33
oligopoly of 3, 26, 31, 32
top 31, 35
Portugal 11, 23
Prague 38, 63–4
U Pinkas restaurant 41–2
premium export 58–9, 119, 127, 142
branding 122–4
Přemysl Ottokar II, King of Bohemia 93
privatization 64, 65, 67, 116, 118
prostitutes *see* Shamhat, tavern-brothels

Protestantism 26–9, 88, 89, 163
  catalyst for the Reformation 87
  see also William of Orange
Protz, Roger 73
Prussia 32
public houses 29, 32, 34, 38, 108–9,
    127, 166
  British pub-goers 125
  dispersed 35
  forced to serve beer to keep license 88
  rural 103
  see also brewpubs
publicity stunts 149
pubs see public houses
Pyramid 153, 154, 159

quality beer 91, 95
  high- 5, 19, 154
  low- 19

Raboch, Tomáš 37, 38, 41
Racerx X 146
Radbuza River 38
Ramses III, Pharaoh of Egypt 8–9
Raskovsky, Pavel 71
Reagan, Ronald 165
Reason TV 148
rebranding 6, 79, 98
Redhook 153, 154
refrigeration 3, 41, 132
  early technology 164
Reinheitsgebot 4, 83–91, 120, 163
religion 74, 104, 161
  major transformations 87
  women and 10, 137
  see also Catholics, monks, Protestantism
restructuring 67, 68–9
Ricardo, David 23, 24
Riepl, Wolfgang 55, 56, 58, 59, 60, 123
Robinson, Jackie 47
Rocheford 10 (beer) 130
Roman Empire 9, 11
  see also Holy Roman Empire
Romans 109
  see also Pliny
Rome 163
Roosevelt University 164
Royal Navy 23–36, 162
Rubens, Hans 137, 138–9, 142, 143
Russia 70, 111, 113–18, 166
  beer stats: consumption 5, 104f, 105,
    106f, 107, 113, 114f, 117; market 4,
    105t, 117, 165
  market share of multinational breweries
    in 68t

sharp fall in vodka consumption 109–10
  see also Soviet Union
Russian River (brewpub) 146

Saaz hops 38, 100
Sabia, Jim 78, 79, 80
SABMiller 59, 60
  AB InBev merger 61, 161
  market share in Eastern Europe
    (2000) 68t
  race to buy up breweries in East European
    post-communist countries 67
Salhofer, Klaus 88
Samec, Petr 95, 99
Samson 98–9
Samuel Adams 77, 78, 154, 156, 159
San Francisco 93, 168
  Anchor Steam brewery 76–7, 144,
    147–8, 151
  Monk's Kettle restaurant 1–2, 130
Sandlot Brewery 78, 80
Saxony see Dresden
scale economies see economies of scale
Scandinavia 12, 67, 116
  see also Denmark, Sweden
Schaefer Brewery 47, 50
Schwarzer Abt 87
scientific revolution 3, 40, 164, 168
Scottish & Newcastle 61
Scythians 10
Seattle 153
Sedlmayr, Gabriel 40–1
Seville 129–30
Shamhat (priestess/prostitute) 8, 9
Shock Top 73, 169
Sierra Nevada brewery 145, 146, 150, 151,
    153, 154, 157–9
Silicon Valley 146
Simpson, Bryan 153, 154, 155, 156,
    157, 158
Slovak Beer and Malt Association 67, 68
Slovakia 68t, 69–72, 95
  barley production 65–6
  see also Bratislava, Heineken Slovensko,
    SUA, Zlatý Bazant
small brewers 75, 76, 133, 136, 138, 142, 159
  capital constraints on 156
  closed 42, 43
  emerging competitive forces from large
    and 79
  exports of 143
  growing again 137
  laws reducing the tax burden on 149
  main struggle for 152
  merged 42

new recipes developed by 81
vanguard for 148
well-respected 140
Smith, Adam 24
socialism 34, 49, 63–72
transition to capitalist state 4
soda water 44
Soenen, Nicolas 139, 140, 142–3, 144
Soufflet-St Petersburg 116
sour beer 5, 133–4, 135, 158, 169
South America 44, 169
see also Argentina, Brazil, Colombia,
Paraguay
Soviet Union 49, 67, 118
control over East Germany 86
disbanded 115, 116
eager to expand communist influence in
Eastern Europe 86
occupations by 63, 95, 98, 101
see also Cold War, Gorbachev, Iron
Curtain, Stalin
Spain 4, 11, 12, 109, 110f, 166
see also House of Bourbon, Seville
Spaten 40–1, 42, 59
specialty beers 59, 78, 119, 131, 136
consumer demand for 5
high-value 137
popularity of 132
rising domestic demand for 138
willingness to pay extra for 127, 166
St Bernardus of Watou 1, 2
St Gall monastery 12
St Louis 42, 57, 93–4, 97
World Fair (1911) 97
St Louis Cardinals 50
Stahl, George Ernst 40
Stalin, Joseph V. 98
Stanford 60, 148
Starbucks 166
Stella Artois 2, 5, 6, 56, 58–9, 60, 75–6,
102, 110, 124, 127, 129, 132, 140–2,
146, 169
big selling point for 133
global spread in sales 131
popularity of 123
stereotypical drinkers 125
stout 30, 146, 164
see also Guinness
Stroh 57
SUA (Slovakian University of
Agriculture) 63, 69, 70
subsidies 64, 66, 71–2, 165
Sumerians 8, 9, 10
SUN brewery 116
Sunshine Beer 50

Sunshine Wheat 77
Super Bowl 46, 55
supply chains 65, 69–70, 165
communist 66
Sweden 32
sweet beer 86, 103, 169
Switzerland 12

takeovers 66–7, 119, 127
foreign 165
unpleasant 80
see also hostile takeovers
tavern-brothels 9, 10
taxation 2, 3, 22, 32, 88, 162
commercial brewing 103
crackdown on fraud 33
efficiency of collectors 28
evading 17, 34, 35
exemption from 4, 13, 74
first records of 16
health concerns and 108
heavy 21
high 33
impetus for major changes in 20
indirect (Britain 1750–1850) 27f
low 109
quadrupling of revenue 27, 74
regressive 17
wine 25, 26, 28
working class disproportionately
burdened by 34
see also excise tax
television 49–50, 57, 124
commercial 53, 54, 116–17, 165
television advertising 3, 5, 47, 51–4, 118,
125, 149
large-scale campaigns 156
sponsored 79
spread of 165
Television Magazine 47, 50
terroir 5, 100, 119, 127
Texas see Austin
Thracians 10
Thrale, Ralph 29, 31
Tigris River 8
Tomsin Brewery 75
top fermentation 38, 73, 88, 129, 132, 141,
146, 163
cloudy, inconsistent recipes 133
hygiene in 135
inconsistent 46
regulations concerning 86
spiced 153
Torpedo 146, 150
Tour De Fat 157

trade *see* beer trade
trademarks 4, 38, 76, 93–102, 123, 169
  court battles over 167
traditional beer-drinking nations 2, 83, 85,
  106*f*, 109
  consolidation in 133
  richer 108
  shakeout in 57, 133
  shrinking markets 105
  trend away from pilsners in 108
  volume consumption decline 140
  see also Australia, Austria, Belgium,
    Canada, Croatia, Czech Republic,
    Denmark, Estonia, Germany, Ireland,
    Latvia, Lithuania, Netherlands, Poland,
    Slovakia, Switzerland, UK, US
Transatlantic Kriek 158
Trappist ales/beers 129–31, 134, 142, 144
  high-end, growing consumer demand for 1
  popularity of 2
  see also Rocheford 10
Tremblay, Victor and Carol 48*f*, 121, 121*f*,
  122, 124–5, 147*f*
Trends in Brewing (conference) 143
Tripel Karmeliet 161
TRIPS (Trade-Related Aspects of International
  Property Rights) 100, 101
Truman, Benjamin 31
TU Munich (Technische Universität
  München) 39, 41, 84, 88
Turkey 116

UK (United Kingdom) 23–4, 27, 140, 162–3
  beer stats: consumption 104*f*, 106*f*,
    110*f*, 166; market 105*t*; production 45*f*
  free trade 24–6
  monastic brewing 12
  number of breweries 43*t*
  tax revenue from alcohol consumption of
    imperialist conquests 35
  see also England, Royal Navy, Scottish &
    Newcastle
Ukraine 67, 68*t*
UNESCO world heritage list 141
Unger, Richard 13, 16–17, 18, 20, 21
University of Antwerp 132
University of British Columbia 16
University of Brussels 78
University of Colorado 150
University of Leuven 64, 107, 114, 129,
  143, 163
University of Michigan 53
Uruk 8
US (United States) 41, 42, 95, 98, 100, 120,
  132, 140, 167, 169

beer stats: consumption 2, 104*f*, 106*f*,
  107, 108, 121*f*; market 4, 104,
  105*t*; production 45*f*;
  style popular in parts of 19
Canadian exports to the north of 126
current market structure 133
historic regional breweries 148
import market 120–2
leader in television and
  macrobrewing 53–4
market share for domestic lagers 76
mass-producing brewers 48
nationwide prohibition of alcohol
  (1919–33) 43*t*, 45
number of breweries 43*t*, 48*f*
popularity of hoppy IPAs 168
suburbanizing 49
top-selling IPA in 146
see also Anheuser Busch, Baltimore,
  Boston, Budweiser, California, Carter,
  Chicago, Colorado, FCC, FTC,
  Michigan, Miller, Milwaukee, New
  York, Pennsylvania, Reagan *also under*
  American craft beers, American South
US Bureau of Alcohol, Tobacco, and
  Firearms 79
US Department of Agriculture 97

Valois 74
Van Breedam, Charles 138
Van Leeuwenhoek, Antoni 40
Van Tongeren, Frank 84, 91
Van Uytven, Raymond 20, 132–3
Vanormelingen, Stijn 129–30, 131, 133
Vedett 140
Velvet Revolution (Czechoslovakia 1989) 99
Verstl, Ina 60
Vervloet, Theo 143
Victoria Bitter 123
Vienna 85, 87, 166
  Commercial Court 101
  Pilsner-loving royal courts 94
Villa, Keith 78–9, 80
Vitus wheat beer 39

Walloons 73
Watson, Bart 152, 159
Watt's steam engine 41
Weihenstephan Research Brewery
  39–40, 158
Weimar Republic 86, 98
weissbier 87–9, 163
  see also white beer
Wenceslaus II, King of Bohemia 38
West Africa 32

Westvleteren 1, 2, 130
Whitbread 119
Whitbread, Samuel 31
white beer 5, 59, 69–70, 73–81, 161, 169
  only remaining brewery brewing 4
  see also Celis
Widmer 159
Wilhelm IV, Duke of Bavaria 83, 84, 87
William III, Prince of Orange 26, 28
wine 4, 10, 12, 24, 102, 110, 111, 145,
  147, 164
  beer as valuable alternative to 166
  cheap 28–9, 32, 33, 34
  elite prefer 9
  exclusive right to market 100
  garbage 23
  high-end 28
  imported 7, 28–9, 109
  low-quality 28
  Pasteur's experiments on 40
  shift toward 166
  sour 135
  strategic regulation and taxation of 28
  tariffs on 26, 33, 36
  see also French wine
wine bars 109
wine consumption fall in 109

  global 5*f*
  moderate 11
winemaking practices 146
WinterÂ s Tale, The (Shakespeare) 32
Wismar 18
Wittenberg (All Saints' Church) 87
World War I 34, 43–6, 75, 86, 97, 98, 139
  German occupation of Belgium 132
World War II 46, 49, 52, 64, 75, 86, 95, 100,
  107, 148

yeast 4, 9, 40, 81, 83, 88
  airborne 134, 135
  bottom-fermenting 41
  commercialized 164
  lager 148
  slow-acting 38
  wild 134, 135
Yuengling (brewery) 148

Zappa, Frank 103, 156
Zarnkow, Martin 39, 40, 84, 158
Zatka, August 96
Zilliak, Steve 164
Zlatý Bazant 66–7, 69
Zymurgy (newsletter-turned-magazine) 151
Zythos Beer Festival 143